The Offense of Love

Publication of this volume has been made possible,
in part, through the generous support and enduring vision of

WARREN G. MOON

The University of Wisconsin Press
1930 Monroe Street, 3rd Floor
Madison, Wisconsin 53711-2059
uwpress.wisc.edu

3 Henrietta Street, Covent Garden
London WC2E 8LU, United Kingdom
eurospanbookstore.com

Printed in the United States of America

Library of Congress Cataloging-in-Publication Data

Ovid, 43 B.C.–17 A.D. or 18 A.D., author.
[Works. Selections. English. 2014]
The offense of love : Ars Amatoria, Remedia Amoris, and Tristia 2 / Ovid ;
a verse translation by Julia Dyson Hejduk, with introduction and notes.
pages   cm — (Wisconsin studies in classics)
Includes bibliographical references.
ISBN 978-0-299-30204-7 (pbk. : alk. paper) — ISBN 978-0-299-30203-0 (e-book)
I. Ovid, 43 B.C.–17 A.D. or 18 A.D.—Translations into English. I. Hejduk,
Julia Dyson, 1966–, translator. II. Ovid, 43 B.C.–17 A.D. or 18 A.D.
Ars amatoria. English. III. Ovid, 43 B.C.–17 A.D. or 18 A.D. Remedia amoris.
English. IV. Ovid, 43 B.C.–17 A.D. or 18 A.D. Tristia. Liber 2. English.
V. Title. VI. Series: Wisconsin studies in classics.
PA6522.A3   2014
871′.01—dc23
2014009152

# The Offense of Love

*Ars Amatoria, Remedia Amoris,* and *Tristia* 2

O V I D

A verse translation by Julia Dyson Hejduk,
with introduction and notes

THE UNIVERSITY OF WISCONSIN PRESS

*In memory of*

JANET KNEIPP *and* JIM TIBBETTS

# Contents

# Preface

When I met Ovid's *Ars Amatoria* my junior year of college, under the expert guidance of Elaine Fantham, I could hardly believe my good fortune. Yes, I had to look up almost every word (I remember translating *conveniat maribus* [1.277], "let it be agreed upon by males," as "let it come together in the seas"), but oh, the payoff when I would finally get the jokes! That the poem was a contributing factor to Ovid's exile made it even spicier. Many elegiac couplets have passed before my eyes since then, but nothing has taken the place of my first Latin love.

It was nearly a decade later when the exile poetry swam into my ken. That, I confess, was a harder sell; my initial inclination, like that of many at the time, was to take Ovid at his word about his declining powers. (Recent scholarship, as I explain in my introduction and notes, has become far more appreciative of Ovid's sophistication in general and exile poetry in particular.) But even before I acquired the taste for his exquisite exilic wit, I always thought *Tristia* 2 was hilarious: what funnier premise could there be than defending one's own dirty poems on the grounds that all poems (even the *AENEID*!) are actually dirty? When the idea came to me of a book that would place Ovid's "offense" and "defense" side by side, I knew somehow it had to be.

Time flies when you're translating Ovid, especially with such good people speeding your chariot along. In particular, I would like to thank Barbara Boyd, Christopher Brunelle, Matthew Cosby, Matthew Hejduk, Sharon James, Raphael Kadushin, Joshua King, Peter Knox, Laura

McClure, Sheila McMahon, John Miller, Scott Mueller, Patricia Rosen-meyer, and Gareth Williams for their helpful comments and encourage-ment. Though I could not possibly acknowledge here all who have helped me to read poetry with delight, this book is dedicated to the memory of two who set me on the right path at the beginning of my journey: my high school English teachers Janet Kneipp and Jim Tibbetts. Naturally, whatever dross remains is my own fault. (Forgive me, Ovid! I tried my best to speak with your voice.)

# Abbreviations

| | |
|---|---|
| *Aen.* | Virgil, *Aeneid* |
| *AJP* | *American Journal of Philology* |
| *Am.* | Ovid, *Amores* (Loves/Love-Affairs) |
| *ANRW* | *Aufstieg und Niedergang der Römischen Welt* |
| *CA* | *Classical Antiquity* |
| *CCJ* | *Cambridge Classical Journal* |
| *CJ* | *Classical Journal* |
| *CP* | *Classical Philology* |
| *CQ* | *Classical Quarterly* |
| *CW* | *Classical World* |
| *G&R* | *Greece and Rome* |
| *ICS* | *Illinois Classical Studies* |
| *IJCT* | *International Journal of the Classical Tradition* |
| *Il.* | Homer, *Iliad* |
| *JRS* | *Journal of Roman Studies* |
| *LCM* | *Liverpool Classical Monthly* |
| *MAAR* | *Memoirs of the American Academy in Rome* |
| *MD* | *Materiali e discussioni per l'analisi dei testi classici* |
| *Met.* | Ovid, *Metamorphoses* |
| *OCD* | *Oxford Classical Dictionary* (3rd ed.) |

OLD      *Oxford Latin Dictionary* (1st ed.)
PCPhS    *Proceedings of the Cambridge Philological Society*
PQ       *Philological Quarterly*
Rem.     Ovid, *Remedia Amoris* (Cures for Love)
RLM      *Rheinisches Museum für Philologie*
TAPA     *Transactions of the American Philological Association*
Tr.      Ovid, *Tristia* (Sad Things)
WS       *Wiener Studien*

# Some Notes on the Notes and the Translations

## SCOPE

The commentator's challenge is to present information essential to understanding the text without bombarding readers with too much information. My imagined audience is a college freshman or general reader with no knowledge of the ancient world beyond, say, one or two Percy Jackson movies. Because the contrast between Ovid's erudite allusions and his sordid subject matter is one of his most delicious sources of humor, I have generally preserved Latin names (plus an actual footnote) rather than slipping into the text the "silent footnotes" most translators prefer; for instance, I translate *Haemonia puppis* (1.6) as "Haemonian ship," not "Jason's ship" or "the Argo." As the poet frequently reminds us, "My art demands difficult toil!" (2.538). But reading and digesting the notes—which are keyed to line numbers and assume familiarity with the introduction (especially the section "Myth and Lit 101")—will provide a first-rate education in Roman literature and civilization, while also giving you a taste of what it means to be a learned reader of a supremely learned poet.

## CROSS-REFERENCES

Another challenge is deciding how often to duplicate information. My working assumption is that the reader will be reading the texts in order and wanting only the occasional reminder of information previously mentioned. For instance, on 1.3–4 "speedy ships . . . chariots," I refer the reader to "Fifty Shades of Metaphor" within the introduction, but I do not do so for subsequent metaphors. On the other hand, for mythological or historical figures not covered in the introduction, I have tended to be generous with cross-references (e.g., for each mention of Jupiter's mistress Io I refer the reader to 1.77 "Memphitic . . . heifer").

### Subheadings

These are mine, not Ovid's; they do not do justice to the poet's subtle and seamless transitions. They do mark off convenient sections, however, so I have taken the liberty of not providing cross-references to notes within a given section.

### Misplaced or Suspected Lines

Because of the vagaries of ancient publishing (see "Ovid's Works" under "Myth and Lit 101" in the introduction), "textual criticism," figuring out what the author actually wrote, is a complex and delicate art. The textual tradition for Ovid is particularly messy: he was popular and easy to imitate, he revised his poems both before and after exile, and our oldest manuscripts of his works are copies (of copies of copies) dating from about a millennium after his death. I indicate with [ ] lines that modern editors believe to have been "interpolated" (inserted by overenthusiastic scribes either importing lines from elsewhere or composing their own in Ovidian style). Sometimes, genuine Ovidian lines get copied in the wrong order; the line numbers that appear in my margins indicate the numbering in the original manuscripts. For instance, for *Ars* 3.485–91, the lines in my edition are numbered 485, 486, 489, 490, 487, 488, 491, showing that modern editors think the couplet 489–90 has been switched with the previous one in the manuscripts.

### Pronunciation

All two-syllable names are accented on the first syllable. In the text (but not the notes), I have placed accents on Latin names of three or more syllables, other than the following common ones: Achílles, Apóllo, Diána, Hércules, Júpiter, Mércury, Théseus, and Ulýsses. In general, "e"/"es" at the end of a word will be pronounced "ee"/"eez" (e.g., "An-dró-mach-e" [An-DRAW-muck-ee], "Pý-lad-es" [PIE-luhd-eez]).

<h1 style="text-align:center">METER</h1>

Like English, Latin has accented and unaccented syllables; unlike English, Latin also has "long" and "short" syllables, with long ones theoretically taking twice as long to say as short ones, like musical half notes and quarter notes. Classical Latin poetry is based on patterns involving this syllable length or "quantity," which is independent of word accent (in some ways analogous to the independence of musical rhythm and pitch). The basic metrical unit for all of Ovid's surviving poetry is the dactyl, a "foot" consisting of three syllables, "long short short" (like a musical measure consisting of a half note followed by two quarter notes; "dactyl" comes from the Greek word for "finger," because a finger has one long bone and two short ones). In most line positions, the dactyl can be replaced by the temporally equivalent spondee ("long long," like two half notes).

Ovid's meter for the poems in this volume, the elegiac couplet (two unequal lines), is extremely regular, with most couplets containing a complete thought. Odd-numbered lines are dactylic hexameters (six feet), in which the first beat of each foot is slightly stressed, like the downbeat of a musical measure. Here is *Ars* 1.1, with long syllables CAPITALIZED, stressed syllables also **BOLDFACE**, and | marking the end of a foot:

**SI** quis in| **HOC AR**|**TEM** popu|**LO NON**| **NO**vit a|**MANDI**

Even-numbered lines are dactylic pentameters, which actually consist of two half-lines (two feet plus one long beat) separated by a strong pause ("caesura," indicated by | |) (*Ars* 1.2):

**HOC** legat| **ET LEC**|**TO** | | **CAR**mine| **DOC**tus a|**MET**

There are other complexities involving smaller pauses in the lines and the interaction of metrical "ictus" (the **STRONG** beat) with word accent, but reading aloud the lines above (and recognizing that there are

Some Notes on the Notes and Translations

no silent letters in Latin, so "**CAR**mine" is three syllables) gives the basic idea.

How best to re-create this feel in English, while producing natural speech rhythms and word order, is one of the translator's many challenges. Rather than "longs" and "shorts," a line of English verse consists, essentially, of unstressed syllables (which I'll call "da") and stressed syllables ("**DUM**"). The most common meter in English is the iambic pentameter, defined as five "iambs" (da **DUM**), but in practice showing tremendous variation: a foot can be "**DUM**," "da **DUM**," "da da **DUM**," or "da da da **DUM**," with a possible additional "da" or two at the end of the line. Even more remarkably, the *same line* can be read in a variety of ways, with its number of feet depending on the author's intent. Consider, for example, the closing lines of Gerard Manley Hopkins's "Hurrahing in Harvest":

> The heart rears wings bold and bolder
> And hurls for him, O half hurls earth for him off under his feet.

My initial attempt to scan these lines yielded something like this (the | marks the end of a foot but should be ignored when reading):

> The **HEART**| rears **WINGS**| bold and **BOLD**er
> And **HURLS**| for **HIM**,| O **HALF**| hurls **EARTH**| for **HIM**| off **UN**|der
> his **FEET**.

But as I began to learn more about Hopkins and appreciate his genius with what he called "sprung rhythm" (basically, the employment of feet with zero or multiple da's), I realized that what looked like a trimeter (three **DUM**s) followed by a heptameter (seven **DUM**s) was actually two pentameters after all. What I had taken for sloppiness was really sublimity:

> The **HEART**| **REARS**| **WINGS**| **BOLD**| and **BOLD**er
> And **HURLS**| for him, O **HALF**| hurls **EARTH**| for him off **UN**|der his
> **FEET**.

Similarly, it looks as if Shakespeare goofed and left out a foot in the third line of this famous passage from *Hamlet* (3.1.74–77):

For **IN**| that **SLEEP**| of **DEATH**| what **DREAMS**| may **COME**
When **WE**| have **SHUFF**|led **OFF**| this **MOR**|tal **COIL**,
Must **GIVE**| us **PAUSE.**| **THERE'S**| the re**SPECT**
That **MAKES**| ca**LA**|mi**TY**| of **SO**| long **LIFE**.

In fact, however, the line's brilliance is enhanced by the realization that it *is* a pentameter, and its middle "foot" consists of a silence, the very "pause" that comes from the contemplation of death's uncertain dreams:

Must **GIVE**| us **PAUSE.**| [**DUM**]| **THERE'S**| the re**SPECT**

To appreciate the music of English poetry, one must occasionally work just a bit to make (say) the pentameter read as a pentameter, but it is worth the effort.

In my translation, every odd-numbered line is a hexameter (six **DUM**s) and every even-numbered line is a pentameter (five **DUM**s). My greatest difficulties tended to come from multisyllabic proper names; "Tyndareus's daughter" and "Thyestes's son" (*Ars* 2.407) are almost as hard on the English hexameter as they were on Agamemnon. Nevertheless, with some concessions to "sprung rhythm," every line does have the appropriate number of **DUM**s. Here is a sample of what I hear when I read my own verses (I think in **DUM**s, not in feet) (*Ars* 1.1–2):

If **AN**y **MAN** in this **NA**tion doesn't **KNOW** the **ART** of **LOV**ing,
    he **NEEDS** to **READ** this **SONG**—read, **LEARN**, and **LOVE**!

Obviously, this is not the only way these lines could be scanned—but as I've tried to show with the examples above from two masters of English verse, scansion is, at least in part, in the ear (and the will) of the beholder. While my verses aren't exactly a threat to Shakespeare or Hopkins, I can promise that you'll have more fun, and a better sense of Ovid's poetry, if you try to feel the hexameter–pentameter rhythm I did my best to convey.

## Sources

The translations are based on the Latin texts of Kenney 1961 (for *Ars* and *Remedia*) and Hall 1995 (for *Tristia* 2). Regarding the notes, I make no claim whatsoever to originality. Rather, I have relied heavily on several excellent commentaries (whose minor changes to the Latin text I have also generally followed): Hollis 1977 for *Ars* 1, Janka 1997 for *Ars* 2 (there is currently no modern English commentary on this book), Gibson 2003 for *Ars* 3, Henderson 1979 for *Remedia*, and Ingleheart 2010 for *Tristia* 2. Christopher Brunelle kindly allowed me to peek at his forthcoming Oxford commentary on *Ars* 3, and Barbara Boyd at her forthcoming Cambridge commentary on *Remedia*. I have also made liberal use of the notes in Green 1982a; Kenney and Melville 1990; *The Oxford Classical Dictionary*; and Apollodorus's *Library* (a summary of mythology attributed to a first-century BC scholar, though it probably comes from the second century AD). For reasons of time and space, I have not provided additional attributions in the notes, but I strongly encourage readers who want to follow up on any facts or ideas to consult these magnificent works.

The Offense of Love

# Introduction

Ovid carried the elegiac couplet to a perfection beyond which it could not
go and his work remains the standard of excellence.

—Gerard Manley Hopkins, letter to R. W. Dixon

Ovid's *Ars Amatoria* (Art of Love) has one of the funniest premises of any
work of literature: namely, that Love—by which he means the initiation
and maintenance of sexual relationships—is a field of study, like chess or
astronomy or agriculture, whose strategies can be analyzed and taught.[1]
Ovid's narrator figures himself as the confident *praeceptor Amoris*, the
"tutor of Love" in complete control of his subject;[2] yet as the power strug-
gle between Art and Love unfolds in the course of the poem, we find the
know-it-all *praeceptor* increasingly incapable of managing his intractable
pupil.[3] The "Remedies for Love" (*Remedia Amoris*), we come to realize, do
not work (despite the Love Doctor's extravagant claims for his own skill).[4]
The poems are masterpieces of irony. In their ruthlessly clinical analyses
of flirtation, self-deception, jealousy, and all the other absurdities of our
species's mating behavior, they also happen to be an insightful exploration
of the human heart.[5] It is both amusing and sobering to see how Ovid's
basic premise that sexual love is teachable powers so many modern maga-
zines and self-help books, which make billions by packaging his tactics for
manipulation, minus the irony, as new and exciting keys to happiness.[6]

3

What makes the *Ars Amatoria* even more enticing is that it was, according to the poet, part of the reason he was exiled by the emperor Augustus.[7] The poem was allegedly said to encourage and teach adultery, an affront to Augustus's moral program, which sought to bolster marriage and procreation (especially among the upper classes) and imposed strict punishments for sexual misbehavior.[8] Yet as Ovid points out in *Tristia* (Sad Things) 2, the longest and most entertaining of his exile poems, *everything* is saturated with illicit sex: why single out the *Ars Amatoria*? His brilliantly mischievous reading of life and literature as one long erotic adventure (what is the *Aeneid* but Virgil sending his "Arms and the Man" into Dido's bedroom? etc. etc.) is so funny partly because, like all funny things, it is partially true. And his ostensibly craven supplication to the emperor—"I'm so very sorry, it was all my fault! I made the mistake of thinking you were an intelligent reader and a decent man with a sense of humor, not the irascible tyrant you obviously are"—is surely one of the cheekiest pseudoapologies ever penned.[9]

The present volume is the first to bring together the offense and the defense. I believe Ovid would have appreciated the ambiguity of those words: Is it OFFense, as in the aggression of a football team (or army or lover), or offENSE, as in the transgression that (allegedly) enraged the emperor? The double meaning captures Ovid's twin roles as the Professor of Love (in the *Ars* and *Remedia*) and the Suffering Artist who ran afoul of a tyrant (in the *Tristia*).[10] In this introduction, after a brief refresher course in classics for the modern reader ("Myth and Lit 101"), I sketch some of the ways our growing understanding of these roles increases our delight in the poems: the Professor's incompetence as a literary critic ("When the *Praeceptor* Reads"), his success (?) in permanently eroticizing the world ("Fifty Shades of Metaphor"), and the consequences of this eroticization for the Augustan program as the Suffering Artist argues from exile that he did nothing but point out what was already there ("The Illicit Sex Tour of Roman Topography and Religion").

The student of Latin literature soon comes to realize that some ambiguities can never be resolved—and some mysteries never solved. I noted above that the *Ars* was "part of" the reason for Ovid's exile; he mentions "a song [poem] and a mistake" (*carmen et error*, *Tr.* 2.207), and despite millennia of eager sleuthing and speculation, the mistake, if there was one, has yet to be definitively identified. The introduction's final section ("Ovid's Exile: Fact and Fiction") gives an overview of various theories, but the reader who hopes to learn from this volume the "real" reason for Ovid's exile will probably be disappointed. On the other hand, if you're looking for a wickedly witty poetic tour of the literature, mythology, topography, religion, politics, and (of course) sexuality of ancient Rome, you'll be 100 percent satisfied or your money back!

## Myth and Lit 101

Ovid's *praeceptor* treats seduction as a respectable science, with mythology and literature its respectable data. The principal researcher's blatant misuse and misinterpretation of that data completes the joke, and it gets funnier the more one knows about his background material. I have attempted in the present section to refresh the modern nonclassicist reader's knowledge of some of the major genres, authors, and characters in our extremely learned poet's universe. As the reader of *Tristia* 2 will discover, the list of authors and genres could go on nearly indefinitely; I have merely tried to hit the highlights here, with others footnoted in the appropriate places.

Unless otherwise noted, like Ovid, I refer to the gods and heroes by their Roman names (even though most of the stories about them are of Greek origin). Authors not designated Greek are Roman (writing in Latin). On common poetic meters, see "Meter" under "Some Notes on the Notes and the Translation."

### MAJOR GODS

In addition to having anthropomorphic appearances and personalities, many of these divinities also function as metonymies for objects or activities (for example, Bacchus = wine). Here is a bare-bones summary of their most important characteristics for understanding Ovid's poetry:

- (*Phoebus*) *Apollo* (same in Greek; Phoebus = Greek "shining"). God of the sun, healing, and poetry (and not bad with a bow and arrow). *Metonymy*: the sun.
- *Bacchus* (Greek *Dionysus*). God of wine, poetry, and ecstatic (sometimes violent) frenzy. *Metonymy*: wine.
- *Ceres* (Greek *Demeter*). Goddess of agriculture. *Metonymy*: grain.
- *Diana/Trivia/Luna* (Greek *Artemis/Hecate/Selene*). Complex goddess with triple function represented by her three names: hunting/the wilderness, the underworld/magic, and the moon (and she is also associated with childbirth). *Metonymy*: the moon.
- *Juno* (Greek *Hera*). Queen of the gods and goddess of marriage (ironically, given her husband Jupiter's lecherous proclivities). Persecutes heroes who are, or are associated with, Jupiter's bastard children. *Metonymy*: none (though she increasingly comes to be associated with Livia, Augustus's wife).
- *Jupiter/Jove* (Greek *Zeus*). King of the gods, the sky, and philanderers; drives his wife Juno insane with his constant infidelities. His thunderbolt represents absolute power. He also increasingly comes to be associated with Augustus. *Metonymy*: the sky/weather (also Augustus, especially in the exile poetry).
- *Mars* (Greek *Ares*). God of war (though Ovid likes to focus on his sex life). *Metonymy*: war.
- *Mercury* (Greek *Hermes*). God of commerce, boundaries, messages, and practical jokes. *Metonymy*: money.
- (*Pallas*) *Minerva* (Greek [*Pallas*] *Athena*). Goddess of weaving, wisdom, and war. *Metonymy*: weaving.
- *Neptune* (Greek *Poseidon*). God of the sea. *Metonymy*: the sea.
- *Pluto/Dis* (Greek *Hades*). God of death and the underworld. *Metonymy*: death.
- *Venus* (Greek *Aphrodite*). Goddess of love, beauty, and, especially, sex. *Metonymy*: sexuality/sexual attractiveness/sexual intercourse.
- *Vesta* (Greek *Hestia*). Goddess of the hearth. *Metonymy*: the hearth/fire.
- *Vulcan/Mulciber* (Greek *Hephaestus*). God of fire and technology; became crippled when Jupiter threw him out of Olympus for trying to protect his mother, Juno. *Metonymy*: fire.

MAJOR HEROES

In addition to the heroes highlighted in the four great epics discussed below—Achilles (*Iliad*), Ulysses (Greek Odysseus, *Odyssey*), Jason (*Argonautica*), and Aeneas (*Aeneid*)—two others recur frequently enough in Ovid's works to merit a billing here. Their individual deeds will be recounted as they occur.

*Hercules* (Greek *Heracles*). This son of Jupiter (who impregnated Alcmena by impersonating her husband Amphitryon) was the greatest of all Greek heroes. He was constantly persecuted by his jealous stepmother, Juno, who forced him to perform numerous labors. He died when his wife Deianira gave him a robe smeared with poison (thinking it was a love charm), but was made a god—one of the few mortals to achieve this distinction (Aeneas, Romulus, and Julius Caesar are others, according to Ovid's *Metamorphoses*).

*Theseus*. This son of Neptune, the greatest hero of Athens (some of his deeds bear a suspicious resemblance to those of Hercules), had a checkered history with women. After accepting the Cretan princess Ariadne's help to navigate the Labyrinth and slay the Minotaur, he abandoned her on an island; he also had a rather troubled marriage with Phaedra (see "Plot" under "*Hippolytus*").

MAJOR LITERARY WORKS AND AUTHORS

Epics

Long narrative hexameter poems telling mainly of wars and journeys.

*Iliad*, by Homer (Greek; Ilium is another name for Troy). But it's complicated. Modern scholars recognize this monumental epic—the beginning of Western literature—as the culmination of a centuries-old oral tradition. Some believe it was written down (or at least composed with the aid of writing) by a single author in the eighth century BC, around the time, not coincidentally, that Greek alphabetic writing came into being. Others see it as the work of many singers, ever changing and perhaps not even

written down in its more-or-less final form until the sixth century BC.
Ovid would simply have viewed it, along with the *Odyssey* (the second
great epic, with pervasive allusions to the *Iliad*), as the work *written* by
*Homer*.

- *Backstory*: In the infamous Judgment of Paris, that son of Priam (the king
  of Troy), tending flocks on Mount Ida (he had been exposed and left to
  die as an infant because of his mother's prophetic dream that he would
  destroy Troy, but shepherds found and raised him), was asked by the
  goddesses Juno, Minerva, and Venus to decide which of the three was
  most beautiful (an apple marked "for the fairest," from the goddess Dis-
  cord, was at stake). Juno attempted to bribe him with power, Minerva
  with wisdom, and Venus with the most beautiful woman in the world,
  who, of course, was Helen (already married to Menelaus of Sparta). In
  the immortal words of Elaine Fantham, "The ninny chose sex, which
  shows how very young he was." After Paris, visiting Menelaus's house,
  took Helen home to Troy with him, most of Greece (which had sworn to
  support whichever man Helen married) went to war against Troy, led by
  Menelaus's brother Agamemnon (see "Backstory" under "*Oresteia*").
- *Plot*: Chryses, a Trojan priest of Apollo, prays to that god to make the
  Greeks return his daughter Chryseis ("daughter of Chryses"), who is cur-
  rently Agamemnon's concubine. When Agamemnon refuses to return
  her to her father, Apollo sends a plague until he does; the Greek leader
  then makes the mistake of taking a replacement prize, Briseis ("daughter
  of Briseus"), from Achilles, the best Greek warrior. Achilles sulks for
  most of the epic and then makes a spectacular comeback after his best
  friend, Patroclus, is killed by Hector, the best Trojan warrior (and hus-
  band of Andromache; their love scenes are among the most moving in
  literature). Achilles goes on a rampage that culminates in his killing of
  Hector. Hector's father Priam comes to Achilles's camp to ransom Hec-
  tor's body, and the poem closes with Hector's burial.
- *Sequels*: The *Odyssey*, the *Oresteia*, the *Aeneid*, and a slew of lost poems.

*Odyssey*, by Homer (see "*Iliad*").

- *Backstory*: While Ulysses is away—fighting for ten years in the Trojan War (see "Plot" under "*Iliad*"), wandering for three, and sojourning for seven on the nymph Calypso's island—his wife Penelope has spent the past two decades fending off her suitors, who are feasting on Ulysses's estate. She's pretty sick of it.
- *Plot*: Ulysses finally leaves Calypso's island (thanks to Jupiter's intervention, via Mercury) and washes up in the quasi-paradisical land of the Phaeacians. There he relates his pre-Calypso adventures, such as blinding the Cyclops (which earned Neptune's wrath), staying with Circe (a witch who changed his men into animals; protected by a magical herb, Ulysses got her to change them back, then enjoyed sleeping with her for a year before finally leaving), and visiting the underworld. After he returns home to Ithaca disguised as a beggar (with Minerva's help), he gradually reveals himself to the people there, last of all to Penelope (once he has slaughtered all the suitors, with some help from his son and father). She tells the servants to move their marriage bed; he gets angry, because their marriage bed is (or should be) drilled into a tree that grew up in their bedroom. By this test, which proves that her cleverness matches his own, she knows he has come home at last. There's some mopping up afterward, but the real highlight is their first night in bed.

*Argonautica*, by Apollonius (Apollonius Rhodius, Greek, third century BC).

- *Backstory*: When their stepmother Ino plotted to sacrifice Phrixus and Helle (to save Boeotia from a famine, which she herself had engineered by secretly roasting all the seed corn), a golden ram (source of the Golden Fleece) was sent by their real mother Nephele, a cloud goddess, to carry the twins across the sea (though Helle fell off and gave her name to the Hellespont). They land in Aia (at the edge of the Black Sea; the region is also called "Colchis," or "[the land of the] Phasis," after its chief river), ruled by Aeëtes (son of Helios, the Sun); Phrixus sacrifices the ram.
- *Plot*: Sent by Pelias, king of Iolcus (in Thessaly), to retrieve the Fleece, Jason and his crew of heroes sail the Argo (supposedly the first ship) to

Aia, having several adventures along the way: dallying with Hypsipyle, queen of Lemnos; killing the Harpies plaguing the blind seer Phineus; getting through the Clashing Rocks; and losing Hercules when he went to look for his boy toy Hylas, who had been abducted by naiads (water nymphs). Aeëtes's daughter Medea falls in love with Jason and assists him in gaining the Fleece by using her magic to help him pass seemingly impossible tests (protecting him from fire-breathing bulls, putting to sleep the dragon guarding the Fleece). She leaves her family (and kills her brother, to slow down pursuit by her father) to marry him.

*Aeneid*, by Virgil (Publius Vergilius Maro, 70–19 BC), the Classic of Classics even before it was completed: as Propertius famously commented, "Step aside, Roman writers, step aside, Greeks! / Something greater than the *Iliad* is being born" (2.34.65–66).

- *Backstory*: The backstory comes mainly from the *Iliad*. A prophecy therein states that Aeneas and his descendants will survive the fall of Troy and continue ruling indefinitely (*Il.* 20.302–8).
- *Plot*: Aeneas, leader of the Trojans who survived the sack of Troy, gets blown off course to Carthage (thanks to his nemesis Juno) as he is attempting to follow prophecies and find his new home in Italy. There the queen Dido falls madly in love with him (thanks partly to manipulations by several gods) as he tells about the fall of Troy (including the story of the Trojan Horse full of Greek soldiers, source of the saying "beware of Greeks bearing gifts") and his wanderings. During a hunting expedition, they end up in a cave together and consummate a weird "marriage" arranged by Juno and Venus. When one of Dido's former suitors blows the whistle on their relationship, Jupiter sends Mercury to tell Aeneas to leave Carthage, which he does. Dido, betrayed and bereft, kills herself with the sword Aeneas had given her as a gift. (And then he visits the underworld and wins a war in Italy and stuff—but the Dido episode is what really matters.)
- *Sequel*: The Roman Empire. As the founder of the city (Lavinium) whose residents founded the city (Alba Longa) whose residents founded Rome, Aeneas is considered the protofounder of Rome.

## Tragedies

Dramas, in a variety of meters, usually about doomed love and dysfunctional families whose members sleep with and/or murder one another (often because of Fate or manipulation by gods). Of the numerous surviving tragedies, the poems in this volume allude most frequently to the ones below.

*Oresteia* (comprising three plays: *Agamemnon*, *Libation Bearers*, and *Eumenides*), by Aeschylus (Greek, ca. 525–455 BC). Sophocles also wrote an *Electra*, Euripides an *Electra* and an *Orestes*.

- *Backstory*: Agamemnon, king of Mycene (in the northeastern Peloponnese), sacrificed his daughter Iphigeneia to gain favorable winds to sail to Troy (see "Backstory" under "*Iliad*"). After the Greeks won the Trojan War, he returned home with Priam's daughter Cassandra, a priestess of Apollo (who, after she rebuffed him, cursed her with always giving true prophecies that would not be believed). Also, Aerope, the wife of Atreus (king of Argos and father of Agamemnon and Menelaus), had an affair with his brother Thyestes and helped him usurp Atreus's kingdom by treachery; when Atreus found out, he killed Thyestes's children (Aegisthus alone survived) and served them to him in a stew. The sun turned back in horror.
- *Plot*: Agamemnon's wife Clytemnestra (Tyndareus's daughter, like Helen) is having an affair with Aegisthus; she kills Agamemnon and Cassandra upon their return from Troy. To avenge their father, Clytemnestra's son Orestes and daughter Electra kill her. Orestes is driven crazy by the Furies (goddesses of vengeance), but eventually regains his sanity when pardoned by Minerva at Athens (after a trial by jury). The Furies (Greek *Erinyes*) become Eumenides ("Kindly Ones") who will safeguard fertility and justice.

*Ajax*, by Sophocles (Greek, ca. 496–406 BC).

- *Backstory*: After the death of Achilles, the Greeks gave his armor to Ulysses as prize for the best (remaining) hero, choosing Ulysses's cunning and verbal dexterity over Ajax's stalwart strength. Enraged, Ajax attempted to slaughter the Greek commanders, but was deflected from this atrocity by Minerva, who created a delusion that caused him to slaughter sheep and cattle instead (thinking they were Greeks).

- *Plot*: When he returns to sanity, Ajax is so horrified and ashamed that he resolves to commit suicide. After some rather nasty speeches to his wife, Tecmessa, he leads her to believe that he will get over it, but in fact goes off and kills himself. Tecmessa's grief is nearly unbearable. The Greeks debate what to do with his body and ultimately grant him burial.

*Hippolytus*, by Euripides (Greek, ca. 480–406 BC).

- *Plot*: Theseus's son Hippolytus insists on worshipping the huntress goddess Diana, scorning Venus, who is not pleased. His stepmother, Phaedra, falls in love with him (through Venus's machinations), attempts to seduce him, and accuses him of molesting her when he refuses her advances. Cursed by his father, Hippolytus dies when his chariot horses get spooked by a sea monster (sent by Neptune, Theseus's father) and drag him to death.

*Medea*, by Euripides.

- *Backstory*: See "*Argonautica.*"
- *Plot*: When Jason abandons Medea to marry Creusa, princess of Corinth, for political reasons, Medea kills their two sons (along with Creusa and her father) in revenge, then escapes to Athens in a chariot drawn by winged serpents. She is the ancient paradigm for the fury of a woman scorned.

## Didactic poems

Longish poems, usually in hexameters, purporting to teach a particular subject (farming, poisonous snakes, philosophy, etc.).

*Works and Days*, by Hesiod (Greek, eighth or seventh century BC). This work on farming, addressed to the poet's good-for-nothing brother, includes much homespun wisdom and several mythological digressions.

Hesiod's other surviving work, *Theogony* (Births of the Gods), is an extended family tree and compendium of Greek mythology.

*De Rerum Natura* (On the Nature of Things/the Universe), by Lucretius (Titus Lucretius Carus, ca. 94–55 BC). This six-book poem explains the atomic theory underlying the philosophical school of Epicureanism, which posited that the gods don't care what humans do and the soul is mortal, so no need to worry about punishment after death. Ovid likes to emphasize his own "scientific" credentials by peppering his work with Lucretian language and mannerisms.

*Georgics* (Working the Land), by Virgil (see *"Aeneid"*). Four books roughly cover field cultivation, viticulture and trees, livestock, and bees (with a long digression on Orpheus and Eurydice in book 4). While ostensibly teaching farming, this work really ponders the great questions of human existence, including the terrible dangers of erotic love. Much of the agricultural imagery in the *Ars* has a mock-serious Virgilian flavor. Virgil's first work, the *Eclogues* (Selections), sometimes called the *Bucolics* (Cowherd Things), sings of life and love among shepherds (and cowherds) in a pastoral setting.

Elegies

Poems of varying length in elegiac couplets. Originally associated with funeral laments, most surviving elegies are first-person accounts of love affairs. The "canon" of Roman elegy, according to Ovid, goes (1) Gallus, (2) Tibullus, (3) Propertius, (4) Ovid.

*Gallus* (Gaius Cornelius Gallus, ca. 70–26 BC), considered the founder of Latin love elegy, though only a few of his lines survive. He was unique among major Latin poets in that he also held high military and political offices: after a victorious generalship in the Alexandrian War (the tail end of the civil war between Augustus and Mark Antony), he was made the first prefect of Egypt in 30 BC. He did or said something to offend Augustus—possibly erecting a statue to himself or otherwise boasting about his accomplishments—and was condemned by the senate in 27/26

BC, which led to his suicide in that year. As a poet punished by the emperor, he was an important model for Ovid.

*Tibullus* (Albius Tibullus, ca. 50–19 BC), author of two surviving books of elegies. His primary love objects are Delia, the boy Marathus, and the menacing woman Nemesis.

*Propertius* (Sextus Propertius, ca. 50–15 BC), author of four surviving books of elegies. His most famous poems are about his mistress Cynthia (the first word of Elegy 1.1, and hence the title of his collection), though later ones veer into other topics involving Roman history, topography, and religion.

*Ovid, Amores* (see under "Ovid's Works").

## Ovid's Works

For completeness, I include here all of the surviving works of Ovid (Publius Ovidius Naso, 43 BC–AD 17), including those written after the ones in this volume.[11] His most important lost work is his tragedy, *Medea* (ca. 12 BC); we also have 100 lines of his *Medicamina Faciei Femineae* (Concoctions for the Female Face), a work on cosmetics that prefigures some of the themes of the *Ars Amatoria*.

The dates are often uncertain, partly because "publication" was a less definitive process in the ancient world. Typically, a poet would recite early drafts at dinner parties and give more polished versions to a few friends (who would perhaps have copies made), but still continue to revise (especially when circumstances changed: many of Ovid's later poems appear to have been revised from exile). The book could be considered "published" at the point when enough friends of friends had made copies that the original author did not know personally all the possessors of his work.[12] A poetry "book" would be anywhere from about 500 to 1,500 lines (most falling in the 700–1,000 range), approximately the length that would fit on a single scroll. Apart from the *Metamorphoses* (which is in hexameters), all of Ovid's surviving works are in elegiac couplets.

*Heroides* (Heroines). The chronology is complicated; the first set—consisting of "single *Heroides*" (1–15)—was written around 20–13 BC, and the second set—consisting of "double *Heroides*" (16–21)—around the time of Ovid's exile in AD 8. (The Ovidian authorship of several of these has been disputed, most of all no. 15, the letter from Sappho, which does not appear in the manuscripts containing the others.) The single *Heroides* purport to be letters from famous abandoned women to their absent lovers; the double *Heroides* are letters with responses (Paris–Helen, Leander–Hero, and Acontius–Cydippe). All of them play off literary models (for instance, no. 1, from Penelope to Ulysses, alludes to Homer's *Odyssey*; no. 4, from Phaedra to Hippolytus, alludes to Euripides's *Hippolytus*, etc.).

*Amores* (Loves/Love Affairs). The chronology is complicated; most likely there were some recitations in the 20s BC followed by the first published edition in 16 BC and the second edition (five books pared down to three) in 8–3 BC. These short first-person poems follow the ups and downs of a lover's progress into and out of love (especially with a fictional woman named Corinna) while simultaneously depicting a poet's progress into and out of love elegy (though does either one ever really graduate?).

*Ars Amatoria* (The Art of Love/The Amatory Art) and *Remedia Amoris* (Remedies for Love). *Ars* 1–2 (to men, on how to catch and keep a girl) was probably published in 2 BC; *Ars* 3 (to women, on how to catch and keep a man) and *Remedia* (on how to unlearn to love) in AD 2.

*Metamorphoses*. The chronology again is somewhat complicated; the poem was probably composed in AD 3–7 and published in AD 8, but also tweaked during Ovid's exile. This sprawling fifteen-book narrative traces human (and divine) history from the origin of the world to the poet's own day, loosely organized around the theme of "metamorphosis," or change of form (such as from human to tree or animal). Though epic in form (that is, a long hexameter narrative), it makes forays into all the generic categories outlined above and then some.

*Fasti* (Calendar; *fasti* literally means "days on which it is right [*fas*] to conduct business"). Composition dates are probably similar to those for the *Metamorphoses*. Though Ovid claims to have written one book for each month of the year (*Tr.* 2.549), only the first six months (January–June) survive, and it is questionable whether he wrote or even intended to write any others (there are many closural elements at the end of book 6). The poem goes through the Roman calendar year, exploring the origins of constellations and religious festivals.

*Tristia* (Sad Things). This five-book collection of letters, prayers, and occasional poems, probably published in AD 9–12, tracks Ovid's exilic journey and settlement in Tomis. *Tristia* 2 is unique in having a named recipient (Augustus) and in taking up an entire book with one long letter; the other four books consist of a series of shorter elegies (like those in the *Amores*) mainly addressed to anonymous friends.

*Ibis* (The bird "Ibis," title of a lost poem by Callimachus cursing a pseudonymous enemy under that name; also Latin for "you will go"). This one-book poem, probably written along with the *Tristia*, is an elaborate and extremely erudite curse addressed to an unnamed enemy; it alludes to just about every bad thing that has happened to anyone throughout history, literature, and mythology.

*Epistulae ex Ponto* (Letters from the Black Sea). This sequel to the *Tristia* was probably written in AD 13 (books 1–3) and 14–16 (book 4). Ovid abandons the commitment to anonymity and addresses these letters to friends back in Rome, begging them to plead with the emperor for his return. By now, the poet has settled into the Tomitan community, learning the languages of the hirsute natives well enough to compose a poetic encomium of Augustus in Getic. (If you believe that, then Ovid has done his work well.)

## Other Important Authors

Remember that "Myth and Lit 101" is just an intro course! Here are a few more authors who should not be left out, with apologies to the many who have been.[13]

*Plato* (Greek, ca. 429–347 BC), the philosopher whose account of his master Socrates's dialogues formed the basis for the Western philosophical tradition. His *Phaedrus*, which has Socrates's defense of passionless sexual pursuit followed by a palinode (a song taking something back) praising passionate love, resembles the *Ars–Remedia* trajectory in reverse. His *Symposium* presents a "ladder" of ascending forms of love culminating in contemplation of The Good; the *praeceptor* depicts a somewhat similar progression, except it culminates in A Good Time.[14]

*Callimachus* (Greek, ca. 310–240 BC) supposedly wrote over eight hundred books, including epigrams, hymns to various gods, and the *Aitia* (Causes, about the origins of various Greek cults, festivals, and cities). He was associated with the court of Alexandria (a city in Egypt founded by Alexander the Great), capital of the kingdom whose Ptolemaic dynasty was fathered by Alexander's friend Ptolemy I and culminated in the famous Cleopatra (VII). He is the poster boy for "Alexandrian" poetry, the name given to the slender, allusive, learned style much admired by Augustan poets like Ovid.[15]

*Cicero* (Marcus Tullius Cicero, 106–43 BC), the most famous of all orators (and after he allegedly retired from politics, not a bad philosopher). Ovid was trained in rhetoric, and his strategies of verbal persuasion have many affinities with Cicero's.[16]

*Catullus* (Gaius Valerius Catullus, ca. 84–54 BC), author of epigrams (short, punchy poems in elegiac couplets), protoelegies, a mini-epic, and lyric love poems (lyric poems, originally sung to the lyre, are generally short, often personal poems in a variety of meters). His most famous poems are those about his affair with Lesbia (a pseudonym for Clodia Metelli ["wife of Metellus"], an aristocratic woman ten years his senior).[17] He is an important precursor of love elegy and a pioneer of Alexandrian poetry in Latin (see "Callimachus").[18]

*Horace* (Quintus Horatius Flaccus, 65–8 BC), author of the *Satires* (Latin *Sermones*, "Conversations" on a variety of subjects), *Epodes* (primarily a mixture of humorous and serious invectives), *Odes* (lyric poems on topics such as love, wine, gods, and death), *Epistles* (verse letters to friends, including one to Augustus [2.1] that is a model for *Tristia* 2[19]), and an *Ars Poetica* (Art of Poetry) that in some ways prefigures Ovid's *Ars Amatoria*.[20] The freedman's son who penetrated Augustus's inner circle and became the poet laureate of Rome, Horace is the model for the kind of success and social status Ovid wishes for, especially in exile—and yet even in the fairly exhaustive list of authors in *Tristia* 2 he is never named.

### When the *Praeceptor* Reads

With the possible exception of Chaucer, it would be difficult to find a more skilled presenter of the art of misreading than Ovid. Such is one of the overarching jokes of the *Ars–Remedia* sequence: the narrator's claim that Love is entirely subject to Art—and hence can be deliberately learned and deliberately "cured"—is undermined by the narrative itself, as well as by the process of constructing it. What he does on a grand scale he also does in miniature. I give here some samples of three things that can happen when the *praeceptor* reads: telling a story that negates its own point, treating "his" previous experience in the *Amores* as a textbook case, and deriving ludicrously inappropriate and bathetic conclusions from mythological *exempla*.

Misreadings provide the punch lines to several of the historical and mythological digressions. The first such set piece, on the Rape of the Sabine Women by Romulus and his crew to bring females to Rome (the founder had neglected that important component), illustrates this phenomenon. The scene functions as an "anti-exemplum," an illustration of the precise opposite of the techniques the poem seeks to inculcate.[21] The Romans had invited their female neighbors to a primitive theatrical show, a crude setup completely lacking in "art" (1.106, 113). Then Romulus's warriors brutally grab the women like predatory animals (117–18). The moral the *praeceptor* derives?

> Romulus, you alone knew how to give soldiers benefits.
>     Give me benefits like that and I'll join the army!

With that precedent, naturally, theatrical shows
   remain a snare for beautiful girls even now. (1.131–34)

Like the other mythological digressions in *Ars* 1, as Alison Sharrock (2006:27) observes, the episode is a "romanticization of force"—hardly the artful seduction that was advertised at the poem's beginning.

Next, the *praeceptor* employs cheap wordplay to segue into the "benefits" (*commoda*) of going to chariot races. The ensuing scene showcases another of Ovid's favorite techniques: turning apparently spontaneous episodes from his own amatory past into normative scenarios.[22] In *Amores* 3.2, a lover's flirtation with a girl at a race takes the form of a passionate monologue addressed to the girl herself: "I've come not to watch the horses (I don't care about those) but to speak with you, to sit by you, to show you the love you inspire in me," et cetera. In *Ars* 1.135–62, every move that that lover made, from flicking an absent speck of dust off the girl's bosom to lifting her robe from the dirty ground so he can peek at her calves, is presented as part of a formula generalizable to all pupils. A. S. Hollis calls the *Ars* passage "a great disappointment" and "a pallid reworking of the brilliant and delightful *Amores* iii.2."[23] This reaction demonstrates that Ovid has accomplished, brilliantly, precisely what he set out to do: to point out both the artificiality of seduction and the absurdity of treating it as a teachable discipline.[24]

The *praeceptor*'s readings of tragedy and epic are even more egregiously boneheaded.[25] For instance, after a catalog of the tragic horrors caused by disordered and thwarted love—including Medea's murder of her children, Clytemnestra's murder of her husband, and Hippolytus's dismemberment through his father's curse—the *praeceptor* interprets this as promising evidence for the strength of the female libido:

So, go on, don't be shy about hoping for girls, all of them!
   There'll barely be one out of many to tell you "No." (1.343–44)

What makes this so funny, of course, is the mixture of truth and lie: the truth that sexual attraction is a prime mover of human behavior, combined with the lie that this force can be wholly controlled and manipulated by a skillful practitioner.

When it comes to full-blown mythological digressions, the longer and more elaborate they are, the more incongruous the *praeceptor*'s reductive conclusions become. The story of Daedalus and Icarus is a case in point (2.21–98). Sharrock devotes over a hundred pages to her analysis of this complex and moving passage, which she sees as, among other things, "a reflection on poetic fame, the artistic process, stylistic levels, and Callimachean artistry."[26] Even apart from the rich intertextuality and metapoetic subtext,[27] readers are seduced by images of the suffering artist struggling to break free from the Labyrinth (itself an incredibly rich and psychologically suggestive symbol),[28] of the pair testing their wings and leaving the earth behind, of the boy discarding safety for a few moments of supreme glory,[29] of the father grieving helplessly, the waters covering all but his son's name. . . . And the *praeceptor*'s takeaway?

> Minos had no power to imprison the wings of a man:
>> *I'm* trying to detain a winged god! (2.97–98)

Like Icarus, we go from soaring sublimity to a sudden cold plunge.

The final mythological digression in the *Ars*, the story of Cephalus and Procris (3.685–746), is a virtuoso display of misreading on every level,[30] as well as a parable about the deadliness of love (and love poetry) and the salvific power of art. But wait, why should I provide here a pallid reworking of my own article on the subject (Hejduk 2011a)? Better to close this section with the *praeceptor*'s teaser, sound advice for anyone subjected to a seducer's—or a poet's—flattering charms: "Don't be too quick to believe" (3.685).

### FIFTY SHADES OF METAPHOR

> How come I know where your face picked up that radiant glow?
>> Keep your door shut! Why publish a rough draft?
>>> *Ars* 3.327–28

This advice to women about the necessity of applying their makeup in private is one of the reasons for the present book. I felt that the last sentence—Latin *quid rude prodis opus*, literally "Why do you bring forth an unfinished work"—simply *had* to be translated "Why publish a rough draft," and it was worth doing the rest of the poem just so I could get that one in.[31] But the idea expressed also encapsulates a crucial theme that animates all of Ovid's work: the analogy between the human body and a work of art, especially the poet's own. One could spin out dozens of examples (and a voluminous bibliography):[32] a "body" of work, the "feet" of a poetic meter, characterization of unpolished verses as "shaggy" and polished ones as "combed." Everything that Ovid says about personal "grooming," *cultus*, flirts with his *ars poetica*. The basic premise of his erotodidactic works is that sexual beings must apply art to their appearance and behavior in order to please, just as a poet must apply art to his poem.[33] Yet paradoxically, the goal of art—whether applied to humans or to actual artwork—is to appear artless: "If it stays hidden, art works" (2.313); "it's through concealment that art makes beauty" (3.210); or, my personal favorite, "gain faith in your genuineness through lots of art" (1.612). The very concept of an *Ars Amatoria*, an Art of Love, rests on the assumption that spontaneous, heartfelt emotion takes meticulous polishing.

Ovid also delights in bringing in metaphors and analogies for amatory pursuit from multiple realms of human endeavor and the natural world.[34] By using many of the same metaphors for his own poetic process—such as the chariot race of poetic composition shading into the chariot race of sexual conquest and consummation—he reinforces the overlap between love and art. Latin *opus*, "work," applies to both an artistic composition and sexual intercourse;[35] near the end of book 2, lover (730) and poet (733) both complete their "work," and Ovid, in praising his own poetic accomplishment, designates himself the champion *amator*, "lover" (738).[36] War also has a way of invading and complicating other metaphors, especially those of hunting and sports: Cupid's arrows could be seen as those of a hunter or a warrior, the *praeceptor* figures himself as the driver of a chariot on both the battlefield and the racetrack, and horses could be used for war, farming, or chariot racing.

In this translation, I have tried my best to preserve these metaphors. To give an idea of their relative prevalence, to avoid clogging the footnotes, and to satisfy my own and (I hope) the reader's curiosity, I present here a list of the principal metaphors Ovid employs in the *Ars*, in descending order of frequency (with [ ] around those used for poetic composition), by book and line number(s).

WAR[37]

1. Love's bow, torches, and wounds: 1.21–23
2. lover as fresh recruit: 1.36
3. Venus quartered in her son's city: 1.60
4. squadron of women: 1.66
5. Romulus gives signal to grab "prize" (could also be hunting metaphor): 1.114
6. "prize" again: 1.125
7. spectator hit by Cupid's arrow (could also be hunting): 1.169–70
8. Trojan Horse: 1.363–64
9. "under my leadership": 1.382
10. Troy captured: 1.478
11. love is a military exercise: 2.233–38
12. jealous woman rushes to fire and the sword: 2.379
13. Venus wages just war: 2.397
14. when she seems your determined foe, go after the pact of sex: 2.461–62
15. love's arrows poisoned: 2.520
16. man besieging girl's door: 2.526
17. endure a rival and you'll be victor in Jupiter's Citadel: 2.539–40
18. shame flees in defeat: 2.556
19. I've supplied arms as Vulcan did for Achilles; Amazons, spoils: 2.741–44
20. I've given arms to Greeks, now time to arm the Amazons: 3.1–6
21. women can't shake off flames or bows: 3.29–30
22. Venus complains that unarmed women handed over to armed men: 3.46
23. Troy should have followed Priam's instructions: 3.439–40
24. law permits bearing arms against armed men: 3.492
25. Cupid ditches blunt weapons for sharp arrows: 3.515–16

26. good leaders station their men well: 3.527–28

27. lover as new recruit and "prize": 3.559–60

28. veteran soldier vs. new recruit: 3.565–66

29. I've opened the gate to the enemy: 3.577

30. time to put away blunt swords: 3.589–90

31. I'm meeting the enemy with chest exposed: 3.667–68

32. inscribe my name on the spoils: 3.812

FARMING/PLANTS/DOMESTIC ANIMALS[38]

1. bull gets accustomed to plow, horses to bridles: 1.19–20

2. Rome's girls more plentiful than crops of Gargara, grapes of Methymna: 1.57

3. theater fertile place for your desires: 1.90

4. women heading to theater like ants and bees: 1.93–96

5. neighbor's grass greener, his cows have fatter udders: 1.349–50

6. crops most luxuriant in fertile ground: 1.360

7. Ceres shouldn't always be entrusted to treacherous fields: 1.401

8. barren field tricks its master by seeming about to produce: 1.450

9. bulls come around to the plow, horses to reins: 1.471–72

10. different grounds bear different things: 1.757–58

11. bull submits to plow: 2.184

12. sow something to reap with full sickle: 2.322

13. bulls and saplings get bigger: 2.341–42

14. let field lie fallow: 2.351–52

15. fields don't always return investment: 2.513

16. grafted sapling gains strength: 2.649–53

17. smell of leather no longer offensive: 2.655–56

18. older woman a field bearing crops, younger a field needing to be sown: 2.667–68

19. new vs. old wine: 2.695–96

20. young plane tree not shady, new meadow hard on feet: 2.697–98

21. flowers wither: 3.67–68

22. pluck the flower before it withers: 3.79–80

23. through childbearing, field wears out through harvests: 3.82

24. wine and crops helped by grooming: 3.101–2
25. hair falls like leaves: 3.162
26. baldness = sheep minus horns, field minus grass, shrubs minus foliage: 3.249–50
27. enclose the crop with a high fence: 3.562
28. older man's love burns slowly like damp straw, green wood: 3.573–74
29. older man's love more fertile, pluck the fruit on its way out: 3.575–76
30. Procris pales like fruit: 3.703–6

SAILING[39]

1. [art moves ships, Ovid the helmsman of Love]: 1.3–8
2. don't have to give your sails to the wind looking for a girl: 1.51
3. maid should help out sails with oars: 1.368
4. don't let the sails go limp: 1.373
5. keels shouldn't always be entrusted to sea: 1.402
6. bad time for sailing if it's her birthday or other gift-demanding day: 1.409–12
7. let a letter test the waters: 1.437
8. [let my anchor be cast here]: 1.772
9. your boat's in the middle of the sea, the harbor I seek is far off: 2.9–10
10. don't use shore wind when on open sea: 2.337–38
11. ships don't always use the same wind: 2.429–32
12. breeze doesn't always help ships: 2.514
13. in bed, don't spread your sails too big . . . : 2.725
14. . . . unless there's time pressure, then use all your sails and oars: 2.731–2
15. [I'm not writing about great women: need smaller sails for my skiff]: 3.26
16. [after that argument, I'm about to encounter a gale]: 3.99–100
17. beautiful don't need to worry; sailor takes greater care during storms: 3.259–60
18. let a letter test the waters: 3.469
19. [spread my sails to the greater task of character]: 3.500

20. favoring winds make a boat sink: 3.584
21. [my weary keel trying to make it to harbor]: 3.748

HUNTING (BY HUMANS AND DOGS)[40]

1. hunter knows where to look for deer and boars: 1.45–46
2. do your hunting in the theater: 1.89
3. (see under "war"): 1.114, 125, 169–70
4. female gatherings ripe for hunting—but hunter becomes hunted: 1.253–58
5. where to place your nets: 1.264
6. need to lay your trap: 1.270
7. boar escapes from net: 1.392
8. women should fall into their own traps: 1.646
9. seasoned doe spots a trap: 1.766
10. prey has fallen into my trap: 2.2
11. woman scorned like boar flinging off hounds: 2.373–74
12. traps, nets, and tracking: 2.593–96
13. hounds wander in vain, stag falls into net: 3.427–28
14. new lover resists if he sees the net: 3.554
15. lover falling into net: 3.591
16. your rabbit will be hunted by others: 3.662
17. doe doesn't teach dogs to run: 3.670

CHARIOT RACING/DRIVING

1. [art drives chariots, Ovid the charioteer of Love]: 1.4–8
2. [this is the course my chariot will mark]: 1.39–40
3. lover's reins still loose: 1.41
4. [Muse borne on unequal wheels]: 1.263
5. steeds like to be patted: 1.629–30
6. [my chariot should hug the post]: 2.426
7. lover should change course: 2.428
8. charioteers sometimes pull reins in: 2.433–34
9. in bed, don't let her pass you in the race: 2.726–28
10. in bed, give free rein: 2.730

11. [Muse, don't be hurled out by whirling wheels]: 3.467–68

12. different bridles for young and old horses: 3.555–56

13. race horse needs rival: 3.595–96

14. [time to get off swan-drawn chariot]: 3.809–10

RELIGION[41]

   1. prophet shooing away respectable women from his mysteries: 1.29–32

   2. Bacchus summoning his prophet: 1.525

   3. more prophetic shooing: 1.607–8

   4. girl came to you with me as prophet: 2.11

   5. more prophetic shooing: 2.151

   6. woman like Bacchant: 2.380

   7. sex like rites of Ceres, Samothrace: 2.601–2

   8. Venus's rites: 2.607

   9. celebrate me as prophet: 2.739

   10. to deceive, approach my rites: 3.616

NATURAL PHENOMENA

   1. wrath melts like ice: 1.374

   2. rocks hollowed out by water: 1.475–76

   3. bank eaten by water: 1.620

   4. compliance swims rivers: 2.181

   5. river gets bigger by picking up waters: 2.343–44

   6. adding sulfur makes weak fire blaze: 2.439–42

   7. time like flowing water: 3.62–64

   8. iron and flint get worn down, but torches and sea inexhaustible: 3.91–94

GAMES/GAMBLING

   1. seducing the maid is a roll of the dice: 1.376

   2. gambler keeps raising the stakes so he won't have lost: 1.451–52

   3. pleasant games: 1.594

   4. in bed, use words to fit the game: 2.724

5. pleasant games: 3.328

6. Venus has a thousand games: 3.787

7. in bed, naughty words in the middle of the game: 3.796

8. [end of my game]: 3.809

THEATER[42]

1. women come to spectate and to be spectacles: 1.99

2. play the supporting role: 1.584

3. you've got to play the lover: 1.611

4. play the role she commands: 2.198

5. let her play the part of the one in control: 2.294

6. play scared, act out a comedy: 3.604–8

FISHING

1. fishermen know which waters have many fish: 1.47–48

2. Rome has as many girls as the sea has fish: 1.58

3. grasp a wounded fish firmly when taking it from hook: 1.393

4. different fish caught by different nets and hooks: 1.763–64

5. keep your hook dangling: 3.425–26

BIRD-CATCHING

1. bird-catchers know the right hedges: 1.47

2. Rome has as many girls as there are birds in the leaves: 1.58

3. Cupid's wings get soggy and stuck with wine: 1.233–35

4. don't let bird go free once its wings are limed: 1.391

5. bird doesn't show bird-catcher best place: 3.669

HUNTING (BY WILD ANIMALS)

1. Sabine women like doves fleeing eagles, lambs fleeing wolves: 1.117–18

2. Menelaus handing Helen to Paris like dove to hawk, sheep to wolf: 2.363–64

3. teaching women like giving poison to vipers, sheep to she-wolf: 3.7–8

4. she-wolf heads for many sheep, Jupiter's eagle for many birds: 3.419–
   20

ANIMALS

1. women like dangerous animals when scorned: 2.373–76
2. doves made up their quarrel and are now nuzzling: 2.465–66
3. animals mating: 2.481–88
4. serpents shed their skin, stags shed their horns and grow new ones:
   3.77–78

DISEASE/MEDICINE

1. like girls, doctors are precise about times: 1.357
2. give her a short time to nurse her wound: 2.455
3. need strong medicines for a wrathful woman: 2.489–92
4. do no harm: 3.52

If nothing else, this quasi-exhaustive list sets up one of the big punch lines in the *Remedia*. Subtracting out from "sailing" the metaphors pertaining to poetic composition rather than sexual conquest shows the three most frequent metaphors for the lover's pursuit to be war, farming, and hunting. So when the Love Doctor wants to recommend some activities to distract his patient from his ailment, what does he choose? You guessed it: war, farming, and hunting—with a side order of bird-catching and fishing. Through his art, he has so thoroughly eroticized the world that there is, in fact, no possibility of escape from the dominion of Love. The *Remedia* has rightly been seen as alluding to works of the Alexandrian poet Nicander of Colophon (writing ca. 130 BC), the *Theriaka* (Poisonous Animals) and *Alexipharmaka* (Antidotes), which catalog poisonous plants and animals and then describe antidotes and cures. Yet as Gianpero Rosati points out, there is a crucial difference between these "cure poems" and Ovid's: "In the case of Ovid, the author himself is responsible for the poisons. Through his teaching he provoked the very illness of his readers whom he now addresses as therapist and saviour" (2006:148).

## THE ILLICIT SEX TOUR OF
## ROMAN TOPOGRAPHY AND RELIGION

If Ovid's overriding joke is the eroticization of everything, part of what makes it funny is that everything is already eroticized. Augustus boasted that he "found Rome a city of brick and left it a city of marble";[43] his construction or refurbishing of monuments, temples, and other public buildings was an important aspect of his political program.[44] By turning all of these locales into potential pick-up spots, Ovid imposes a humorous veneer of sexuality—but he also points out the sexuality already latent in them.[45] In the exile poetry, he archly turns the pansexuality of Roman topography and religion brought out by the *Ars* into an argument in his defense.

Take the problem posed by Jupiter, for instance. The increasing concentration of power into the hands of one man led to a natural analogy between the Father of Gods and Men (Jupiter) and the Father of the Country (Augustus). What began as a tentative, implicit analogy in the earlier Augustan poets becomes almost an equation in Ovid, who refers quite openly to the edict sending him into exile as the thunderbolt of Jupiter.[46] But Ovid also uses Jupiter as a chief role model for adulterers, which obviously creates some tension with Augustus's War on Adultery. The poet's warning about women visiting Jupiter's temple—especially with its sneaky adjective "august"[47]—makes this tension clear:

> What place is more august than temples? She should avoid
>    these too, unless she's ingeniously plotting her sin.
> She's standing in Jupiter's temple: in Jupiter's temple, it will
>    occur to her how many women that god made mothers!
> Going to worship at Juno's temple next door, she'll be thinking
>    how that goddess fumed about her copious rivals. (*Tr.* 2.287–92)

Such passages make it hard not to see subversive hints in Ovid's ostensible flattery of the emperor, and his wife Livia, as the manifestations of Jupiter and Juno on earth.[48] They also remind us that religious monuments are subject to the same vagaries of "reader response" as written texts—that attempts to control morality through the manipulation of images will inevitably run up against both the unpredictability and the intractability of human desire and imagination.[49]

Or consider Ovid's mischievous fun with the temples of Mars Ultor ("The Avenger," commemorating Augustus's vengeance on the killers of his adopted father, Julius Caesar), in the Forum of Augustus, and Venus Genetrix ("The Mother"), in the adjacent Forum of Julius Caesar. Both deities played important roles in the mythical genealogy of Augustus's family, Mars as the father of Romulus and Venus as the mother of Aeneas.[50] Yet the aspect of Mars and Venus that Ovid consistently brings up is their adulterous affair—not to mention the illicit sex with mortals that gave rise to Rome's founders.[51] He reduces the carefully planned temples to the dynamics of an adultery mime, with Mars the clever lover and Vulcan (whose temple stood at some distance) the cuckolded husband:[52]

> She's come into the temple of great Mars, your gift:
>     the Avenger's coupled with Venus, her man's outside! (*Tr.* 2.295–96)

The poet can't be held responsible for planting dirty ideas in anyone's mind, since the message conveyed by the monuments themselves is there for all to see! On one level, this brings to mind the rejoinder of the man criticized for perceiving obscenities in every Rorschach inkblot: "You're the one who keeps showing me these dirty pictures!" Yet on another level, some might argue that it reveals a deep truth about the sexual aggression lurking within Augustus's architectural performance of Roman power.[53]

### OVID'S EXILE: FACT AND FICTION

Evidently, so long as the secret exists, the fascination [Ovid's exile] exerts will continue to encourage scholars to combine the available facts of history with the amorphous and cryptic allusions of Ovid to form a coherent answer to the enigma.

John C. Thibault, *The Mystery of Ovid's Exile*

Fifty years ago, John Thibault made a heroic effort to assemble all the available evidence for the reason(s) behind Ovid's exile—and as the quotation above indicates, no compelling solution to the enigma emerged.[54] Aside from the poet's own words, we have almost no evidence that the exile even happened, and none at all about its cause. Nevertheless, I shall attempt in this section to give a brief overview of Ovidian Exile Studies in the early twenty-first century: the reasons, the reality, and the rewards.

## THE REASONS

Some of the relevant facts are (we think) these. First, what Ovid tells us: (1) the reasons are "a poem" (*carmen*), which he elsewhere clearly indicates is the *Ars Amatoria*, and "a mistake" (*error*); (2) the "mistake" was nothing criminal, but involved "seeing" something; (3) people knew what the "mistake" was, but Ovid refuses to name it in his poetry; (4) after a private meeting with him, Augustus banished the poet to Tomis, a small town on the Black Sea (Latin *Pontus*),[55] without trial or decree of the senate; (5) his exile was technically a *relegatio* (banishment), which involved leaving Rome but without loss of property or citizenship; (6) the *Ars Amatoria* was removed from the three public libraries in Rome, but not burned (which would require a decree of the senate). From other sources, we know that Augustus banished his granddaughter Julia the Younger (call her "J2") for adultery at or around the time Ovid was banished (AD 8); he had banished his daughter, Julia the Elder (call her "J1," J2's mother),[56] for adultery about ten years earlier (2 BC)—around the time *Ars* 1–2 was published (*Ars* 3 and *Remedia* were probably published about four years later). This tantalizing scenario has given rise to any number of speculations about the "mistake," theories that could be characterized loosely as political intrigue, sexual scandal, and "other."

The most vigorous and eloquent modern proponent of the "political intrigue" theory is Peter Green.[57] Augustus's unusual longevity meant that he outlived almost all of his desired heirs;[58] the question of who would be his successor, either after his natural death or through the expediting of that process, did in fact give rise to various plots and machinations, according to the ancient historians. Green starts from the assumption that what Ovid says about the reasons for his exile is basically true (an assumption I shall examine below), then searches for a solution that fits the "clues" (1982b:212–13):

We are looking, to recapitulate, for an indiscretion that took place in high society, was unpremeditated but part of a complex and dangerous situation, was not *per se* indictable yet could have brought Ovid a death sentence (not, perhaps, quite so paradoxical a claim as might at first sight appear to be the case), brought Ovid no profit, and in fact consisted simply of his having witnessed—perhaps without full understanding at the time—an offense committed by others. In particular he stresses the fact that he had taken no treasonable action against Augustus, that he was innocent of murder or forgery. Had he reported the incident he might have remained a free man, but he was afraid to do so. He was also, he admits, naïve and gullible. Further, his error wounded Augustus deeply and was, indeed, a direct offense against him.

He situates Ovid's mistake amid the "deadly factional struggle" between the "Julians" (Scribonia, Julia, and their descendants/adherents) and the "Claudians" (Livia, Tiberius, and their descendants/adherents); he sees the sexual promiscuity of the two Julias, and the alleged immorality of the *Ars Amatoria*, as a smokescreen. He speculates that Ovid "saw" or otherwise had knowledge of a Julian coup against Augustus, and that by refusing to name names when interrogated the poet incurred the emperor's lasting displeasure.

But the "sexual scandal" theory has an equally vigorous advocate in George Goold. Goold demolishes the idea that Ovid was in possession of some secret threatening to Augustus: "Certainly, to banish the most articulate of living Romans to a place beyond instant control and from which he could, and did, send a spate of missives to Rome was no way to keep his mouth shut" (1983:96). He sensibly argues that the two charges against Ovid were probably related: "If, possessing absolute power, you are minded to inflict summary punishment on a man who has mortally offended you, it hardly makes sense to charge him, for example, with (*a*) running away with your wife and (*b*) poisoning your cat ten years earlier" (103). He suggests that the "mistake" most likely involved Ovid's abetting J2's adultery in some way, such as offering his house for her affair. J2's lover, Junius Silanus, got off relatively light; he went into voluntary exile, but was allowed to return when Tiberius became emperor in AD 14. Ovid was not so lucky: "Augustus's special animosity against Ovid is adequately explained by the latter's immoral verse and the pander's role he played, and it may well have been kept alive by his perpetual whining, whereas Silanus, for all his adultery, had the sense to accept exile and keep quiet" (106). We should also note that adultery by the emperor's direct female descendants did more than set a bad moral example: to a man obsessed with ensuring the succession of his own bloodline, J2's affair—negating the legitimacy of her children, who otherwise could have been her grandfather's successors—had serious political consequences. If Ovid had in some way colluded in this affair, then the *carmen* that teaches adultery (and yes, let us be honest, that is what it does) and the *error* of encouraging a politically charged adultery would dovetail quite nicely.

Yet somehow the idea of the fifty-year-old Ovid, whose life was poetry, being a major player in either a political intrigue or a sexual scandal among the super-elite just does not quite fit. We must also take seriously the argument of Peter Knox (2004) that the motivating force behind Ovid's exile was not Augustus, but his stepson Tiberius. Augustus displayed both taste—witness his patronage of "Augustan poets" like Horace and Virgil—and tolerance: when Tiberius reported to him a slander by one Aemilius Aelianus, Augustus responded, "[Don't] take it too much to heart if anyone speaks ill of me; let us be satisfied if no one can *do* ill to us."[59] Tiberius, it seems, had neither. Not a single major poet flourished during his reign, and he famously killed or forced suicide on many writers whom he perceived as critical of him. Knox argues that, in the last decade of Augustus's reign (he died in AD 14 at the age of 77), Tiberius's influence was increasingly felt; this could explain why the punishment for the *Ars* occurred so long after its initial publication. Most tellingly for our purposes, in AD 8, a historian named Titus Labienus, who had praised the younger Cato (the paradigmatic defender of the Republic against Julius Caesar during the civil war that brought Caesar to power in 49–46 BC), was forced to commit suicide; in the same year, an orator named Cassius Severus, who admired Labienus and was known for his sardonic wit, was exiled for libel of Augustus. Ironically, the *Ars* may well have been a key factor in Ovid's punishment, but not for the reasons usually supposed: the poet would have run afoul of Tiberius with his lavish praise of Gaius as the emperor's heir apparent (*Ars* 1.177–228). In that hostile climate, any blunder could have precipitated the punishment.[60]

## THE REALITY

Amid all this speculation, we should be clear about one thing: Ovid makes nothing clear, if by "makes clear" we mean that his words have any necessary connection to objective truth. The goal of rhetoric is to persuade, not to inform. Ovid's rhetorical training would have included, among others, these time-honored strategies: (1) package lies in as much truth as possible, (2) engage sympathy with a moving story, (3) divert attention with an entertaining display, and (4) use sex.[61] One of Ovid's most successful ploys is to argue that the *Ars Amatoria* should not be singled out for censure, since *all* of life and literature is saturated with sex—a topic he has no trouble expounding on for hundreds of lines. Scholars have taken him at his word about the "poem and mistake" because they have nothing else to go on, and because they assume that he "could not have dared to publish [certain things] if they were untrue."[62] But elegiac poets, and Ovid especially, dare to publish all sorts of things about "their" lives and loves that are of dubious veracity, to say the least; the personae and situations they create suit the demands of a good story, not those of an accurate autobiography. What if Ovid's goal was not, in fact, to secure his recall, but to capitalize on his exile as an opportunity to pioneer a new and exciting poetic genre, one starring himself as a martyr and hero surpassing all others?[63]

What is also clear is that, in many demonstrable respects, his account of his exile is pure fiction.[64] Even a superficial reading suggests this: for instance, his long, elegant poem describing the violent storm pitching the ship he's on (*Tristia* 1.2) is self-refuting.[65] The "Scythian" landscape is a frozen wasteland where wine must be served in chunks; the enemy arrows sticking out of the roof have turned his house into a sort of hedgehog; when he finally learned the native tongue and composed a long encomium of Augustus in Getic (!), the hirsute natives (who resemble bears more than humans) came to the poetry reading with quivers full of poisoned arrows; and so on. In fact, Tomis has (and had) a climate fairly similar to that of Central Italy, and in Ovid's day the Greek culture there was thriving.[66] When the poet Catullus served in a governor's retinue not far from there, his complaint was of insufficient opportunities to extort money from the natives, not of skin-clad barbarian hordes with poisoned arrows threatening him day and night. The fact that Ovid's copious letters survive at all indicates that the mail service was decent, and his protestations of failing powers are so artfully executed (as has been increasingly recognized in recent years) that he must have had plenty of leisure to refine them. Ovid may have been "exiled" from New York City, but it was hardly to Siberia.

In addition to the obvious hyperbole and literary construction of his poetry, suspicions are raised by the near absence of references to Ovid's exile in the ancient historical record. Tacitus (ca. AD 56–118), a historian cynically alert to the harsh exercise of power by Augustus and other emperors, could be expected to make at least a passing reference to the exile of Rome's leading poet, but he does not; Suetonius, whose life of Augustus refers openly to the emperor's exile of members of his own family, is similarly silent about Ovid. Writing several decades after Ovid's death, the court poet Statius (AD 48–96) in a wedding song says that on such an occasion "Ovid wouldn't have been sad [*tristis*, playing on his title *Tristia*] even in Tomis" (*Silvae* [Material] 1.2.254–55); but this would be equally applicable whether Ovid's setting were factual or fictional.

The other ancient reference to Ovid's time in Tomis, however, indicates that one of the greatest scholars of the ancient world believed that Ovid did indeed live his final days there. The immensely learned natural historian Pliny the Elder (AD 23–79), who was born just six years after Ovid's death, refers to the eleven species of fish named in a poem he believed to be by Ovid, "On Fishing" (*Halieutica*): "We'll add to these [species previously named] the animals mentioned by Ovid, which are found in no one else, but perhaps are native to the Black Sea, where he began that work in his final days: the sea-ox, [etc.]" (*Natural History*

32.152). Most modern scholars agree that the *Halieutica* was not by
Ovid,[67] but that is irrelevant here.[68] Pliny clearly believed that Ovid died
in Tomis, and though many of the natural phenomena he describes may
seem incredible or ridiculous to us, the man was no fool. The "argument
from silence" cuts both ways; to my mind, it beggars belief that, if one of
Rome's greatest poets had truly written his decade-worth of "exile poetry"
from his armchair in the City or an Italian villa somewhere, not a single
ancient source would have remarked on that fact.[69]

On the other hand, when Ovid insists that his "mistake" involved
inadvertently "seeing" something, I think we should take this with more
than a grain of salt. He compares himself to Actaeon, a hunter who acci-
dentally came upon the goddess Diana bathing in a woodland pool and
was punished by being turned into a deer and massacred by his own dogs:

> Why did I see that—something? Why did I make my eyes guilty?
>     Why was that fault made known to me, all unawares?
> Actaeon didn't mean to see Diana naked;
>     that didn't make him a prey for his dogs any less.
> Yes, among the gods even Fortune must be atoned for;
>     wounded divinity shows no mercy to Chance. (*Tr.* 2.103–8)

The reason I am inclined to think Ovid is fibbing here is this: *no one
can justly be punished for inadvertently seeing something.*[70] Ovid spells this
out in the Actaeon episode in the *Metamorphoses* (a poem at least tweaked
from exile) in a way that sounds just like his own self-justification in the
exile poetry: "If you investigate carefully, you'll find a reproach to For-
tune in him, not a crime [*scelus*]; for what crime was there in a mistake
[*error*]?" (*Met.* 3.141–42). It follows either that Ovid was *unjustly* pun-
ished (which he would have us believe), or that his punishment did *not*
arise from him just seeing something. If what Ovid "saw" were dangerous
or embarrassing information that needed to be kept under wraps, then
he would have been killed or forced to commit suicide, not sent, pen in
hand, somewhere beyond the emperor's control. But suppose, instead,
that Ovid wanted to engage our sympathy and divert our attention.

What better way could he have chosen than to identify himself with Actaeon, punished by a cruel divinity for an involuntary mistake? In one stroke, he turns himself into the paradigm of an innocent sufferer and us readers into sleuths and voyeurs (WHAT DID HE SEE???).[71] By cloaking the reason for his exile in tantalizing mystery, he tempts us irresistibly to search for clues—and his very insistence on the need for secrecy testifies implicitly to the authoritarianism and injustice of the Augustan regime.[72]

Many arguments asserting Ovid's truthfulness tend to fall apart when we recognize that his "plea for recall" is actually a thinly veiled act of defiance. Thibault remarks that "Ovid estimated the delicacy of his situation well enough to employ a politic and psychologically sound appeal, through slavish protestations of his guilt, to the mercy of the despot who had personally condemned him" (1964:2). This very formulation in fact reveals that Ovid's strategy is the opposite of "politic and psychologically sound": instead, he has succeeded magnificently in casting Augustus as a capricious despot whose subjects must grovel slavishly, even when their "offenses" really are benign (as anyone with a sense of humor, proportion, and literary acumen could easily see!). By constantly harping on how he must remain silent about his "mistake" so as not to cause Augustus pain, Ovid aggravates the wound—a variation on the rhetorical device of *praeteritio* (passing by), through which one underscores something by saying one won't mention it.[73]

The hypothesis that Ovid's aim was to needle the emperor rather than to mollify him, and at the same time to exonerate and exalt himself, helps to make sense of many puzzling facts. Most obviously, it would explain why the exile poetry, for all its ostensible flattery of that most wise and beneficent prince, consistently makes Ovid look as good and Augustus as bad as possible.[74] *Tristia* 2 alone states or implies that (1) Augustus did not in fact read the poems (and so his condemnation is completely unfair); (2) if he had read them, he would have realized that they are meant to be playful and are actually no more offensive than anything else (as anyone with literary knowledge and taste would recognize); (3) Ovid has strong support and popularity among educated people (so the only ones turning against him are doing so to kowtow to a tyrant); (4) Ovid himself and his house have always been blameless and virtuous (unlike a certain adultery-ridden family); and (5) he alone is being punished as an old man for a peccadillo of his youth (a blatant act of caprice and inclemency).[75] In teaching Augustus both how literature should be read and how a ruler should behave, *Tristia* 2 is, in many ways, as didactic as the "real" didactic poems in this volume, with all that that implies about the power dynamics of teacher and student.[76] This does not exactly constitute contrition. The hybrid apology, "I'm sorry if I offended you" ("What I did was trivial and you're a loser for blowing it out of proportion"), is effective approximately zero percent of the time. I have to think that Ovid—and Augustus, one of the shrewdest politicians in history—was smart enough to realize this.

THE REWARDS

Whatever the truth behind Ovid's exile may be, his poetry adopts it seamlessly into a coherent and compelling narrative of his life.[77] Though the *Remedia* was probably published in AD 2, six years before Ovid's exile, its rhetoric seems uncannily prescient:

> For recently certain people have criticized my books;
> according to their strict standard, my Muse is a slut.
> But as long as I'm this charming, and sung all over the world,
> the one or two who want to can pick at my work! (*Rem.* 361–64)

> Envy strikes peaks: winds blow through the highest points;
> thunderbolts sent by Jupiter's hand strike peaks. (*Rem.* 369–70)

> If my Muse is appropriate for frivolous material,
> I've won my case—she's being tried on false charges.
> Devouring Envy, eat your heart out! I've got a great name now—
> and greater, if its feet just keep the same path. (*Rem.* 387–90)

Jupiter's thunderbolt happens to be Ovid's primary metaphor for the edict sending him into exile. Sergio Casali suggests that "Ovid wrote the

*Ars*, and then he devoted the rest of his poetic career, starting from the sequel itself of the *Ars*, the *Remedia*, . . . to constructing that poem as a poem that excited Augustus' anger" (2006:220). The epic struggles of the elegiac hero[78]—himself—offer limitless opportunities for the play of wit and shuffling of genres that contribute to his unique charm.[79] The inefficacy of the *Remedia* proved that the *Ars* had worked too well; similarly, the exile poetry shows the poet's repeated attempts to employ the *Remedia*'s strategies for "unlearning to love" his mistress Rome, all in vain.[80] As in his hilariously lugubrious poem on his own sexual impotence (*Amores* 3.7), Ovid succeeds through failure.[81]

Perhaps most importantly, the isolation and loneliness he describes connect him to the lived experience not merely of actual exiles, but (at some times, anyway) of every thinking person. Surrounded by Latin-less barbarians, he has "unlearned how to speak"; his response is to pour out volumes of poetry, to cling ever more desperately to the Muses who got him into this mess and with whom he has a love-hate relationship as tempestuous as the most passionate elegiac affair.[82] His exile poetry, as Gareth Williams notes, "is without parallel in classical Roman literature as a meditation on the state of exile itself" (2002a:338). The exile's poverty opens up a treasure trove of ironic possibilities: the paradoxes of speechless eloquence, of isolation that unites him with all fellow sufferers, of a body chained to a wasteland while the mind soars beyond the limits of the known world. I have argued that the Jesuit priest and Christian poet Gerard Manley Hopkins, enduring near the end of his life a spiritual "exile" in Ireland from his native England, found Ovid's late works a source of inspiration and solace in the darkness of his own "winter world" (Hejduk 2010). I believe both poets recognized that exile, fundamentally, is not an accident of geography, but a characteristic of the human condition.

As Aristotle famously remarked, "Poetry is something both more philosophical and more serious than history, for while history deals with the particular, poetry deals with the universal."[83] Exile gives Ovid's poetry a universal appeal even more compelling than that of his already universal theme of love. Jo-Marie Claassen expresses beautifully the importance of this timeless reach, to which the facts of the case are largely irrelevant:

Whether he was exiled (and why) or not is as immaterial to his poetic purpose as it should be to our purpose as readers of his poetry. What Ovid's poetry of exile conveys, the anguish of loss and the alienation felt by all exiles everywhere and in every era, is even more relevant in the twentieth century with its *final solutions*, its *ethnic cleansings*, its *total onslaughts* and its aeronautical mobility than ever it was in an era of ships and swords and the emperor's displeasure. (1994:110)

If Ovid's purpose was to persuade Augustus to let him return, then, obviously, he failed. But if his purpose was to persuade his readers that he was the innocent victim of a despot, a poetic genius whose alienation led to a triumph of art and the human spirit, then he succeeded. His exile poetry combines the allure of a mystery (what *was* that "mistake"?) with the excitement of an epic (how will the suffering hero overcome the wrathful god's persecution?) with the poignancy of a love story (will boy Ovid ever be reunited with girl Rome?), animated by a sly wit and verbal dexterity unequalled before or since. His courtship may not have won the emperor, but it did win everyone else.

## NOTES

1. So vast is the scholarship on Ovid that I can give only a taste of it in this introduction. For those who want to delve deeper, Watson 2002 (on *Ars* and *Remedia*), Gibson 2009 (on *Ars*), Boyd 2009 (on *Remedia*), and Claassen 2009 (on *Tristia*) provide useful overviews and bibliographies. Gibson et al. 2006 (and especially its introductory essay, Green 2006) is a must-read for anyone interested in the *Ars* and *Remedia*. For detailed commentaries on individual books, see "Sources" under "Some Notes on the Notes and the Translation." On the reception of Ovid—after Virgil, probably the most influential of all Latin poets (sorry, Horace!)—the essays in Knox 2009 (McNelis 2009, Fyler 2009, James 2009, Braden 2009, Ziolkowski 2009, and Martin 2009) and Ingleheart 2011 are a good starting place; see also the timeline in Lively 2006:338–40.

2. See on 1.17 "tutor of Love" for a fuller explanation of the term. The artificiality of the *praeceptor*'s persona has long been recognized as one of the poem's chief sources of humor (see, e.g., Durling 1958). Wright 1984:1 observes that "the poem is finally, we may conclude, as much about the narrator and his deceptions as it is about the lovers and their deceptions." On the *lena* (procuress) as alter ego of the *praeceptor* and other male elegiac narrators, see Myers 1996.

3. See Kennedy 2000:165–67 on the irony of love as a rational choice that can turn into an irresistible force when one "plays the lover" too well; Miller 1993:232 on the "increasing ironization of the teacher *qua* teacher"; and Myerowitz 1985:198n78 on passages that point up the "*praeceptor*'s failure at total artistic control." James 2008:138 points out that, in addition to the many obvious failings of the *praeceptor*, his "imaginary audiences . . . are not merely improbable but impossible." Although the occasional admission of fallibility can be an effective didactic strategy that enhances rather than diminishes the teacher's authority (Volk 2002:165), Watson 2007 argues persuasively that Ovid's *praeceptor* in general meets the many criteria for the stock comic character of the "bogus teacher," contesting Volk's claim that "both teacher and students of the *Ars amatoria* are unequivocally successful" (2002:186). Clearly, modern scholars are not entirely in agreement, and one of the reasons to read these poems is to decide for yourself.

4. The dates of composition and the relationship of *Ars* 3 and *Remedia* both to one another and to *Ars* 1–2 are controversial; see Murgia 1986a and 1986b; Anderson 1990; Gibson 2000 and 2003:37–43; Nickbakht 2005; Miller 2006 (and below, "Ovid's Works"). But whatever Ovid's original plan may have been, the poems as they stand form such a coherent narrative (in my opinion) that it makes sense to treat them as such. On the "failure" of the *Remedia*, see Davisson 1996; Brunelle 2000–2001; Sharrock 2002:160–61; Fulkerson 2004; Hardie 2006; Rosati 2006. On different treatments of "love as illness" by poets and philosophers, see Caston 2006.

5. Myerowitz 1985:25: "We may admire the tragic intensity of Virgil's Dido, the passionate abandon of Catullus, the wholeness of the elegists' exclusive devotion, but it is Ovid's lover with the voice of his mean-spirited *praeceptor*, like the voice in our head forever directing us to choose one role or another, that must remind us most of our own secret selves."

6. Downing 1990 argues that the *praeceptor*—especially in book 3, addressed to women (books 1 and 2 are addressed to men)—functions as a sort of "anti-Pygmalion," turning living women into lifeless works of art. His striking phrase "artefaction of the self" (238) occurs to me sometimes as I peruse magazine covers in the grocery store checkout line (e.g., "The Making of Kim Kardashian"). On the crafting of women to conform to male desires in the *Ars* and *Remedia*, see James 2003a; Gardner 2008; Merriam 2011.

7. Rosati 2006:157: "Ovid was well aware that prohibition sharpens desire (*quod licet, ingratum est; quod non licet, acrius urit*, 'what is allowed is unwelcome; what is forbidden burns more fiercely,' *Am.* 2.19.3); and he also knew that proclaiming oneself a victim of censorship is the most effective tool of self-promotion that an artist can possess (anticipating the advertising techniques of modern mass media)." In the exile poetry, Ovid tells us that the *Ars* was banned from Rome's public libraries.

8. In 18 BC, Augustus had enacted the "Julian Law about the orders (socioeco-nomic classes) marrying" (*lex Iulia de maritandis ordinibus*), which prescribed ages between which citizens were expected to marry, and the "Julian Law about restrain-ing adultery" (*lex Iulia de adulteriis coercendis*), which made adultery a criminal offense. The laws were, on the whole, unpopular and unsuccessful. See Treggiari 1991:277–98; Galinsky 1996:128–40; McGinn 1998. On the disingenuousness of Ovid's claims not to be undermining Augustus's moral reforms, see Davis 1995.

9. See Fulkerson 2012:339 on Ovid's presentation of "an extremely irrational Augustus, and a wholly victimized poet."

10. Discussing Ovid's reception in the Middle Ages, Dimmick 2002:264 observes, "It is in this powerfully ambivalent role of the *auctor* [author] at odds with *auctoritas* [authority], just as much as (and indeed inseparable from) his expertise on mythology and sexuality, that he is most precious to the poets." Ovid's persona in the exile poetry is sometimes referred to as the *relegatus* (banished man), though not so universally as the *praeceptor* in the erotodidactic ("teaching love") works, partly because the distinctness of the *relegatus* from "Ovid himself" is not quite so obvious. In addition to the Suffering Artist, the *relegatus* figures himself as a dead man, an *exclusus amator* (locked-out lover) of Rome, an epic hero persecuted by a wrathful god, and various other sorts of victim (see Nagle 1980:19–70 and Claassen 1999b on the "vocabulary of exile").

11. For a fuller chronology and a parallel list of important events in Roman history and literature, see the helpful table in Knox 2009:xvii–xviii.

12. On this complex process of "publication," see Starr 1987; Holzberg 2002:27–31.

13. I've provided just a bit of bibliography on these "extra" authors; the task of providing it for everyone above was too daunting for my meager powers.

14. See Lev Kenaan 2008. Dillon 1994 stresses the importance of the (to us) less famous *Alcibiades* in the formation of a "Platonist *Ars Amatoria*."

15. See Miller 1983; Sharrock 1994a, esp. 198–204, 253–56, and 294–95; Acosta-Hughes 2009.

16. On Ovid's debt to Cicero and forensic oratory in general, see Ingleheart 2010:12–21.

17. See Dyson 2007; Hejduk 2008; Skinner 2011.

18. See Miller 2007.

19. See Barchiesi 2001b; Ingleheart 2010:8–10.

20. See Toohey 1996:146–74.

21. For this interpretation and a nuanced discussion of the episode, see Labate 2006.

22. See Davis 2006:105–8 on the three passages (*Ars* 2.169–74, 2.545–54, and 3.659–66) in which the *praeceptor* specifically recalls "his" experiences in the *Amores*.

23. Hollis 1977:58. Wilkinson 1955:143 laments, "how could the author of the brilliant monologue at the races in *Amores* III, 2 bring himself to introduce a gar-bled summary in didactic form at *Ars* I, 135–62?" Otis 1970:18 characterizes the *Ars* as a "warmed-up and inferior version of the *Amores*."

24. Modern scholars tend to be more willing to give Ovid (the actual person) credit for knowing what he's doing. See Downing 1993:39: "The lifeless and mechanical is not *supposed* to be preferred to the natural and spontaneous, and if Ovid has instilled this attitude in his reader, then he has succeeded in the *Ars* pas-sage, that is, succeeded in showing the failure of the system even in its success"; Dalzell 1996:141: "The comedy in the *Ars* lies in the very lack of liveliness, in the banal, matter-of-fact way of dealing with something which the poet and the reader both know cannot be reduced to a formula"; Greene 1998:113: "In refusing to per-petuate the illusions and self-deceptions that he believed were so much a part of love and love poetry, Ovid's poems reflect a deep commitment to the moral responsibility of the poet to show the cruelty and inhumanity perpetrated in the name of culture, in the name of *amor*"; James 2003b:157: "Ovid does not add hypocrisy, exploitation, and pretense to Roman love elegy—he lays them bare." Ironic and allusive writers can be particularly prone to misreading, however: as Sharrock 2012:77 rightly notes, "Ovid's entanglement with the poetic tradition and exposure of its potential for shallowness forms part of his poetic-erotic pro-gram in the elegiac works—which is that you never quite know how to take it."

25. Watson 1983:120 observes how the brief mythological exempla in the *Ars* generally "fail to fulfill their ostensible, corroborative function, either because the myths themselves are not taken seriously, or because they are essentially inappro-priate to the context." On continuities between Ovid's amatory and exilic works in their (ab)use of mythological exempla, see Davisson 1993; on Ovid's use of myth in general, see Graf 2002.

26. Sharrock 1994a:87–195 (quotation from p. 128).

27. That is, references to other texts ("intertextuality") and coded discussion about the nature of poetry ("metapoetic subtext"). It would be impossible to give a full account of Ovidian intertextuality in the limited space of the present book, but those who wish for a taste of that kind of scholarship might take a look at Hinds 1998; Myers 1999:194–95 (for an overview); Kennedy 2006; Miller 2006; Casali 2009.

28. On resonances of the Cretan Labyrinth in everything from an ancient epic to a modern blockbuster, see Hejduk 2011b.

29. Anne Sexton's (1928–74) brilliant poem "To a Friend Whose Work Has Come to Triumph" is my favorite modern reflection on the myth of Icarus, espe-cially the ending:

> Feel the fire at his neck and see how casually
> he glances up and is caught, wondrously tunneling

into that hot eye. Who cares that he fell back to the sea?
See him acclaiming the sun and come plunging down
while his sensible daddy goes straight into town.

30. Bowditch 2005:283 notes that "Procris, inscribed as a reader within the poem, becomes emblematic of a reader's experience of subjectivity as effected by the actual process of reading."

31. An unsympathetic critic might object that the *rude opus* here refers more to visual than to verbal art. But since Ovid frequently uses visual art as a *mise en abyme* for his poetry—for instance, Arachne's tapestry (*Met.* 6.103–28) as a *Metamorphoses* in miniature—it's only fair that I should get to substitute a verbal image for a visual one. *Mise en abyme* (French for "placement in the abyss"), a trendy but useful term for "a work of art depicted within a larger work of art and reflecting on the 'framing' work," derives from the heraldic practice of depicting a coat-of-arms shield at the center of a larger shield (*abyme* is the technical term for a shield's center). French author André Gide (1869–1951) brought the term into use in literary theory.

32. For starters, see Helzle 1988; Keith 1994; Farrell 1999; Fear 2000; Hinds 2006.

33. As Solodow 1977:127 felicitously observes, "Venus is only nominally the subject of a poem that might instead of 'The Art of Love' be more fitly entitled 'The Love of Art.'"

34. On the totalizing impulse of love elegy, Conte 1989:445 remarks, "the greater the closure of the world represented, the greater the effort language must make to reduce to its model all that would remain excluded from it, recuperating and converting it any way it can." The *Ars* takes this "converting" process to its logical, if absurd, extreme.

35. See Kennedy 1993:58–63.

36. See Volk 2002:173–88 on "poetic" and "mimetic simultaneity," as the writing of the poem coincides with the progress of the lover's affair.

37. See Cahoon 1988; McKeown 1995; Gale 1997.

38. See Leach 1964.

39. See Murgatroyd 1995.

40. See Murgatroyd 1984; Green 1996.

41. See Ahern 1990.

42. Though no single author or work stands out as a clear model eligible for inclusion in "Myth and Lit 101," the conventions and stock characters of comedy have a tremendous influence on Roman elegy in general and the *Ars Amatoria* in particular. See McKeown 1979; Currie 1981; Fantham 1989; Ingleheart 2008; James 2012.

43. Suetonius (Gaius Suetonius Tranquillus, ca. AD 70–130), *Life of Divine Augustus* 28. Much of our knowledge of the Roman emperors comes from his biographies.

44. On the transformative ideological implications of Augustus's building program, see Zanker 1988; Galinsky 1996; Favro 1996; Pollini 2012. Boyle 2003 helpfully collects (with translation and commentary) all of Ovid's references to Roman monuments.

45. Welch 2012:103 insightfully detects a quasi-erotic "rivalry": "Indeed so frequent is mention of the monuments, in Propertius and Ovid at least, that one might call Rome the poet's true beloved, whose affections are also sought by the poet's supreme rival—the Princeps himself. At no other time in ancient Roman history was the city so lavishly wooed as it was during Augustus' reign." Welch 2005 provides an extended analysis of Propertius's elegiac appropriation of the Roman cityscape, an important model for Ovid. See also Armstrong 2005:115–39.

46. On Augustus as Jupiter, see Mader 1991:145–48, esp. n. 18.

47. On the simultaneously flattering and ironic implications of this pun on Augustus in the context of Jupiter's temple (one of the many religious monuments the emperor had restored), see Edwards 1996:24–25; Miller 2004:230–31.

48. On the delicate problem of Livia as Juno, who is generally portrayed as jealous and shrewish in Augustan literature, see Johnson 1997; Barchiesi 2006.

49. See Gibson 1999:37 on *Tristia* 2 as an elaborate demonstration that "it is not possible for Augustus to control interpretation."

50. On the importance of Venus and Mars in "The Mythical Foundations of the New Rome," see Zanker 1988:195–201.

51. See Miller 1997:386–87; Richlin 1992:156–58.

52. Sharrock 1994b:121–22 sees in Vulcan and Venus possible shades of Augustus and his daughter Julia: like Julia, Venus departs to an island after the discovery of her adultery (see the next section of this chapter).

53. See Kellum 1997.

54. Modern scholars have, alas, hardly fared better in settling anything definitively; see, e.g., Claassen 1994; Ezquerra 2010.

55. Tomis is "usually identified with Constanza, a Milesian Greek settlement on a small Pontic peninsula. Its hinterland is the Dobroudja, a flat stretch of coastal Romania bounded on the west and north by the coils of the Danube, and on the south-east by the Black Sea itself" (Claassen 1999a:29).

56. Before settling down with Livia, Augustus had a rather checkered history with women—not uncommon in a society where marriages were often determined by political convenience. Reading between the lines of Suetonius's straightforward summary of Augustus's "love life," we can imagine why adultery in such an environment would be common: "In his youth he was betrothed to the daughter of Publius Servilius Isauricus, but when he became reconciled with Antony after their first quarrel, and their troops begged that the rivals be further united by some tie of kinship, he took to wife Antony's stepdaughter Claudia [43 BC], daughter of Fulvia by Publius Clodius, although she was barely of marriageable age; but

because of a falling out with his mother-in-law Fulvia, he divorced her before they had begun to live together. Shortly after that he married Scribonia [40 BC], who had been wedded before to two ex-consuls, and was a mother by one of them. He divorced her also, 'unable to put up with her shrewish disposition,' as he himself writes, and at once took Livia Drusilla from her husband Tiberius Nero [38 BC], although she was with child [with Drusus, brother of Tiberius] at the time; and he loved and esteemed her to the end without a rival" (*Augustus* 62; translation by Rolfe 1914). His daughter Julia by Scribonia was his only biological child.

57. Green 1982b expands on the basic thesis of Sir Ronald Syme (from the chapter "The Error of Caesar Augustus" in Syme 1978), the great historian whose writings channel the acerbic spirit of the Roman historian Tacitus (ca. AD 56–118). A sample of Syme's reasoning and rhetoric: "Was it a matter of politics or of morals? The political aspect has been firmly discounted in some standard manuals. A false dichotomy. The two things are not easily dissevered, immoral conduct being normally alleged to disguise a political offence—or to aggravate it" (1978:219).

58. These included his sister's son Marcellus (d. 23 BC), his henchman and son-in-law Agrippa (d. 12 BC), and his daughter's sons Lucius (d. AD 2) and Gaius (d. AD 4). Agrippa Postumus, J2's brother, was banished to an island in AD 7, allegedly for his bad character.

59. Suetonius, *Augustus* 51.3.

60. During the reign of Tiberius himself, in AD 21, one Clutorius Priscus was killed for a "poem and mistake": he composed and recited a premature eulogy of Tiberius's mortally ill son Drusus, and when the boy (unfortunately, from Priscus's point of view) unexpectedly recovered, the senate voted and carried out the death penalty—not expressly with the emperor's consent, but anticipating his wishes (Knox 2004:11).

61. To readers of Cicero's *Pro Caelio* (Defense of Caelius), these strategies will seem eerily familiar (see Hejduk 2008 for a translation and bibliography). On rhetoric in Ovid's poetry, see Fantham 2009, esp. 42–44; on the formal rhetorical structure of *Tristia* 2, see Ingleheart 2010:15–21, an elaboration of Owen 1924:48–62.

62. Wilkinson 1955:734, quoted by Green 1982b:203.

63. On Ovid's exile poetry as an "invention without parallel," see Claassen 1999a:32–35.

64. On the "unreality" and literary aims of Ovid's exile poetry, see Fitton Brown 1985; Williams 1994:3–49. Rosenmeyer 1997:51 observes that "truth and fiction for Ovid function less as polar opposites and more as points on a continuum."

65. See Ingleheart 2006c on the literary and political implications of this extremely complex poem.

66. Habinek 1998:158: "One would never guess from Ovid's account that Tomis boasted a gymnasium and richly decorated civic buildings, that its epitaphs

give evidence of its inhabitants' familiarity with Euripides, Theocritus, and other Greek authors, or that it served as religious and civic center of the five Greek city-states in the immediate Danube delta."

67. See Knox 2009:212.

68. Many famous authors in antiquity had various spurious works attributed to them—a sort of reverse plagiarism in which a name brand was slapped on imitation goods.

69. There is also something in the argument of Holzberg 2002:26 that "if the theme of the poor banished poet had been a fiction, Ovid could hardly have held his readers' interest with it through nine books of verse containing a total of 6,726 lines."

70. Entertaining the possibility that Ovid may not be entirely truthful does unsettle the certainties of previous generations. Even if we cannot affirm the conclusions, we can still enjoy the rhetoric of passages such as Alexander 1958:321: "Can any one, on reflection, seriously question that Ovid saw, by an evil piece of luck, a goddess in the nude, a great lady, in all likelihood—in practical certainty, rather—a member of the imperial house (*O dea certe!*), and that the princess was, considering Ovid's political and social ties, the younger Julia? What else can justly be inferred from this passage? Who else upon whom Ovid unexpectedly and disastrously looked, could be rationally viewed as a goddess?" (Alexander appears not to have heeded the counsel of Avery 1936:100: "It has been seriously advanced that the poet had accidentally seen the empress Livia bathing. Anyone who can find in verse 105 of the poem, a verse in which Ovid compares his fate to that of Actaeon, any support for such a theory ought, for his own peace of mind, to close his Ovid and confine his reading henceforth to safer and more serious authors, such as Vitruvius or the *Auctor ad Herennium*.")

71. See Ingleheart 2006a and 2006b.

72. Hinds 2007. On Ovid's sly hints that people should read between the lines, see Casali 1997; Barchiesi 1997:15–44 and passim. On his fearful suppression of his friends' names in the *Tristia*, see Oliensis 1998.

73. On Ovid's extremely noisy "silence," see Forbis 1997.

74. Even Ovid's most lavish praise of the emperor can be seen to contain a barb and a challenge. As Mader 1991:149 points out, "Augustus is stylized as the kind of man whose continued animosity towards the exiled poet would be in contradiction to his own nature and publicly advertised persona." Nugent 1990 traces the growing scholarly recognition that *Tristia* 2, rather than being an unsuccessful attempt to secure the poet's recall, is actually a stunningly successful attempt to elevate himself and his art at the emperor's expense—a thesis also eloquently expounded by Johnson 2009:137–44. Green 2005:xxxix–xl gives a succinct list of Ovid's "snide hints" at Augustus's shortcomings, noting that the poet's "fury, contempt, and seething sense of injustice are unmistakable."

75. Such is a (partial) list of Augustus's shortcomings relating directly to Ovid; as Wiedemann 1975:217 notes, the poem also makes "embarrassing references to famine, wars, and unpopular legislation."

76. Davis 1999:802 observes that "Ovid's aim is not so much to flatter and cajole as to instruct and inform the emperor concerning the nature of literature and his own achievements"; Barchiesi 2001b:92 notes that Ovid figures Augustus as a "novice to be initiated into the reading of poets."

77. See Holzberg 2006:68 on the various ways Ovid "plays with the facts of his life and the facts of the background of his poetry."

78. See Claassen 2001:14 on Ovid's creation in the exile poetry of a coherent mythical world in which "Augustus takes the place accorded to the king of the gods in [Ovid's] other works."

79. On Ovid's complex and mischievous manipulation of genre and generic expectations throughout his works, see Harrison 2002; Farrell 2009. In his discussion of Ovid's affinity (but not identity) with satire, Brunelle 2005:154 remarks, "Generically speaking, Ovid is not a citizen of the world; he simply runs a lucrative import business."

80. See Fish 2004. O'Gorman 1997:120–21 discusses the parallel between the lover "unlearning to love" in the *Remedia* and the poet "unlearning to speak" in the exile poetry.

81. See Sharrock 1995; Hallett 2012.

82. See Hejduk 2009:57–58; Williams 2002b:241–42.

83. *Poetics* 9. Like the *praeceptor Amoris*, the great Greek philosopher who attempted to systematize all human knowledge was tutor to a headstrong boy bent on world domination (Alexander the Great, 356–323 BC).

# Ars Amatoria

BOOK I

If any man in this nation doesn't know the art of loving,
   he needs to read this song—read, learn, and love!
Art (and sails and oars) is what makes speedy ships move,
   art drives light chariots: art is the thing to steer Love.
Autómedon was handy with chariots and pliant reins,         5
   Tiphys was pilot of the Haemónian ship:
Venus has put me, the artist, in charge of tender Love;

2. **song:** Latin *carmen* (pl. *carmina*) can mean "song," "poem," or "magical incantation"; I have translated it throughout as "song," the only English word that will do for all of these meanings. (The Twelve Tables, Rome's first written law code [449 BC], declares that to sing or compose an evil *carmen* against someone is punishable by death.) The poet likes to contrast his own fail-safe, all-powerful *carmen* with the feckless *carmina* of (other?) enchanters.

3–4. **speedy ships . . . chariots:** The sea voyage and the chariot race are among Ovid's favorite metaphors for poetic composition (and also for sexual conquest), appearing especially at points where his poem is about to change course or enter dangerous waters. On these and other metaphors in the *Ars*, see "Fifty Shades of Metaphor" in the introduction.

5. **Automedon:** Charioteer of Achilles. On common mythological and literary references in Ovid's works, see "Myth and Lit 101" in the introduction.

6. **Haemonian ship:** The Argo. Haemonia = Thessaly (in northern Greece; Haemon was the father of Thessalus), birthplace of Jason.

7. **Love:** Cupid, son of Venus, was usually pictured by the Romans as a young man or an adolescent boy (not the cherubic toddler of Renaissance paintings and modern Valentines).

they'll call me "The Típhys and Autómedon of Love"!
He's wild, of course, and bound to keep rebelling against me;
    but still, he's a boy, a soft and steerable age.          10
Phíllyrus's son polished up the boy Achilles with a lyre,
    and crushed down his wild spirit with gentle art.
He who was the terror of his allies, the terror of his foes—
    they say he was scared to death of that old codger!
The hands that Hector was to feel—he offered them up     15
    for beatings, on demand, when his master asked!
A Chiron to that son of Aéacus, I am the tutor of Love:
    each a fierce boy, each the son of a goddess.
But, nevertheless, the bull's neck is weighted down with the plow,

8. **"The Típhys and Automedon of Love"**: By associating himself with two of the great Greek epics (the *Argonautica* and the *Iliad*), the poet marks himself as, if not a great epic hero, at least great epic support staff.

11. **Phíllyrus's son**: Chiron, the centaur (man above, horse below) who taught Achilles and other heroes.

14. **old codger**: Despite his equine nether half, Chiron is referred to with the word for a human "old man" (*senex*).

15. **hands that Hector was to feel**: In one of the *Iliad*'s most moving scenes, king Priam goes to Achilles to ransom Hector's body, declaring at the end of his speech, "I have done what no other mortal on earth has done: I have touched my lips to the hand of the man who slew my son" (*Il.* 25.505–6). With typical bathos, Ovid depicts the hands of man-slaying Achilles as those of a naughty schoolboy. Achilles's hands play several unheroic roles in the *Ars*: see 1.693–96 and 2.713–16.

17. **son of Aeacus**: Achilles, grandson of Aeacus (descendants are often referred to as "son" or "daughter") and son of the sea goddess Thetis.

17. **tutor of Love**: Latin *praeceptor Amoris*, the name modern scholars often give to the narrator of the *Ars*, whose views should not be equated with those of the man who actually held the pen! See "Why Read This Book (and This Introduction)?" and "When the *Praeceptor* Reads" in the introduction. Here "tutor of Love" ostensibly means "tutor of (the boy named) Love" (like "Johnny's tutor"), though the phrase can also mean "tutor of (the subject of) Love" (like "Math tutor").

and spirited horses grind bridles in their teeth.                    20
Love will yield to me, too, even if he wounds my heart
   with his bow, and shakes and tosses around his torches;
the more he pierces me, the more violently he burns me,
   the better avenger I'll be of the wound he's made.

## BOTH POET AND PROPHET

Phoebus, I won't pretend that you've endowed me with arts,          25
   nor is my source the voice of high-flying birds,
nor did Clio and Clio's sisters appear to me,
   Ascra, as I tended my flocks in your valleys.
Experience is what inspires this work! Obey the skilled prophet:
   I'll sing truths. Be present, Mother of Love, for my project!    30

24. **the wound he's made:** At the opening of Ovid's poetic oeuvre (*Amores* 1.1), the poet claims that, while he was attempting to sing a martial epic, Cupid stole a foot from his second line, thus turning the meter of epic (hexameters) into the meter of love poetry (elegiac couplets); see "Meter" under "Some Notes on the Notes and the Translation." When the poet complained, Cupid shot him with one of his infamous arrows. Though the *praeceptor* claims here to be avenging that wound, it will eventually become clear that Cupid in fact has the last laugh.

27–28. **Clio . . . valleys:** Hesiod, at the opening of his *Theogony*, claims that the Muses appeared to him at Ascra, a village in the valley of the Muses on Mount Helicon in Boeotia (in central Greece). Though Hesiod does not mention Clio (the Muse of history) specifically, Callimachus, in the original prologue to his *Aitia*, alludes to this Muse visitation scene and also makes Clio the first to answer the poet's question. Ovid is showing off his learned credentials by conflating these two models.

29. **Experience:** The poet's reliance on human skill (as opposed to divine inspiration, though he claims that too when it suits him) owes much to the tradition of scientific didactic poetry pioneered by Lucretius.

29. **prophet:** Latin *vates* literally means "prophet" or "divine mouthpiece," but in Ovid's day was often used to mean simply "bard" or "poet." He likes to activate its religious meaning in order to endow himself with (pseudo-) divine authority.

Get ye far hence, slender fillets, badges of modesty,
    and you, long hem, who reach halfway down the foot:
safe Venus is what I'll sing, and permissible affairs,
    and there will be nothing criminal in my song.

## The Three Tasks

First, your task is to figure out something you'd want to love,    35
    you fresh recruit just taking up your new arms;
the second task is to proposition a girl who excites you;
    the third, to make sure love lasts a good long time.

31–32. **Get ye . . . foot:** With a stock religious formula used to shoo away the profane from sacred rites, the "prophet" playfully banishes respectable married women, who wore the fillets (headbands) and long hems described, from his "mysteries." (Fillets and hems are metonymies for the women who wear them. Surely the *praeceptor* could have no other motivation for ordering women's clothes to go away!)

33. **safe Venus:** "Safe" here refers not to disease but to the complications arising from affairs with aristocratic women, whose fidelity was important because it ensured the legitimacy of their offspring (and thus the proper transmission of property). Such women were subject to strict punishments under Augustus's adultery legislation: see "Why Read This Book (and This Introduction)?" in the introduction. The *praeceptor* protests that his poem concerns the seduction only of lower classes of women, such as slaves, freedwomen (former slaves), and courtesans ("escorts" who frequented dinner parties and were often highly educated, but not of aristocratic Roman families). The issue of precisely whom he is instructing men how to seduce will be of great importance in his later defense of his poem.

36. **fresh recruit:** The idea of love as military service (*militia amoris*) is one of the dominant metaphors in Roman love elegy. Though related to the idea of the "battle of the sexes" (which Ovid also exploits frequently), it is not quite the same; the lover is a soldier in Venus's or Cupid's army, but his unspecified enemy is more the forces preventing him from winning the girl than the girl herself.

38. **the third:** The first and second tasks are the subject of the present book; the third (and most challenging) will be the subject of book 2.

This is the way; this is the course my chariot will mark;
    this is the goal my speeding wheel will head for.        40

## STEP ONE: FINDING THE GIRL

While you still can—your reins are loose, you can go where you want—
    pick out one you can tell, "You alone turn me on!"
She's not just going to drop in your lap out of thin air;
    you've got to use your eyes to pick out the right girl.
The hunter knows well the best place to put his nets for deer,    45
    knows well in what valley the gnashing boar hangs out;
bird-catchers know the right hedges; the one who dangles hooks
    knows which waters are swum by many a fish:
you, too, who are after material for a long love,
    figure out first which spot is thick with girls.    50
I won't be making you give your sails to the wind in your quest;
    you won't have to go very far to make your find.
So what if Pérseus filched Andrómeda from the black Indians,
    and the Greek girl was snatched by a Phrýgian man:
Rome will give you so many girls—and such beauties, too—    55

42. **"You alone turn me on!"**: Latin *tu mihi sola places*, an exact quotation of Propertius 2.7.19 (in a poem that elevates passion for Cynthia over marriage, politics, and war). Will the pick-up line be more effective, one wonders, if the girl recognizes the allusion or if she doesn't?

49. **material**: Latin *materia* has roughly the same range of meanings as our word "material," including the subject matter for poetic composition—one of many overlaps between the art of love and the art of poetry.

53. **Perseus . . . Indians**: Perseus, wearing the winged sandals of Mercury, rescued the Ethiopian princess Andromeda when she was chained to a rock and about to be devoured by a sea monster. Indian and Ethiopian are often used interchangeably in Latin poetry.

54. **Greek girl . . . Phrygian man**: Helen and Paris (Phrygian often = Trojan; Phrygia, a kingdom in modern Turkey, was one of Troy's main allies in the Trojan War). In holding up as a model the disastrous adultery of Paris and Helen (see 2.5–6, 359–72), a married noblewoman, the *praeceptor* tends to undermine his claim not to be offering instruction in unlawful affairs.

that you'll say, "Whatever the world has to offer, She's got!"
The crops that Gárgara's got, the grape clusters of Methýmna,
    the fish that lurk in the sea and birds in the leaves,
the stars in the sky—your Rome has got that many girls!
    Aenéas's mother is quartered in her son's city.                      60
If it's those first, still-ripening years that turn you on,
    a genuine girl will come before your eyes;
if it's twenty-somethings you hanker for, a thousand will tempt you:
    you'll be forced to throw up your hands about which to choose!
Or if by chance it's the older and wiser that appeal to you,            65
    believe me, the squadron of those will be even more packed!

## RECOMMENDED VENUES

You just go sauntering leisurely in Pompey's shade,
    when the sun's coming up to the back of Hercules's lion,
or where the mother has added games of her own to those
    of her son, a monument rich in foreign marble;                      70
and don't avoid the colonnade, studded with ancient paintings,
    that bears the name of Lívia, its author;
or where the daughters of Belus dared to murder their wretched

57. **Gargara:** A town at the foot of Mount Ida (near Troy), known for its rich harvests.

57. **Methymna:** A town on the island of Lesbos, known for its vintages.

60. **Aeneas's mother:** Venus (thanks to her affair with the Trojan mortal Anchises).

67. **Pompey's shade:** The colonnade of Pompey, often frequented by elegant women.

68. **sun's . . . Hercules's lion:** In July; the constellation Leo represented the Nemean lion, killed by Hercules.

69–70. **mother . . . marble:** The portico of Augustus's sister Octavia adjoined the Theater of Marcellus, her son.

72. **Livia:** Wife of Augustus; her magnificent colonnade was in the Subura, actually a rather crowded and seedy neighborhood of Rome.

73. **daughters of Belus:** The fifty granddaughters of Belus, daughters of Danaus (hence usually called the Danaids), married their cousins, the sons

cousins, and their fierce father stands with drawn sword;
and don't let Adónis, wept by Venus, pass you by,                    75
    and the seventh-day rites observed by the Syrian Jew;
and don't flee the Memphític temple of the linen-clad heifer
    (she turns many girls into what she herself was to Jove!).
Even the Fora (who could believe it?) are conducive to love,
    and flame often blazes up in the noisy Forum,                    80
where, placed beneath the temple of Venus, made of marble,
    Áppias strikes the air with her jets of water.
Often that's where the lawyer is entrapped by Love,
    and one who drafts safeguards for others lets his own guard down;
often that's where the glib orator is at a loss for words—           85
    he has to plead an unprecedented case *pro se*!
Venus has a good laugh at this man from her temple nearby:
    he was just a patron; now he wants to be a client!

---

of Aegyptus; Danaus ordered them to murder their bridegrooms on their
wedding night, and all but one (Hypermestra) did so. The portico of the
Danaids adjoined Augustus's magnificent temple of Palatine Apollo.
75. **Adonis:** Switching from places to occasions, the *praeceptor* refers to the
Adonia, the festival of Venus's lover Adonis (who was killed in a hunting
accident; she redeemed him from the dead for part of each year).
76. **seventh-day rites . . . Syrian Jew:** Romans were fascinated by the large
Jewish community living among them, and especially the Sabbath (though
they frequently misunderstood its purpose).
77. **Memphitic . . . heifer:** Io, a nymph who was raped by Jupiter, turned
into a cow, and ultimately transformed into the goddess Isis (Memphis is a
city in Egypt); her priests wore linen (they were, understandably, forbidden
to wear animal products).
81–82. **temple of Venus . . . water:** The temple of Venus Genetrix ("The
Mother") was near the fountain of the Appiades (water nymphs) in the
Forum Iulium ("Forum of Julius Caesar"), site of law courts.
88. **patron . . . client:** The patron/client relationship in Rome involved
intangibles like a patron's advocacy for the client in court in exchange for
political support; the simple transfer of money was frowned on. That a man

## THE THEATER

But be sure most of all to do your hunting in the curved theater;
    that's a place that's fertile beyond your dreams.                    90
There you'll find something to love, something to fool around with,
    something to touch once, and something you'll want to hold onto.
As the officious ant comes and goes throughout the long column,
    lugging with grain-bearing mouth its accustomed food,
or as bees, taking possession of their groves and fragrant            95
    meadows, flit through blossoms and blooming thyme,
so the most cultured women rush to the crowded shows;
    often the abundance has stymied my judgment.
They come to spectate, they come to be spectacles themselves;
    that place has occasioned the loss of chaste modesty.               100

## THE RAPE OF THE SABINE WOMEN

You, Rómulus, first made the games a scene of turmoil,
    when ravished Sabines cheered up wifeless men.
Back then, there were no curtains hanging in the marble theater,
    nor had the stage been reddened by liquid saffron;
there, whatever foliage the wooded Pálatine offered,                  105

---

would be a woman's "client" is a joke involving inverted gender and power
roles, but not a reference to prostitution.

89. **theater:** Theatrical performances and sporting events were held in Rome's
three permanent theaters, those of Pompey (55 BC), Balbus (13 BC), and
Marcellus (13 or 11 BC).

101–2. **Romulus . . . wifeless men:** When Romulus founded Rome (753 BC),
there were no women, so he invited the neighboring Sabines to a show and
then had his men abduct their women. Won over by their new husbands'
love (so the story goes), these women intervened in the ensuing war and
established peace between the two peoples.

104. **liquid saffron:** Pounded saffron, mixed with sweet wine, was sprayed on
the stage to produce a pleasant smell.

105. **Palatine:** One of the hills of Rome. For what would become of that
primitive woodland, see on 3.119 "Palatine . . . leaders."

simply arranged, became an artless backdrop;
the people took their seats on risers made of turf,
    with random foliage draping their shaggy locks.
Each one picks out and marks with his eyes the girl he wants
    for himself, and his silent heart harbors many thoughts;                    110
and while the Tuscan flautist provides crude accompaniment
    for the dancer thrice striking the leveled ground with his foot,
in the midst of the applause (the applause was artless back then)
    the king gives his people the signal to grab their prize.
At once they jump out, broadcasting what's on their mind with
        a shout,                                                                115
    and lay their greedy hands upon the maidens.
As doves, a very timid crowd, flee from eagles,
    and as the young lamb flees at the sight of wolves,

111. **Tuscan flautist:** Tuscan = from Etruria, a region in central Italy (of which the Tiber forms the eastern boundary); the Etruscans were said to have introduced dancing accompanied by the flute in 364/363 BC as a remedy for plague.
112. **thrice striking . . . with his foot:** This nonerotic method of dancing recalls the ritual dance of the Salii ("Leapers"), an ancient priesthood associated with Mars.
114. **prize:** Latin *praeda*, cognate with our "predator" and "prey," can mean "prey/quarry" or "war prize/booty." There are two distinct senses of English "prize," one of which comes from Latin *pretium*, "price/reward," the other from Latin *pre(he)ndo*, "seize"; only the latter (as in "war prize," something seized in war) is related to *praeda*. It is difficult to choose a single English word that conveys, as *praeda* does, something *either* sought *or* attained in *either* hunting *or* war ("prey" and "prize" come closest, but the translator's choice between them is difficult).
116. **lay their . . . hands:** Latin *manus iniciunt*, a legal term for claiming a piece of property.
117. **doves . . . eagles:** Stock characters (along with lambs and wolves) in martial epic similes—but such descriptions generally apply to men fighting against men.

so those girls were afraid of the men rushing lawlessly;
    not one retained the color she'd had before.                          120
There's just one fear, but not just one appearance of fear:
    some tear their hair, some sit there out of their minds;
this one is silent and gloomy, that one calls "Mother!" in vain;
    one complains, one freezes; one stays, one flees.
The girls are snatched and led off, a prize for the marriage bed,         125
    and it's possible fear itself made many attractive.
If anyone fought back too much and refused her companion,
    the man himself lifted her to his greedy bosom
with words like these: "Why mar your tender eyes with tears?
    What father is to mother, I'll be to you."                            130
Romulus, you alone knew how to give soldiers benefits.
    Give me benefits like that and I'll join the army!
With that precedent, naturally, theatrical shows
    remain a snare for beautiful girls even now.

## How to Flirt at Sporting Events

Don't miss the competition of noble horses, either:                       135
    the Circus—so many seats!—offers lots of benefits.
You don't need fingers to communicate secret messages,
    nor do you have to receive a signal through nods.
No one is stopping you—sit down right next to your mistress!
    Join your side to her side just as close as you can!                  140

---

135. **competition of noble horses:** See "When the *Praeceptor* Reads" in the
introduction.
136. **Circus:** Chariot races, Rome's most popular sport, were held in the Cir-
cus Maximus ("Biggest Racecourse"), which could hold about 150,000 people.
136. **benefits:** Latin *commoda*, which in lines 131–32 referred specifically to
"fringe benefits." Ovid delights in abrupt transitions that depend on a word's
double meanings.
139. **mistress:** Latin *domina*, literally, "woman who owns slaves." Thanks to
the metaphor of the "slavery of love" (*servitium amoris*) inaugurated by Roman

Good thing that, like it or not, the rope forces you to be joined—
    that conditions are such that you *have* to touch the girl.
At this point, find some opening for friendly chat,
    and start your speech with a general remark:
be sure to inquire whose horses are running as if you care;        145
    whichever one she applauds for applaud for at once.
But when the parade comes, crowded with ivory statues of gods,
    applaud for Lady Venus with eager hands.
If by chance—it does happen—a speck of dust falls into
    the girl's bosom, your fingers must brush it away;        150
even if there's no speck, brush away the absence of speck:
    take any and every excuse to offer your services.
If her cloak's hanging down too low and lying on the ground,
    officiously gather it up off the dirty soil:
right away, as payment for services rendered, the girl        155
    will let you get an eyeful of her calves!
Also, be on the lookout that whoever's sitting behind you
    doesn't press his knee into her soft back.
Trivial things capture frivolous minds: many have found
    it useful to smooth out a pillow with skillful hand;        160
it's also been helpful to stir up a breeze with a slender tablet
    and place a round footstool beneath her tender foot.
The Circus will present these openings to a new love,

---

elegiac poetry, which casts the lover as a woman's slave, *domina* comes to take on our sense of "mistress" as "long-term extramarital love object." Yet aside from this word *domina*, some slave-like behaviors recommended in 2.209–32, and a mention of slavery at 2.435, the love-as-slavery metaphor is largely absent from the *Ars*. The *Remedia*, on the other hand, continually employs the language of slavery and liberation.

141. **rope:** Blocks of seats were marked off by a line or rope, apparently under rather cramped conditions.

147. **statues of gods:** Before the races, statues of gods were carried in a procession around the Circus, with spectators applauding for their particular favorites or patrons.

as well as the grim sand strewn in the anxious Forum.
In that sand, the boy of Venus has often fought,                          165
    and the spectator of wounds has gotten wounded:
while he's chatting and touching her hand and getting a program
    and asking who's winning, since he placed a bet—
he's been hit! He's groaned! He's felt the flying shaft,
    and now he's part of the spectacle himself!                          170

## The Mock Naval Battle

How about that mock naval battle Caesar just put on
    where he brought in the Persian and Cecrópian ships?
Yes, from coast to coast came the youths, from coast to coast
    came the girls, and the whole world was in the City.
Who didn't find something to love in a crowd like that?                    175
    Oh, how many were tortured by a foreign love!

## Caesar's Upcoming Eastern Campaign

Behold, Caesar's preparing to add the one missing piece
    to the conquered world: furthest Orient, now you'll be ours!

164. **grim sand . . . Forum:** Sand (Latin *harena*, whence our "arena") to absorb the blood was strewn in the Forum for gladiatorial games.

171. **mock naval battle:** In 2 BC, as part of the festivities for the dedication of the Temple of Mars Ultor (see "The Illicit Sex Tour of Roman Topography and Religion" in the introduction), Augustus staged a re-creation of the Battle of Salamis (a decisive Greek victory that took place in 480 BC, near the end of the war between Greece and Persia, in the straits between Athens and the island of Salamis; had the Persians won this war, who knows what would have become of Western civilization). The Roman re-creation took place in an artificial lake on the right bank of the Tiber and involved more than thirty large vessels, many smaller ones, and over three thousand gladiators, plus rowers.

172. **Cecropian:** Athenian; the name comes from Cecrops, a mythical king of Athens.

174. **the City:** Rome, of course; Latin *urbs* (city) often means Rome (cf. modern New Yorkers).

Párthian, you're going to pay! Rejoice, O buried Crassi
    and flag ill-treated at barbarian hands! 180
The Avenger is here, and in his first years claims the title of leader—
    as a boy, handling wars that are not for boys.
Stop being timid and counting the birthdays of the gods:
    Virtue mantles the Caesars before their time.
Celestial character rises up more swiftly than 185
    its years, and can't stand the expense of lazy delay.
Hercules was a baby when he squeezed the two serpents
    in his fists, and was worthy of Jupiter in the cradle;
how big were you, Bacchus, you who remain a boy even now,
    when India was conquered and cringed at your thyrsi? 190
You'll take up arms, boy, with your father's authority and years,
    and with your father's authority and years you'll conquer.

177. **the one missing piece:** The rhetoric in this passage implies that Caesar was about to launch a great expedition, led by his eighteen-year-old adopted son Gaius (actually his daughter Julia's son). In fact, the great expedition seems to have boiled down to successful negotiations at two dinner parties.

179–80. **O buried Crassi and flag:** The Parthians (a proverbially devious people in what is now Iran) had captured the Roman standards (Latin *signa*, poles with an eagle on top, which I translate as "flags" for their similar symbolic implications) in 53 BC, when the triumvir ("one of three men," third member of the coterie that included Julius Caesar and Pompey) Marcus Licinius Crassus, along with his son Publius, was defeated and killed at an ill-omened battle at Carrhae (a small town in modern Turkey); but Augustus, through diplomatic negotiation, had already achieved the return of the standards in 20 BC.

187. **the two serpents:** Jealous Juno had sent these in an attempt to nip the baby Hercules in the bud, to no avail.

189. **you who remain a boy even now:** Bacchus was depicted as an eternal adolescent (in looks and, often, behavior).

190. **thyrsi:** Ivy-wreathed wands (which could become deadly weapons) carried by Bacchus and his followers.

191. **authority:** Latin *auspicia*, literally (or at least etymologically) "bird-watching"; the leader of an army was required to "take the auspices" before

Under so great a name, you owe a great battle debut;
   now leader of young men, soon to be leader of old.
You have brothers, so avenge the brothers that have been wronged;   195
   you have a father: protect a father's rights.
The Father of the Fatherland, and your own, has armed you;
   the enemy's snatching his unwilling father's kingdom.
You will bear righteous shafts, he, accursed arrows;
   justice and righteousness will march as your flag.            200
The Párthians lose their case; let them lose in battle, too!
   Let my leader bring Eastern wealth to Latium!
Grant him divine power as he goes, Father Mars, Father Caesar—
   for one of you is a god, the other will be.
I prophesy: Behold, you shall win, I will sing votive songs       205
   and with a loud voice will I have to proclaim your name:
you shall stand firm, and encourage your battle line with my words
   (oh, that my words may not fall short of your spirit!);
I'll sing of the Párthians' backs and of the Romans' breasts

---

a campaign by observing the behavior of birds to determine the gods' atti-
tude, and the army/campaign would thus be "under his auspices."
194. **leader of young men**: In 5 BC, Augustus had given Gaius (and his
brother Lucius) the title Leader of the Youth (*Princeps Iuventutis*).
194. **soon to be leader of old**: Though Augustus had high hopes that Gaius
would be his heir, they were disappointed when Gaius died in AD 4 (Lucius
had died in AD 2); he had to settle for his stepson Tiberius.
195. **the brothers**: Phraataces V of Parthia had supplanted his father Phraa-
taces IV, against the wishes of Phraataces IV and his sons (the brothers of
Phraataces V).
197. **Father of the Fatherland**: The title *Pater Patriae*, one of Augustus's favor-
ites, was bestowed on him by the senate in 2 BC, shortly before the present
poem was written.
202. **Latium**: The region of central Western Italy containing the city of Rome.
204. **the other will be**: Predictions of Augustus's divinity always need to be
tactfully handled, insofar as they entail his death ("Become a god—just not
too soon!").

and the shafts the foe shoots from his horse turned away
   in retreat. 210
You flee to conquer, Párthian: What will be left you when conquered?
   Párthian, your Mars is ill-omened even now.

## THE PARADE

And so that day will come when you, loveliest of all,
   golden, will be drawn by four snow-white horses;
the leaders will march in front, their necks loaded down with
   chains, 215
   so that they can't find safety in flight as before.
Happy youths, mixed together with girls, will be spectators,
   and that day will bring release to everyone's spirits.
And when some one of those girls will ask the names of the kings,
   what regions, what mountains or waters are carried along, 220
give all the answers—whether or not she's asked the questions;
   and what you don't know, declare as if you knew well.
Here's the Euphrátes, a crown of rushes encircling his brow;
   the one with blue floppy hair must be the Tigris;
make these Arménians; this one's Persia, descended from Dánaë; 225

210. **shoots . . . in retreat:** The Parthians were famous for pretending to re-
treat, then shooting backwards from their horses (though since this trick was
so well known one wonders how effective it could have been).
212. **Mars:** Here, as often, = "warfare" (the god Mars would never actually
help Rome's enemies!).
213. **you:** Gaius. The *praeceptor* imagines his "triumph," a formal parade
marching into Rome, in which conquered leaders, along with people dressed
up as the conquered land's geographical features, preceded the victorious
general riding in a four-horse chariot.
225. **descended from Danaë:** Danaë was a princess from Argos imprisoned by
her father, Acrisius, who had heard a prophecy that her son would overthrow
him; Jupiter visited her in a "shower of gold" (a magical sunbeam? a bribe to
the guard?), and she bore him Perseus (who gave his name to Persia).

that's a city in the Achaeménian valley;
this and that guy are leaders, you can find names to call them—
    the right ones if possible, plausible ones if not.

DINNER PARTIES

Dinner parties, too, when the table's set, give you openings:
    you can get something out of them besides wine!                     230
Often at these, when Bacchus is laid out, glowing Love
    has forced his bowed horns down with tender arms,
and when the wine has sprinkled Cupid's absorbent wings
    he gets weighted down and stuck in the place of capture.
Of course, he's very quick to shake out his soggy feathers—             235
    but even a sprinkling by Love is bad for the heart.
Wine gets the spirit primed and makes it ready for heat;
    care flees and is diluted by much pure wine.
Then there's laughter, then the pauper puts on a bull's horns,
    then pain and cares and wrinkles depart from the brow.              240
Then simplicity—very rare in our age—reveals
    the heart, since the god has shaken off all arts.
Often at these have girls snatched away the hearts of young men,
    and Venus in wine was fire in a fire.
Here, don't put too much confidence in the treacherous lamp:           245
    night and pure wine wreak havoc on judgments of beauty.
In the clear light of day did Paris observe the goddesses,
    and said to Venus, "Venus, you beat them both."
At night, blemishes hide and every fault is forgiven,
    and that hour makes any and all of them beauties.                   250
When judging gems, when judging purple murex-dyed wool,
    when judging faces and bodies—consult the daylight.

226. **Achaemenian:** Persian, from the ancient Persian king Achaemenes.
232. **forced his bowed horns down with tender arms:** This appears to be a description of an actual allegorical picture, but the details are a bit obscure.
239. **puts on a bull's horns:** That is, becomes fearless and aggressive.

## OTHER LIKELY SPOTS

Why should I count out for you the female gatherings
    ripe for hunting? My count will be more than the sand!
Why should I mention Baiae, and the shores fringed with sails,    255
    and the water giving off hot sulfurous steam?
Some man bearing from here a wound in his heart has said,
    "This healing water's not what it's cracked up to be."
Look! There's the woodland temple of suburban Diana
    and the kingdom won by the sword with deadly hand;    260
she—although she's a virgin, although she hates Cupid's arrows—
    has dealt many wounds and will deal many wounds to the people.

## STEP TWO: CATCHING THE GIRL

Thus far, Thaléa, borne on unequal wheels, has instructed you
    where to find something to love, where to place your nets.
Now, I strive to explain what arts you should use to catch    265
    the one who excites you (a work of extraordinary art).

255. **Baiae:** A posh hot springs resort on the Bay of Naples, where much questionable behavior took place (the ancient Las Vegas).
259. **woodland temple of suburban Diana:** The Grove of Diana Nemorensis at Aricia (about sixteen miles southeast of Rome) was a popular spot for everything from healing pilgrimages to romantic trysts. The Rex Nemorensis ("King of the Wood"), a fugitive slave who "reigned" as Diana's priest-king and gained office by breaking off a bough from her sacred tree and then slaying his predecessor, added to the mystique.
261. **although:** Latin *quod*, which could also mean "because"; there are good arguments for either meaning, and I change my mind periodically.
262. **many wounds:** The "healing" goddess, like the "healing" waters of Baiae, can (counterproductively) inflict the wounds of love.
263. **Thalea:** A Muse (especially associated with comedy), as metonymy for poetry.
263. **unequal wheels:** Ovid likes to liken the unequal lines of his elegiac couplets (see on 24 "the wound he's made") to vehicles with unequal wheels or people with a shortened leg—a (mock-)self-deprecating gesture.

Men, everyone, everywhere—pay docile attention;
    come and hear my promises, throng of fans!

First, you've got to believe in your heart that they all can be caught:
    you'll catch them, you just need to lay your trap!        270
Birds will sooner keep quiet in spring, cicadas in summer,
    the Maenálian hound sooner show his back to the hare,
than a woman will fight back when assailed by a young man's flattery;
    even the one you might think doesn't want it will want it.
Just like a man, a girl thinks secret Venus is fun;        275
    the man's bad at hiding it, her lust is more concealed.
If we males could make a pact not to ask anyone first,
    women, defeated, will take on the role of askers!
In soft meadows, it's the female who moos to the bull;
    the female always whinnies to the horn-hooved stallion.        280
Our libido is thriftier and not so furious;
    the masculine flame remains within civilized bounds.
Why should I mention Byblis, who burned with forbidden love
    for her brother, and bravely punished her crime with a noose?
Myrrha loved her father, but not as a daughter should,        285
    and now lies hidden, squeezed by a covering of bark;
by her tears, which she pours forth from the fragrant tree,
    we're anointed, and the drops bear their mistress's name.

---

272. **Maenalian hound:** Hunting dogs from Arcadia (= Maenalia, from the Maenalus mountain range in Arcadia, in the central Peloponnese) were especially skilled.

283. **Byblis:** After she sent her brother a letter confessing her love and he rejected her, she killed herself and metamorphosed into a spring (according to *Metamorphoses* 9.450–665).

285. **Myrrha:** After she slept with her father under cover of darkness and became pregnant by him, he discovered her identity and she fled before he could kill her; she metamorphosed into a myrrh tree (according to *Metamorphoses* 10.298–502).

## PASIPHAË AND THE BULL

By chance, beneath the shadowy glades of wooded Ida,
    there was a bull, shining white, the glory of the herd,      290
distinguished by a slender black mark between his horns;
    a single spot there was, the rest was like milk.
Him did the Cnossian, him did the Cydónian heifers
    desire to have carried on their backs.
Pasíphaë was happy to become the bull's slut;      295
    she envied and hated the beauties among the cows.
I sing a well-known tale! Crete, with its hundred cities,
    no matter what lies it tells, cannot deny it!
She herself, for the bull, is said to have harvested
    new leaves and tender grass with unpracticed hand;      300
she's an escort to the herd, she's not held back by care for her
    husband: Minos had been conquered by cattle.
Pasíphaë, why are you putting on expensive clothes?
    That lover of yours has got no nose for riches.
Why bother with a mirror when heading for mountain flocks?     305
    Why keep fussing with hair that's been done, you dope?
And yet, believe your mirror when it says you're no heifer.
    How you're longing for horns to sprout from your forehead!

289. **Ida:** A mountain in Crete, not to be confused with the mountain of the same name near Troy where the Judgment of Paris took place.
290. **bull:** In the backstory the *praeceptor* suppresses here, King Minos was supposed to sacrifice this bull to Neptune, but refused because of its beauty; Neptune cursed the king by making his wife fall in love with the animal. Every woman who gets involved with Minos—in the *Ars* and *Remedia* we see Pasiphaë, Scylla (331–32), and Procris (3.685–746, *Rem.* 453)—undergoes some terrible fate, as does the artist Daedalus (2.21–98).
293. **Cnossian . . . Cydonian:** Cnossos and Cydonea were major cities of Crete.
298. **lies:** It was proverbial that "Cretans are liars" (cf. Titus 1:12: "One of themselves, even a prophet of their own, said, The Cretians are alway liars, evil beasts, slow bellies").

If Minos turns you on, there's no need to look for a lover;
    if you'd rather cheat on your man, cheat with a man!       310
Her bedroom abandoned, the queen is swept along through the woods
    and groves like a Bacchant stung by the Aónian god.
Ah, how often with hateful glance she spied a cow
    and said, "Why does *that* one turn my master on?
Look how she's showing off for him in the tender grass;      315
    I wouldn't be surprised if the fool thinks she's pretty!"
She spoke, and ordered her to be led from the great herd at once
    and dragged, undeserving, under the crooked yoke,
or forced her to fall at the altar in a phony ritual
    and happily held her rival's guts in her hand.      320
How often she would appease the gods with slaughtered rivals
    and hold their guts and say, "Go turn *mine* on now!"
And now she's longing to turn into Európa, now Io,
    since one was cattle, the other carried by cattle!
Still, the leader of the herd did get her pregnant, deceived      325
    by a maple-wood cow, and the birth revealed the author.

---

310. **your man . . . with a man:** A play on the two senses of Latin *vir* as "husband" and "adult human male" (emphasis on "human").

312. **Aonian god:** Bacchus (Aonia = Boeotia, the region of Greece containing Thebes, Bacchus's place of origin). The sometimes violent frenzy of the Bacchants, his female worshippers, became paradigmatic for women under the influence of extreme passions.

323. **Europa:** This Theban princess was seduced by Jupiter in the form of a bull and carried over the sea to Crete.

323. **Io:** See on 77 "Memphitic . . . heifer."

326. **maple-wood cow:** The master craftsman Daedalus created this contraption, which enabled Pasiphaë to consummate her unnatural passion and subsequently give birth to the Minotaur (whose bull head made it obvious who the father ["author"] was).

## OTHER EXAMPLES OF FEMALE LUST

If the Cretan had restrained herself from loving Thyéstes
    (is it so hard to do without just one man?),
Phoebus wouldn't have halted midjourney and wrenched back
      his chariot,
    turning his horses around to approach Auróra.         330
The daughter of Nisus, since she stole his purple lock,
    is housing rabid dogs on her loins and groin.
Átreus's son, who dodged Mars by land and Neptune by sea,
    became his wife's grim sacrificial victim.
Who hasn't wept at the burning of Ephýrean Creúsa       335
    and the mother drenched in the blood of her murdered sons?
Phoenix, son of Amýntor, wept from blinded eyes;
    maddened horses, you tore apart Hippólytus!
Phíneus, why gouge out the eyes of your innocent sons?


327. **the Cretan:** Aerope.
330. **Aurora:** Goddess of the dawn.
331. **daughter of Nisus:** In love with Minos, who was at war with her father Nisus, Scylla betrayed her father by cutting off the purple lock of hair that made him invincible and handing it to Minos. See on 290 "bull."
332. **housing rabid dogs:** Scylla the sea monster who threatens Ulysses is conflated here with Scylla the daughter of Nisus, who metamorphosed into a bird. The conflation has a long pedigree and seems to have been something of a learned joke, as Virgil does the same thing in *Eclogue* 6.74–77.
333. **Atreus's son:** Agamemnon.
335. **Ephyrean Creusa:** The Corinthian (Ephyre = old name for Corinth) princess whom Jason was about to marry.
336. **the mother:** Medea.
337. **Phoenix, son of Amyntor:** Phoenix was accused, either falsely or truly depending on the version, of sleeping with his father's concubine; his father blinded him in punishment. (This is the first of three stories of sons punished by fathers who believed they had slept with the father's wife or concubine.)
339. **Phineus:** This unfortunate Thracian seer blinded his sons because he believed they had slept with his second wife (Idaea; in some versions, she blinds them herself), then was blinded himself. (As punishment for revealing

That punishment's going to rebound on your own head!          340
All of those crimes were set in motion by women's lust:
    it's fiercer than ours and has more madness in it.
So, go on, don't be shy about hoping for girls, all of them!
    There'll barely be one out of many to tell you "No."
The ones who say "Yes" and the ones who say "No" still like to
        be asked;                                                345
    even if you're disappointed, rejection's not dangerous.
But why should you be disappointed, when a new pleasure's most fun,
    and the heart craves someone else's things more than its own?
The grass is always greener in someone else's field,
    and the neighbor's cattle have got the fatter udders.        350

### Strategy Tip: Get to Know Her Maid

But your first concern is to get to know the maid of the girl
    to be caught: she'll grease the skids for your approach.
Be sure she's one who's in on her mistress's private plans,
    a trusty accomplice in her secret affairs.
Seduce her with promises, seduce her with propositions;          355
    you'll get what you want quite easily if she's willing.
She'll choose the time (doctors, too, are precise about times)
    when the mistress's mind is at ease and fit to be caught;
the mind will be fit to be caught when it's happiest with the world,
    as crops will be most luxuriant in fertile ground.           360
When hearts are rejoicing and not constricted by any pain,
    they're open: then Venus sneaks in with flattering art.

---

the gods' secrets, he also had his food stolen or defiled by Harpies, very nasty
bird-women.)
343. **don't be shy about hoping for girls, all of them!**: See "When the *Praeceptor* Reads" in the introduction.
357. **doctors**: Here the *praeceptor* may be anticipating his role as Love Doctor, which comes to full bloom in the *Remedia* (though in this poem he is still primarily the Prophet or Professor of Love).

When Ílium was in mourning, it was defended by arms;
  when happy, it brought in the Horse pregnant with soldiers.
She also should be tried when she's grieving, hurt by a rival;    365
  your efforts will make sure she's not unavenged.
The maid, while busy combing out her morning hair,
  should egg her on and help out the sails with oars,
and, muttering to herself, with a little sigh, should say,
  "But, I suppose, you couldn't pay him back."    370
Then she should tell about you, then she should add persuasive
  words, and swear you're dying of crazy love.
But hurry, lest the sails go limp and the breezes die down;
  like fragile ice, wrath gradually melts away.

## ON SEDUCING THE MAID

Would it help, you ask, to seduce this servant herself?    375
  There's a big roll of the dice in crimes like that.
One gets officious after sex, another more sluggish;
  one serves you up for her mistress, another for herself.
It's all how the gamble turns out; it might reward your risk,
  but my advice would still be to hold back.    380
I'm not the one to walk along cliffs and jagged peaks;
  under my leadership, no young men will be caught.
If, however, while she's going back and forth with the tablets,
  her body—not just her officiousness—turns you on,
be sure you obtain the mistress first and she follows behind:    385
  the maid mustn't be your starting point for Venus.
This one thing I warn you, if art's to be trusted at all
  and the thieving wind doesn't carry my words out to sea:

382. **under my leadership . . . caught:** In *Amores* 2.7, the poet vehemently protests to his girlfriend that he would never dream of sleeping with her slave; in 2.8, he asks the slave, "How did she find us out?"
383. **tablets:** Wooden tablets smeared with wax and inscribed with a metal stylus, used for nonpermanent written communications.

Get it right, or don't try; the informer's out of the way
　　as soon as she herself takes part in the crime.　　　　　　390
Having a bird go free when its wings are limed is no use;
　　for a boar to escape from a bulging net is not good;
a fish that's wounded from chomping a hook should be firmly grasped;
　　keep pressing the one you've tried and don't leave till you win.
[Then—since she's guilty of your shared crime—she won't
　　betray you,　　　　　　395
　　and you'll know all that your mistress says and does.]
But let it be kept secret: if your informer's kept secret,
　　you'll always be in on what your girlfriend is up to.

## The Importance of Timing

If anyone thinks that times must be watched only by those
　　who work laborious fields, and sailors—he's wrong.　　　　400
Not always should Ceres be entrusted to treacherous fields,
　　not always the hollow keel to the waves of green,
nor is it always safe to make plays for tender girls:
　　at the right time, the same thing often turns out better.
If her birthday is coming around, or the first of the month　　405
　　in which Venus likes to snuggle up to Mars,
or if the Circus is not, as before, decked out with little
　　statues, but has kings' treasures on display,

391. **limed:** The Romans caught small birds by smearing birdlime (a sticky substance) on twigs.
405–6. **the month . . . Mars:** That is, April 1 (March was Mars's month, April Venus's); the *praeceptor* never misses a chance to allude to the adultery of Mars and Venus (see 2.561–92 and "The Illicit Sex Tour of Roman Topography and Religion" in the introduction). Though April 1 is not mentioned elsewhere as a gift-giving opportunity, there was a festival of Venus on that day, which could well have been a Valentine's Day–like occasion for romantic blackmail.
407–8. **Circus . . . statues:** This appears to be a reference to the Sigillaria, a December festival in which little clay statues (*sigilla*) used to be displayed for

put off the task: then an ugly storm, then the Pleíades threaten;
    then the sea's waters drown the tender Kid;                              410
then it's a good time to stop; then whoever's consigned to the deep
    can barely hold onto his mangled boat's shipwrecked timbers.
Here's when you should begin: that day when the tearful Állia
    ran with the blood that poured from Latin wounds,
and the day the Sabbath festival observed by the Syrian                     415
    from Palestine returns, no good for business.
Your girlfriend's birthday should be for you a great object of dread,
    and any day that requires a gift should be black.
But she'll pull it off, no matter how well you avoid it: a woman
    finds arts to pilfer her longing lover's riches.                         420
Some slovenly salesman will come to your bargain-hungry mistress
    and spread his merchandise out while you're sitting there;
she'll ask you to look it over, so you can appear in the know;
    then she'll give kisses, then she'll ask you to buy.
She'll swear that she'll be content with this for years to come;             425
    she needs it now, now (she'll say) it's a steal!

---

sale, but which now boasts more expensive items. "Circus" could refer to the
Circus Maximus (see on 136 "Circus") or to the smaller Circus Flaminius (at
the southern end of the Campus Martius near the Tiber).

409. **Pleiades:** A cluster of seven stars that set in winter, thus marking the
end of the sailing season. The *praeceptor* is speaking metaphorically of the
lover's quest as a sea journey (the actual season of the year is irrelevant to his
point).

410. **tender Kid:** Another constellation that set in winter.

413. **tearful Allia:** The defeat of the Romans by the Gauls (Celtic tribes liv-
ing in northern Italy, France, and other parts of modern Europe) at the river
Allia (which flows into the Tiber about eleven miles from Rome) on July 18
(390 BC) was a national day of mourning, a "black day" (*dies atra*) on which
no business could be conducted—and thus no presents bought.

415. **Sabbath festival:** See on 76 "seventh-day rites . . . Syrian Jew." The Sab-
bath as a no-business day was observed by many Gentiles in Rome.

If you make an excuse that you haven't got the cash on you?
    "Put it in writing!" (You'll wish you'd never learned how.)
How about when she demands a gift with fake birthday cake
    and is born for herself as often as she needs?       430
How about when she weeps bitterly over the phony loss
    of the gem she pretends has slipped from her pierced ear?
They ask to be given lots "to use," won't return it when given;
    you lose, and you get no thanks for what you've lost!
For me to expound on the sacrilegious arts of whores     435
    ten tongues in as many mouths would not be enough.

## LETTERS AND LIES

Let wax spread over well-erased tablets test the shallows,
    let wax go first as the confidant of your heart;
let it bear your sweet nothings and words that sound like a lover's,
    and no matter who you are, throw in lots of prayers.     440
Moved by prayer, Achilles bestowed Hector on Priam;
    a wrathful god is moved by a pleading voice.
Be sure to make promises, for what harm can it do to promise?
    Anyone can be a big spender with promises.
Hope, if she's once believed, holds on for a good long time;     445
    she's a treacherous goddess, but handy nevertheless.
If you've given something, you'll be a candidate for rejection:
    she will have gained what's past and not lost a thing.
But what you haven't given, always seem on the point of giving:
    thus has a barren field often tricked its master.     450

435. **sacrilegious arts of whores:** Much vitriol in Latin "love" poetry is spent on denigrating women who expect gifts in exchange for their favors.
436. **ten tongues:** The *praeceptor* rises to epic grandeur as he warms to his theme (wishing for additional mouths, generally in denominations of ten or a hundred, to sing a particular topic is typical of high epic style since Homer).
441. **Achilles bestowed Hector on Priam:** See on 15 "hands that Hector was to feel." (The *praeceptor* seems to have forgotten that quite a bit of gold was offered as well.)

Thus, so he won't have lost, the gambler keeps on losing,
   and the dice keep calling back his greedy hands.
This is the task, this the labor: to score without that first gift.
   So she won't have given *her* gift for free, she'll keep giving.
Therefore, have a letter engraved with flattering words     455
   go first, sound out her feelings, test the road;
a letter delivered on an apple deceived Cydíppe,
   and the girl, unaware, was caught by her own words.

## BE ELOQUENT (BUT NOT TOO OBVIOUS)

Roman youth, I'm telling you, go learn the good arts
   not only to protect trembling defendants:     460
like the people, and the serious judge, and the chosen senate,
   the girl will surrender, defeated by your fluency.
But hide your strength—don't wear your eloquence on your sleeve;
   your speech should flee from words that sound affected.
Who but a total dunce would declaim to a tender girlfriend?     465
   Often a forceful letter was reason for hatred.
Your diction should inspire trust, using everyday words—
   flirtatious, though, so you seem to be speaking in person.
If she won't take it and sends what you've written back unread,
   hope that she's going to read it, and stick to the plan.     470

453. **This is the task, this the labor:** An exact quotation of *Aeneid* 6.129, where the Sibyl (priestess of the entrance to the underworld) tells Aeneas that the doors *into* the underworld lie open day and night, but getting *out* again? "This is the task, this the labor" (*hoc opus, hic labor est*).
457. **letter . . . Cydippe:** The "letter," inscribed on an apple by Acontius, read, "I swear by Diana to marry Acontius": reading aloud (as the ancients did) can be dangerous.
466. **a forceful letter was reason:** The Latin could also be construed as "a letter was a forceful (or valid) reason"; both translations have merit.

### PERSISTENCE

In time, difficult bullocks come around to the plow;
    in time, horses are taught to bear pliant reins.
An iron ring is wasted away by incessant use;
    a curved plow is ruined by incessant earth.
What is there that's harder than rock, what's softer than water?    475
    Yet by soft water hard rocks are hollowed out.
Just be persistent, in time you'll defeat Penélope herself:
    you see Pérgamum captured late, but captured still.
She's read it and she doesn't want to write back? Don't force it;
    just be sure she keeps reading your sweet nothings.    480
She who wished to have read them will wish to write back when she's
    read them;
    these things come by degrees in their own good measure.
Maybe, at the first attempt, a grim letter will come to you
    asking that you desist from soliciting her.
She fears what she asks, she wants what she doesn't ask:
    your persistence.    485
    Press on, and eventually you'll get what you want.
Meanwhile, if she's being carried along reclined on a couch,
    with a cunning pretense approach your mistress's litter;
and so no one will lend disagreeable ears to your words,
    cloak them slyly as you can in ambiguous signs.    490
Or if her feet are treading a spacious colonnade
    in a leisurely way, here again, make a friendly detour,
and be sure to go in front sometimes, sometimes fall behind,
    sometimes hurry along, sometimes go slowly.
And you mustn't be ashamed to drift a bit past the center    495
    of the columns, or to nudge her side with your side.
A pretty girl mustn't sit in the curved theater without you:

---

477. **Penelope herself:** Ulysses's wife did not, in fact, succumb to twenty years
of wooing by her throng of suitors.
478. **Pergamum:** The citadel of Troy (often simply = Troy).

she'll bear on her shoulders the show for you to watch.
You'll be allowed to look around at her, admire her,
    speak volumes with your eyebrow, volumes with signs;          500
and you should applaud when the actor's dancing some girl's part,
    and be a fan of whoever is playing the lover.
Whenever she stands, you'll stand; whenever she sits, you'll sit;
    fritter away your time at your mistress's whim.

## GROOMING FOR MEN (NOT TOO MUCH!)

But don't think it's good to torture your tresses with hot iron          505
    or smooth your calves with biting pumice-stone;
tell them to do such things whose Phrygian rhythms accompany
    Great Mother Cýbele with shrieks and howls.
For men, a careless appearance is fitting; Theseus's head was
    untouched by a comb, but he swept away Minos's daughter;          510

502. **playing the lover:** In an adultery mime, Rome's most ancient (and immensely popular) genre of drama. These farces generally involved a woman and her lover bamboozling her stupid husband—precisely the sort of immorality that the *praeceptor* protests he is *not* teaching (one of many indications that his protest is disingenuous).

506. **smooth your calves with biting pumice-stone:** While it was considered appropriate for Roman men to pluck their armpits, depilating their legs was seen as effeminate. Such choices could have both moral and aesthetic implications. Seneca the Younger (ca. AD 1–65; philosopher, dramatist, and adviser to the emperor Nero) comments on different writing styles, "the one sort grooms itself more than is right, the other neglects itself more than is right; the former plucks even its legs, the latter not even its armpits" (*Epistle* 114.14).

507. **Phrygian rhythms:** The priests of Cybele, the Great Mother goddess imported from Phrygia (near Troy, and representing the decadent, luxurious East) to Rome in 203 BC, were eunuchs; their worship involved loud clanging instruments and howling.

510. **Minos's daughter:** Ariadne; the story of her abandonment by Theseus is about to be told at line 525.

Phaedra loved Hippólytus, and he wasn't well groomed;
   Adónis, fit for the woods, was a goddess's sweetheart.
Bodies should please by their neatness and be tanned on the Campus;
   the toga should be spotless and fit well.
Your tongue should not be stiff, your teeth should not be rusty,     515
   nor your rambling foot be swimming in baggy leather.
A bad hairdo shouldn't make your tresses stand out stiffly:
   your hair and your beard should be trimmed by a practiced hand.
Your nails should not protrude and should be without defilement;
   no hair should stand in the hollows of your nose.     520
The breath of your mouth should not be of grim and evil odor,
   nor the man and father of the herd smite the nose.
Grant that everything else is for wanton girls to do,
   and whoever, scarcely a man, is looking for a man.

511. **Hippolytus:** Naturally, the *praeceptor*'s takeaway from this tragedy is that the Rugged Hunter Look is attractive to women.

512. **Adonis:** See on 75 "Adonis." Venus even dabbled in hunting to indulge her crush on this young hunter.

513. **Campus:** The Campus Martius ("Field of Mars"), a large field outside of Rome where athletic and military exercises took place.

515. **tongue . . . teeth:** It appears from the next line that the *praeceptor* here means parts of a shoe, though he teases us with terms that would also apply to the mouth.

522. **man and father of the herd:** A goat, whose proverbial bad smell was associated with that of human armpits. Using the word *vir* (man) here for a nonhuman "husband" is somewhat ironic, especially given the following couplet; see on 310 "your man . . . with a man."

524. **scarcely a man, is looking for a man:** Though the Romans condoned sexual liaisons between men and adolescent boys (before the growth of body hair marked them as "men"), homosexual relationships between grown men were an object of extreme scorn and ridicule. "Scarcely a man" here means "effeminate," not "young."

ARIADNE AND BACCHUS

Look, Liber's calling his prophet! He, too, is helpful to lovers:            525
    he's a fan of the flame that heats his own blood.
The Cnossian girl was wandering madly on unknown sands,
    where narrow Dia is struck by the waters of the sea.
She'd just woken up—was wearing her tunic without a belt,
    barefoot and with her saffron locks unbound—                          530
and was crying out "Cruel Theseus!" to the heedless waves,
    an innocent shower wetting her tender cheeks.
She was crying out and weeping at once, but both were attractive;
    she was not made uglier by her tears.
And now, striking again her soft, soft breast with her palms,             535
    "That traitor has left," she said. "What will become of me?"
"What will become of me?" she said: cymbals sounded all over
    the shore, and drums, hammered by frenzied hand!
She fainted from fear, and broke off the words she had been saying;
    there wasn't a drop of blood in her lifeless body.                    540


525. **Liber:** Bacchus (Latin *Liber* = "Free"), conveniently here as god of both wine and poetry.
526. **he's a fan of the flame:** The translator's job would be a piece of cake if all puns were this easy. Latin *favet* really means "favors, supports"—"fan" in the sense of "enthusiast"—but I'm certain Ovid would have approved of the play on "fan" as "device that moves air toward a fire."
527. **Cnossian girl:** Cnossos was the major city of Crete, Ariadne's home. Latin *Cnosis* means "female from Cnossos"; English forces one to choose a noun like "girl," "maiden," "woman," etc., which can be tricky, given the connotations of each of those words, only some of which are appropriate in any given context. Ariadne ran away with Theseus after helping him navigate the Labyrinth and kill her half brother (the Minotaur; see on 326 "maple-wood cow").
528. **Dia:** An island in the Aegean, identified with Naxos. Whether Theseus, heading back to Athens from Crete, left Ariadne there accidentally or intentionally depends on the version one follows. In any case, Ariadne is the quintessential "abandoned woman."

Look, the Mimallónides, hair scattered down their backs!
   Look, the frisky satyrs, the god's advance guard!
The old drunk (look!) Silénus, on his swaybacked ass,
   can barely sit up—but he's artfully holding the mane.
When he goes after the Bacchants, the Bacchants flee and
      come back;                                                                        545
   a lousy horseman, he prods his steed with a rod;
he's slipped off his long-eared ass and tumbled onto his head!
   The satyrs shout, "Come on, get up, Dad, get up!"
Now the god in his chariot (he'd covered the top with grapes)
   was giving golden rein to his yoke of tigers.                               550
Color, and Theseus, and speech—they all deserted the girl;
   thrice she tried to flee, thrice fear held her back.
She shuddered, like dry ears of grain rustled by the wind,
   like a light reed trembling in a sodden swamp.

541. **Mimallonides:** The Macedonian term for Bacchants (Bacchus's frenzied female followers).

542. **satyrs:** These rambunctious, goat-legged male inhabitants of the wild were always drinking and chasing nymphs (think *Animal House* [1978]).

543. **Silenus:** The middle-aged leader of the satyrs, a "wise fool" figure who, in Virgil's sixth *Eclogue*, is tied down (after a bender) and forced to sing a song that encompasses all of poetry. Ovid may glance at this paradox in the next line with "artfully" (Latin *arte*, literally "by art"); his references to "art" are seldom without point.

550. **tigers:** In line with Bacchus's exotic Eastern origin (and potentially predatory inclinations), he substitutes these large cats for the usual horses (in contrast to Silenus's ludicrous horse-substitute).

551. **Color, and Theseus, and speech:** A choice example of the rhetorical figure called *syllepsis* (placing together) or *zeugma* (yoking), in which a verb or preposition governs objects that are both literal and figurative (my favorite—with thanks to Elaine Fantham—is "She left in a temper and a taxi"). Here "Theseus deserted her" means "Theseus left her mind," but ironically, of course, Theseus has also deserted her in fact.

552. **thrice . . . thrice:** The repetition of "thrice," like the simile in the following couplet, gives the passage a (mock-)epic flavor.

The god told her, "See, I'm here, a more faithful sweetheart
    for you.                                                                  555
   Fear not: you, Cnossian, will be Bacchus's wife!
Take heaven as your gift. You'll be watched as a star in heaven;
    you'll often guide doubting ships as the Cretan Crown."
He spoke, and—so the tigers wouldn't scare her—jumped down
    from his chariot (the sand sank at the weight of his foot),            560
and enfolding her in his bosom—she had no strength to fight back—
    he swept her away: everything's easy for a god.
Some shout "Hymenaéus!"; some shout "Eúhion, Euhoe!"
    Thus bride and god are joined on the sacred couch.

## DINNER PARTIES

Therefore, when Bacchus's gifts are laid out and given to you,            565
    and the woman is on part of the couch you share,
pray the Nyctélian father and his nocturnal rites
    not to command his wine to go to your head.

558. **you'll often guide doubting ships:** Some editors read "The Cretan Crown
will often guide doubting ships" (Latin *reget*, "it will rule," vs. *reges*, "you will
rule"). Normally, Ariadne's crown (*corona*) is made into the constellation;
Bacchus, however, implies that the star(s) will be Ariadne herself.
560. **the sand sank:** A humorous realistic detail: gods are larger, and heavier,
than life.
563. **"Hymenaeus!"** . . . **"Euhion, Euhoe!":** Cries appropriate to a wedding
(from the marriage god Hymen) and Bacchic rituals (Euhius was a cult title
of Bacchus), respectively: all bases are covered.
565. **Bacchus's gifts:** For this sort of abrupt transition (Bacchus as lover →
Bacchus as wine at a dinner party), see on 136 "benefits."
566. **part of the couch:** Romans ate reclining on couches (they would have
considered sitting in chairs to eat meals a strange barbarism).
567. **Nyctelian father:** Bacchus, probably from his ceremonies taking place
at night (*nyx* = Greek "night," *telein* = Greek "perform"); "nocturnal rites"
glosses this etymology.

Here, with covert conversation, you can say lots of secret
    things she'll know are said to her alone.                                        570
Write frivolous sweet nothings in a film of wine
    so she can read on the table that she's your mistress,
and gaze into her eyes with eyes confessing fire:
    often a silent face has speech and words.
Make sure to be the first to grab the cup that's been touched            575
    by her lips, and to drink from the side where the girl will drink.
Whatever food she's taken a bit of with her fingers,
    get—and while you're getting it, touch her hand.
You should also want to be pleasing to the man of your girl:
    he'll be more useful to you if you make friends.                           580
If you're throwing dice to drink, let him go first;
    give him the garland that has slipped off your head.
Your inferior or your equal, let him take everything first,
    and don't hesitate to play the supporting role.

569. **Here:** In this entire passage, the *praeceptor* is replaying a scene from *Amores* 1.4, in which the narrator imagines to his girlfriend all the ways they will outwit her husband at a dinner party. The poet's transformation—from eager, jealous lover in that scene to self-confident know-it-all, teaching a fail-safe procedure, in this one—exhibits his determination to "tame" and "steer" that rebellious boy called Love, even as it reminds us (through the young lover's jealousy) of the impossibility of doing so. See "When the *Praeceptor* Reads" in the introduction.

579. **the man:** Latin *vir*, which would almost certainly be read as "husband" (see on 310 "your man . . . with a man")—once again, belying the *praeceptor's* protest that he is not counseling adultery.

581. **throwing dice to drink:** It is not entirely clear what this means (the Latin, like the English, could mean either "throw first" or "drink first"). Romans threw dice to determine who would be the *symposiarch* (master of drinking), who would decide how strong the wine would be for all the guests (Romans generally diluted their wine with varying proportions of water); or it may be that the guests are throwing dice to see who drinks first.

[It's a safe and well-worn path to deceive through the name
    of "friend";                                                                585
  but though it's safe and well-worn, it's still a fault.
That's also how a manager "manages" a bit too much
  and thinks more needs "looking after" than he was told.]

My recommendation to you is to have a fixed measure for drinking:
  both mind and foot should continue to do their jobs.                     590
Be especially on guard against quarrels spurred on by wine
  and hands too easily stirred to savage wars.
By drinking the wine he was served, Eurýtion fell like a fool;
  table and wine are more suited for pleasant games.
If you've got a voice, sing; if you've got supple arms, dance;                   595
  whatever gifts you've got to charm with, charm with.
Though real inebriation is harmful, phony will help:
  make your sly tongue trip over stammering words,
so whatever you do or say that's naughtier than you should,
  the cause will be set down as too much wine.                             600
And drink a health to your lady, a health to the one she sleeps with—
  but pray for the man's ill health in the silence of your heart.

585–88. **It's a safe . . . he was told:** Though these lines do have an Ovidian
feel, they do not seem quite appropriate here, as pointing out that "it's still a
fault" to deceive would be contrary to the amoral and self-serving point of
the previous lines. Some editors suggest that they may fit better after line
742.
593. **Eurytion:** A centaur killed in the famous brawl between Lapiths (a
Thessalian clan) and centaurs, when the latter got drunk at the wedding
feast of Pirithoüs (king of the Lapiths); the incident, which represented civ-
ilization vs. untamed Nature, was also proverbial in warnings against the
dangers of excessive drinking.
595. **supple arms, dance:** For the Romans, erotic dancing was characterized
primarily by arm movements, while religious dancing seems to have involved
mainly the stamping of feet: see on 112 "thrice striking . . . with his foot."
602. **the man's:** Or "her husband's."

Now, when the tables have been cleared and the guests are leaving,
    the very crowd will give you a place and an opening.
Squeeze into the crowd and, sidling up as she's leaving,        605
    brush her side with your fingers and touch foot to foot.
Now is the time for speech: rustic Modesty, begone
    far hence: Chance and Venus assist the bold.
Your eloquence should not be subject to my conditions;
    just want her, and you'll be an orator on your own.        610
You've got to play the lover and mimic wounds with your words;
    gain faith in your genuineness through lots of art.
It's not hard to be believed: each seems lovable to herself;
    no one's not charmed by her own looks, even the ugliest.
Often, though, the imposter has started to love for real;        615
    often what he'd pretended at first he became.
(All the more then, O girls, you should go easy on fakers;
    the love that just now was phony will become true!)
Now is the time to catch a heart, stealthily, with sweet nothings,
    as the hanging bank is eaten away by clear water.        620

607. **rustic:** Latin *rusticus*, a word whose connotations are impossible to convey with any single English word. The *rus* (whence our "rural") was the countryside, as opposed to the *urbs* (city); whereas "urbanity" conveyed sophistication, suavity, and wit, "rusticity" conveyed boorishness, clumsiness, and—this is the main point here—prudishness. A Roman man unsuccessful in seducing a woman would be likely to call her *rustica*.

607. **Modesty:** Latin *pudor*, which could also be translated "shame." If appropriately applied, *pudor* is a good and necessary thing; to be "shameless" was no more a virtue for Romans than it is for us.

607–8. **begone far hence:** The *praeceptor* as prophet again (see on 31–32 "Get ye . . . foot").

608. **Chance and Venus assist the bold:** The *praeceptor* as epic warrior giving a stirring pep talk. Aeneas's nemesis, Turnus, declares, "Fortune assists the bold" (*Aen.* 10.284); here Venus is thrown in for good measure.

612. **gain faith in your genuineness through lots of art:** Here, in a nutshell, is Ovid's irony, *ars poetica*, and insight into the human condition. See "Fifty Shades of Metaphor" in the introduction.

Don't let it bother you to praise her face, and her hair,
   and her well-shaped fingers, and her dainty foot:
even chaste women like to have their beauty proclaimed;
   virgins enjoy and care about their own beauty.
Why else are Juno and Pallas ashamed, even now, to have lost     625
   the beauty contest in the Phrygian woods?
The bird of Juno shows her feathers off if they're praised;
   she hides her riches if you look on in silence.
Steeds, amid the contests of the rushing racetrack,
   like you to comb their manes and pat their necks.     630

## More Helpful Hints: Perjury, Tears, and Rape

Don't be shy about promising: promises suck girls in.
   As witnesses to your promise, throw in lots of gods.
Jupiter laughs from on high at lovers' perjuries, ordering
   Aéolus's South Winds to dispose of them, voided.
Jupiter got in the habit of swearing falsely to Juno     635
   by the Styx: now, he smiles on his own example.

626. **Phrygian:** See on 54 "Greek girl . . . Phrygian man."
627. **bird of Juno:** The peacock, the "eyes" in whose tail were said to be from
Juno's hundred-eyed watchman Argus (killed by Mercury at Jupiter's request).
Peacocks are of course more resplendent and likely to show off than peahens,
but a female bird works better for the *praeceptor's* point here.
634. **Aeolus's South Winds:** Aeolus was king of the winds. Any wind could
blow words away, but it was the South Wind's (*Notus*) specialty.
634. **voided:** Latin *inritus*, commonly used in poetry to mean "unfulfilled" or
"in vain"; here the *praeceptor* activates its etymological and legal sense of "not
ratified, null and void."
635–36. **Jupiter . . . Styx:** It is not entirely clear whether the *praeceptor* has
his facts straight. A pseudo-Hesiodic fragment does show Jupiter swearing a
false oath to Juno about never having touched Io; on the other hand, break-
ing an oath by the *Styx*, most dreadful river of the underworld (and often
standing metonymically for death itself), was supposed to incur an unendur-
able punishment for gods and mortals alike. Here, "by the Styx" appears to
be the *praeceptor's* enhancement.

For gods to exist is convenient, and since it's convenient, let's think it:
  let incense and wine be offered on ancient hearths.
Nor does a carefree quietude, similar to sleep,
  restrain them: live a clean life, the divine is at hand!          640
Return what's entrusted to you; let loyalty keep its pacts;
  let there be no fraud; keep your hands free from slaughter.
Take my advice and deceive only *girls* with impunity:
  faith should be kept except for this one deceit.
Be traitors to the traitors: they're a dirty lot,                   645
  on the whole, and *should* fall into the traps they've laid.

It's said that Egypt was deprived of the rains that nourish
  fields, and that it was in drought for nine years,
when Thrásius goes to Busíris and shows him that by shedding
  the blood of a guest, Jupiter can be appeased.                    650
Busíris says to him, "You'll be Jupiter's first victim,
  and you yourself, a guest, will bring water to Egypt."
Phálaris, too, roasted the limbs of violent Períllus

---

637. **For gods to exist is convenient, and since it's convenient, let's think it:**
This cynical line is sometimes quoted as if it represented Ovid's real view.
But have I mentioned that the *praeceptor* has his own axe to grind?

639. **carefree quietude:** This refers to the Epicurean doctrine that the gods
exist, but live a blissful life off in the sky somewhere paying no attention to
humans.

641. **Return what's entrusted to you:** Since Roman society had no high-
security banks, people left their money and valuables with friends for safe-
keeping; returning this *depositum* when asked was a sacred duty.

649. **Thrasius:** A seer from Cyprus.

649. **Busiris:** A mythical king of Egypt with a penchant for slaughtering for-
eigners. When he attempted this on Hercules, however, he got a taste of his
own medicine—a sequel the *praeceptor* does not care to mention.

653. **Phalaris:** A tyrant of Syracuse (ca. 570–554 BC). When Perillus con-
structed a bronze bull as a torture/murder device—the victim roasted in it
would cause the bull to bellow realistically—Phalaris made the artist the first
victim (his one just act).

in a bull: the unhappy author baptized his work.
Both men were just, nor is there any fairer law                    655
   than for artificers of murder to die by their art.
Therefore, so perjuries deceive perjurers, as is right,
   let women be wounded and hurt by their own example.

Tears are helpful too: you'll move adamant with tears;
   make sure, if you can, she sees your cheeks dripping wet.           660
If tears (and it's true that they don't always arrive on time)
   are lacking, touch your eyes with a greasy hand.
What wise man would not mix kisses with flattering words?
   So she doesn't give them. Take them without her giving!
She'll fight back, perhaps, at first, and call you "Monster!"        665
   Fighting back, she still wants herself to be conquered.
Only take care that kisses snatched the wrong way don't injure
   her tender lips, that she can't complain they were hard.
Anyone who's grabbed kisses and doesn't grab the rest too
   deserves to forfeit even what he *has* been given.                  670
After the kisses, you almost made it to the grand prize!
   Ah me—that wasn't modesty, it was rusticity!
Call it force if you will, that force is pleasing to girls;
   what they like, they often want to have given "unwilling."
Whoever's been violated by a sudden snatching of Venus              675
   rejoices, and wickedness is considered a service.
But she who, when she *could* have been forced, departs untouched?
   Though she simulates an expression of joy, she'll be sad.
Phoebe suffered force, force was used on her sister,
   and both the snatchers were pleasing to the snatched.             680

672. **modesty . . . rusticity:** See on 607 "rustic" and 607 "Modesty."
679. **Phoebe:** In *Fasti* 5.669–720, Ovid tells the story of how Phoebe and her sister (Hilaira), engaged to Idas and Lynceus, were abducted by twin brothers Castor and Pollux; in the ensuing battle, only Pollux survived (and he and Castor became the constellation Gemini). There is no indication there that the sisters enjoyed the abduction.

## ACHILLES AND DEIDAMIA

The story is well known, of course, but still worth telling:
　　Scýrian Girl Hooked Up with Haemónian Man.
The goddess (worthy to beat two under Mount Ida) had already
　　given an evil reward for the praise of her beauty;
Priam's daughter-in-law had already come from afar,　　　　　　685
　　and a Greek wife dwelt within the Ílian walls;
everyone was swearing an oath for the jilted husband,
　　for one man's pain had become a national cause.
Achilles had concealed his manhood beneath a long robe
　　(shameful, if he weren't honoring his mother's prayers).　　　690
What are you doing, Aéacus's son? Weaving's not your job!
　　You're to seek fame through another of Pallas's arts!
What's with the baskets? Your hand is fit for bearing a shield!
　　Why's the right hand by which Hector will fall holding wool?
Throw away those spindles wrapped around with worked thread!　695
　　That hand of yours should be shaking the Pélian spear!
By chance, the royal maiden was in the very same bedroom:
　　through rape, she figured out that he was a man.
She was conquered by strength, of course (so we're meant to believe!),
　　but still, she wanted to be conquered by strength.　　　　　700

682. **Scyrian Girl Hooked Up with Haemonian Man:** Achilles's mother (the sea goddess Thetis), knowing that her son would die in battle if he fought at Troy, sought to protect him by hiding him in drag on the island of Scyros (in the Aegean). Haemonian = Thessalian (see on 6 "Haemonian ship").

691. **Aeacus's son:** Grandson, actually. The epic-style appellation contrasts nicely with Achilles's embarrassing position.

692. **another of Pallas's arts:** Pallas (Minerva) was the goddess of both weaving and warfare (not to mention wisdom).

693. **Your hand:** See on 15 "hands that Hector was to feel."

696. **Pelian spear:** The famous spear cut from an ash tree on Mount Pelion (in Thessaly), a gift from Chiron (see on 11 "Phillyrus's son"), was so heavy that only Achilles could wield it.

"Wait!" she'd often cry, when Achilles was in a hurry—
    for he'd ditched the spindle and taken up brave arms.
Where's that "force" now? Why, with wheedling voice, do you cling
    to the author, Deidamía, of your "rape"?
Of course, it's shameful to be the one to initiate things,      705
    but when someone else makes the first move it's fun to "endure" it!

## BE AGGRESSIVE (OR NOT)

Ah, that youth has got too much confidence in his own looks
    who's waiting around until she asks him first.
The man should approach her first, the man should pour out praying
       words;
    she should graciously receive his flattering prayers.      710
To get what you're after, ask! She only wants to be asked;
    give an excuse and an opening for your desire.
Jupiter used to go groveling to the heroines of old;
    there was no girl who put the moves on great Jupiter.
However, if you sense that your prayers are making her puffed-up   715
    with scorn, break off the attack and beat a retreat.
Many desire what flees, but hate what presses on:
    dispel any boredom with you by pressing more gently.
Nor should the asker always confess that he's hoping for sex:
    let love sneak in undercover with the name of "friendship."   720
I've seen this approach give the slip to a girl who was downright severe;
    he who had been her attendant became her lover.

## THE LOVER'S PROPER APPEARANCE: PALE AND SKINNY

A white complexion's disgraceful for a sailor: he ought to be
    dark from the waters of the sea and the rays of the sun;

701. **when Achilles was in a hurry:** This could mean hurrying off to war,
or . . . a little too eager to reach the finish line in their mutual race.
713. **groveling:** Latin *supplex*, "suppliant"; the god did sometimes attempt
entreaty first, though he did not, even once, take no for an answer.

disgraceful, too, for the farmer, who ever with crooked plow          725
    and heavy hoe turns the earth under open sky;
and you who seek the fame of the Palládian crown—
    if *your* body is white, you'll be a disgrace.
But let every lover be pale: that's the right color for lovers;
    though many may think it's not so great, it is.          730
Pale over Sidë, Oríon used to wander the forests;
    pale was what Daphnis was for the stubborn naiad.
Let leanness, too, prove your feelings, and don't think there's any shame
    in placing a dark hood on your gleaming hair.
All-night vigils whittle down the bodies of youths,          735
    and care, and the pain arising from great love.
In order to obtain your desire, be a wreck,
    so anyone who sees you can say, "You're in love!"

### Your Worst Enemy: Your Best Friend

Should I complain or warn you that right and wrong are mixed up?
    Friendship is but a name, faith an empty name.          740
Alas, it isn't safe to praise what you love to a comrade:
    when he believes your praises, he sneaks in himself.
"But Actor's son did not defile the bed of Achilles;

---

727. **Palladian crown:** The crown of olive leaves (from the sacred tree of Pallas), the prize in the Olympian games.
729. **let every lover be pale:** Apparently the *praeceptor* has forgotten the advice he gave in line 513 to sport a healthy tan.
731. **Orion:** A gigantic mythical hunter and lothario who became a constellation. Sidë seems to have been his first wife.
732. **Daphnis:** A Sicilian shepherd who died for love; he was one of the mythical founders of pastoral poetry. He figures prominently in the two most famous exemplars of that genre, Theocritus's *Idylls* (early third century BC) in Greek and Virgil's *Eclogues* in Latin.
732. **naiad:** A sexy water nymph.
743. **Actor's son:** Patroclus (actually Actor's grandson); Achilles and Patroclus, whose relationship was passionate but (apparently) platonic in Homer

as far as Piríthoüs went, Phaedra was chaste.

Pýlades used to love Hermíone as Phoebus loved Pallas—                    745
  was like twin Castor to you, Tyndáreus's daughter!"

If anyone hopes for the same, he should hope for tamarisk trees
  to drop apples, and look for honey in the middle of a river.

Nothing is fun but what's foul; each cares only for his own pleasure,
  and even this gets its charm from another man's pain.                    750

Oh, the evil! An enemy's not to be feared by a lover;
  fly from the ones you trust and you'll be safe.

Beware of your kinsman, and your brother, and your dear comrade;
  this is the crowd that'll give you real grounds for fear.

## FINAL ADVICE: BE FLEXIBLE!

I was just about to wrap up, but . . . girls have a great variety                    755
  of hearts! Catch a thousand souls a thousand ways!

Not every land bears all the same things; that one's suited
  for vines, this one for olives; here, grains ripen well.

Hearts have as many characters as faces have shapes;
  the wise man will adapt to countless characters;                    760

like Próteus, he'll dissolve himself now into fickle waves,

---

and eroticized in later authors and artists, were a paradigm of male friend-
ship. Patroclus did not put the moves on Achilles's concubine Briseis.

744. **Pirithoüs . . . Phaedra:** The best friend and wife, respectively, of The-
seus. (Phaedra was decidedly *not* chaste in her passion for Theseus's son
Hippolytus.)

745. **Pylades . . . Pallas:** The friendship of Pylades and Orestes was also prover-
bial; Pylades (the *praeceptor* asserts) had no more sexual interest in Orestes's
wife Hermione (daughter of Menelaus and Helen) than Phoebus Apollo did
in his sister Pallas.

746. **Tyndareus's daughter:** Helen, the sister of twins Castor and Pollux.

761. **Proteus:** A shape-shifting god of the sea; he would deliver true informa-
tion only to those who could hold him fast until he returned to his true
(humanoid) form. Is there a hint here that the steadfast may finally attain
something true, or it this merely advice to keep shifting?

now be a lion, now a tree, now a bristling boar.
Some fish are caught by a casting-net, others by hooks,
    others the bulging nets drag in with taught rope.
A single style won't work for you for every age;            765
    the seasoned doe will spot a trap further away.
If you seem learned to the simple, or aggressive to the chaste,
    she'll lose confidence in herself at once, poor thing.
Thus it happens that one who's afraid to entrust herself to
    a decent man goes cheap to a worse one's embrace.        770

Part of the task I've undertaken is done, part remains;
    here let the anchor be cast and hold my ship.

# Ars Amatoria

BOOK 2

Sing "Io Paean!" Sing "Io Paean!" Sing it again!
   The prey I've been stalking has fallen into my trap!
The happy lover has given the verdant palm to my songs,
   which trump the Ascran and Maeónian old men.
Like this did Priam's son, the guest, having snatched the wife,    5
   set gleaming sail from heavily armed Amýclae;
like this was he who bore you in his victorious chariot,
   Hippodamía, conveyed by foreign wheels.
Not so fast, young man! Your timber's afloat in the middle
   of the waves, and the harbor I seek is a long way off.    10

1. **"Io Paean!":** Paean was originally a healing god, then an epithet for Apollo and Asclepius as gods of healing, and finally (along with "io" or "ie") a ritual cry of thanks for well-being and/or salvation—somewhat analogous to our "alleluia."
2. **prey:** Latin *praeda*; see on 1.114 "prize."
3. **palm:** A palm branch was given to the victor in an athletic or artistic competition.
4. **Ascran and Maeonian old men:** Hesiod (see on 1.27–28 "Clio . . . valleys") and Homer (from Maeonia, in Asia Minor), considered the authors of the most ancient and finest poetry.
6. **Amyclae:** City in Sparta where Helen and Menelaus lived; see on 1.54 "Greek girl . . . Phrygian man."
8. **Hippodamia:** Oenomaus of Pisa, father of Hippodamia, would allow her to marry only a man who beat him in a chariot race; Pelops won by trickery and carried off his prize.

It's not enough that (with me as prophet) the girl has come to you;
    my art is what caught her, my art is what must keep her.
Nor does it take less prowess to keep what you've got than to find it:
    that was luck, but this will be a work of art.
Now, if ever, Cytheréa and son, take my side;                    15
    now, Érato, for you've got the name of Love.
I'm ready to speak great things: what arts can make Love stay,
    the boy that strays throughout such a wide, wide world.
He's flighty, and he's got two wings to fly away with;
    it's very hard to set a limit on those.                      20

## THE STORY OF DAEDALUS AND ICARUS

Minos had done everything to keep his guest from escaping,
    but he managed to find a daring route through wings.
Daédalus, when he'd enclosed what the mother's crime had conceived—
    the semi-bovine human, semi-human bovine—
said, "Minos most just, let there be an end to the exile;         25
    let my ancestral land receive my ashes,
and since, driven by unfair Fate, I had not the power
    to live in my fatherland, grant me the power to die there.
If an old man's thanks are too cheap, grant return to the boy;
    if you don't want to spare the boy, spare the old man."       30

15. **Cytherea:** Venus (from her shrine on the island of Cythera, said to be her birthplace, southeast of the Peloponnese).
16. **Erato:** The Muse of erotic poetry (from Greek *erōs*, "sexual love"). Virgil famously invokes Erato near the beginning of the *Aeneid*'s second half (7.37); the *praeceptor*'s invocation of her here signals the second half of his two-book advice to men.
21. **Minos:** He was peeved with Daedalus for facilitating his wife Pasiphaë's affair with a bull (for the story, see 1.289–326).
24. **the semi-bovine human, semi-human bovine:** Seneca the Elder (writer on oratory, ca. 50 BC–AD 40) relates an anecdote in which Ovid's friends chose his three worst lines, Ovid his three favorite lines; naturally, they turned out to be the same three lines, and this was one of them (*Controversiae* [Debates] 2.2.12).

These things he'd said, but he could have said these things and much
    more—
    *that* one wasn't giving the man a way out.
As soon as he realized this, he said, "Now, Daédalus, now
    you've got some material for your genius to work with.
Minos has got control of the land and control of the sea;        35
    neither the earth nor the waves will let us escape.
What's left is a path through the sky: through the sky we'll try our
    journey.
    Grant permission, high Jupiter, to my attempt.
It's not that I'm aspiring to touch the seat of the stars;
    yours is the only way I can flee my master.        40
If there's a path through the Styx, we'll swim through Stygian waves;
    I'm going to have to change the laws of my nature."
Evils often inspire genius: who'd ever believe
    that a man was able to take a path through the air?
To make the oars of birds he arranges feathers in order        45
    and weaves a delicate work with linen bands;
the bottom part is attached by wax made supple by fire—
    and now the labor of his new art was finished.
The boy, beaming, kept fingering the wax and the feathers,
    unaware that these arms were made for his shoulders.        50
His father told him, "These ships will sail us to the fatherland;
    with this device we'll escape the clutches of Minos.
Minos has closed off everything else, but not the air;
    break through the air, which we can, through my invention.
But the maiden of Tégea, the comrade of Boötes,        55

41. **Styx:** See on 1.635–36 "Jupiter . . . Styx."
50. **arms:** Latin *arma*, "armor" or "equipment" rather than human "arms"—
but Ovid *would* have made this pun had he written in English. (Latin *armus*,
though from a different root than *arma*, does mean "shoulder.")
55. **maiden of Tegea, the comrade of Boötes:** Callisto, a nymph from Arcadia
(of which Tegea is a district) who was raped by Jupiter, turned into a bear
by Juno, and became the constellation Ursa Major ("Bigger Bear"). The

Oríon wielding his sword—you must not visit these;
stay behind me on the wings I've given you. I'll go in front.
    You follow; under my leadership, you'll be safe.
For if we get too close to the sun, going through the ethereal
    breezes, the wax won't be able to take the heat;                    60
or if we flap our wings down low too close to the waves,
    the supple feathers will get waterlogged by the sea.
Fly between the two—and fear the winds too, my son,
    and spread your sails wherever the breezes bear you."
Amid these warnings he fastens his work on the boy and shows
        him                                                             65
    how to move, like a mother bird teaching her chicks;
then he puts on the wings he's fashioned for his own shoulders
    and timidly poises his body for the new journey;
and now—about to take off—he kissed his little son,
    and the father's cheeks could not contain their tears.              70
There was a hill, lower than a mountain, higher than a plain:
    here the two bodies were launched on their wretched flight.
Daédalus moves his own wings himself and also looks back
    at his son's, and keeps his course in the same direction.
And now, delighting in the new journey, shedding his fear,              75
    Ícarus soars more boldly with daring art.
(Some man, while he was angling for fish with a quivering rod,
    saw them: his hand left behind the work it had started.)
Now Samos was on the left (Naxos had been left behind,

---

constellation Boötes ("Ox-Driver") comes (according to Ovid) from her son
Arcas, raised to the stars at the moment he was about to shoot his mother,
the bear. Together, these constellations roughly correspond to our Big Dipper.
56. **Orion:** See on 1.731 "Orion."
79–80. **Samos . . . Naxos . . . Paros . . . Delos:** Islands in the Aegean Sea.
Heading roughly northeast from Crete, Daedalus and Icarus have nearly made
it to Asia Minor (Samos is just off the coast).

and Paros, and Delos, loved by the Clárian god),                    80
Lebínthos was on the right, and Calýmne, shady with forests,
    and Astypaláea, ringed with shoals full of fish,
when the boy, excessively reckless in his unwary years,
    pushed his path too high and deserted his father.
The bindings fail, the wax liquefies from the god too near,          85
    and his waving arms can't hold the wispy winds.
Terrified, he looks down to the sea from the height of the sky;
    night rose and covered his eyes in his trembling dread.
The wax had melted away; he shakes his naked arms,
    and panics, and has nothing to hold him up.                      90
He plummets, and says, "Father, father, I'm carried away!" as he falls;
    the green waters closed his mouth as he was speaking.
But the unhappy father, a father no more, shouts, "Ícarus!"—
    shouts, "Ícarus! Where are you? What sky do you fly in?"—
was shouting, "Ícarus!" . . . He saw the feathers in the waves.      95
    The earth covers his bones, the sea has his name.
Minos had no power to imprison the wings of a man:
    *I'm* trying to detain a winged god!


80. **Delos, loved by the Clarian god:** Apollo (who had an oracle and grove at
Claros, in the Greek city of Colophon in Asia Minor) retained a fondness for
the island of Delos, his birthplace.
81–82. **Lebinthos . . . Calymne . . . Astypalaea:** More islands in the Aegean
not far from the Asia Minor coast.
85. **the god:** The Sun.
95. **was shouting, "Icarus!":** The switch from "shouts" to "was shouting" sug-
gests that in the very act of saying his son's name Daedalus learns the answer
to his question. The threefold "shouting" (*conclamatio*) of a dead loved one's
name was part of Roman funerary ritual; that Daedalus unwittingly per-
forms this ritual while still hoping to find his son alive adds to the pathos of
the scene.
96. **the sea has his name:** The Icarian Sea (near Icaria, an island southwest of
Samos).

### Magic Won't Work: Just Be Lovable

He's on the wrong track, whoever scurries to Haemónian arts
    or gives what he's plucked from the brow of a newborn horse.    100
It's not the herbs of Medéa that will make love live,
    or Marsian chants mixed with magic incantations:
the Phasian would have kept Aeson's son, Circe kept Ulysses,
    if only love could be held onto by song!
Nor will it do any good to give pale philters to girls;    105
    philters are bad for the mind and can lead to madness.
Let every wickedness be far hence! To be loved, be lovable,
    something a handsome face alone won't give you.
Even if you're a Níreus, beloved of ancient Homer,
    and a tender Hylas, snatched by the naiads' crime,    110
to keep your mistress and not be stunned that she's left you behind,
    add your endowment of wit to the goods of your body.
Beauty's a fragile good; the more the years pile up,
    the smaller it gets, and it's ravaged by its own length.
Neither violets nor yawning lilies are always in bloom;    115
    the thorn hardens, left behind by the rose it's lost.
Grey hairs are coming for you soon, you beautiful man;
    the wrinkles are coming soon to plow your body.
Now build your mind to make it last and add on to your beauty:
    the mind alone remains till the funeral pyre.    120

99. **Haemonian arts:** Thessaly (see on 1.6 "Haemonian ship") was famous for its witches.
100. **plucked from the brow of a newborn horse:** This substance, called *hippomanes* (horse-madness), was believed to be a powerful aphrodisiac.
102. **Marsian chants:** The Marsi, a tribe of central Italy, were famous for miraculous snakebite cures and other magical practices.
103. **Phasian . . . Aeson's son:** Medea and Jason.
104. **song:** See on 1.2 "song."
107. **be far hence:** See on 1.31–32 "Get ye . . . foot."
109. **Nireus:** Called by Homer the handsomest of the Greeks after Achilles, and proverbial for his beauty.

Take no small care to have cultivated the liberal arts
   in your breast and to have thoroughly learned two tongues.

## ULYSSES AND CALYPSO

Ulysses was no beauty, but eloquent he was—
   and he still tormented sea goddesses with love.
Oh, how often Calýpso grieved at his hurrying away,           125
   and claimed that the water wasn't fit for sailing!
She kept asking for The Fall of Troy again and again;
   he kept telling the same story different ways.
They were standing on the shore; there, too, lovely Calýpso
   demanded the Odrýsian chief's bloody death.           130
He, with a slender stick (for by chance he was holding a stick)
   depicts the work she asks for in the dense sand.
"This" he said "is Troy" (he made the walls on the shore);
   "here's your Símois; pretend this is my camp.
There was a field" (he makes a field) "which we spattered with
     Dolon's           135

121. **liberal arts:** Latin *ingenuae artes*, literally "freeborn arts," the studies appropriate for a free person (Latin *liber* = "free"), as opposed to the "servile arts" appropriate for slaves (*servi*). Political correctness (which might flinch at such class snobbery) was millennia away.

122. **two tongues:** Latin and Greek (which was the language of high culture, flirtation, and showing off, as French used to be among the English).

127. **asking for The Fall of Troy:** Throughout this scene, the Roman reader would be reminded of Virgil's Dido, who similarly begged her lover to keep retelling his own Fall of Troy story and later tried to talk him out of entrusting himself to the stormy waves.

130. **Odrysian chief:** Rhesus, a Thracian king (Odrysia = Thrace) allied to the Trojans. A prophecy stated that if his horses drank from the Xanthus river and ate Trojan grass, then Troy would never fall. Ulysses and Diomedes captured his horses and killed him on their night raid of the Trojan allies' camp.

134. **Simois:** A river of Troy.

blood, while he stays up hoping for Haemónian horses.
The tents of Sithónian Rhesus had been over there;
  that night the captured horses carried me back—"
he was drawing more, when suddenly Pérgamum was swept
  away by the tide, and the camp, with Rhesus its leader.                    140
Then the goddess said, "These waves you think will be faithful to you
  when you go—do you *see* what great names they've destroyed?"
The moral: beware of trusting in a treacherous figure,
  whoever you are—or have something more than your body.

## Be Obsequious

Skillful indulgence is excellent for capturing hearts;                       145
  harshness stirs up hatred and savage wars.
We hate the hawk, because it lives constantly under arms,
  and wolves whose habit is to attack timid sheep;
the swallow, though, because it's gentle, is free from men's traps,
  and the Chaónian bird has turrets to roost in.                             150
Get ye far hence, quarrels and battles of bitter tongue!
  Soft love is to be nourished by sweet words.

136. **Haemonian horses:** The horses of Achilles (who was from Thessaly: see on 1.6 "Haemonian ship"). Ulysses and Diomedes intercepted and killed Dolon on their night raid.
137. **Sithonian:** Thracian (Sithon was an old name for Thrace).
139. **Pergamum:** See on 1.478 "Pergamum."
143. **figure:** Latin *figura*, like our "figure," can refer to human shape or to a drawing. This is surely one of the *praeceptor*'s most outrageous concluding aphorisms.
150. **Chaonian bird:** The dove. The oracle of Jupiter at Dodona (in Chaonia, a region in Epirus in northwest Greece) was the oldest and one of the most famous in the Greco-Roman world. Prophetic messages issued from the rustling of the god's oak tree and from the doves that nested in its branches. Ovid likes to draw parallels between himself and nice birds, especially prophetic ones.
151. **Get ye far hence:** See on 1.31–32 "Get ye . . . foot."

Brides should drive off their men, grooms drive off brides through
    disputes,
    both constantly thinking the other one is suing;
this is what's fit for wives, the dowry of wives is disputes;      155
    a girlfriend should always hear the sounds she wants.
It wasn't the law that ordered you to come into one bed:
    in your case, the function of law is performed by Love.
Have soft sweet nothings and words that are pleasing to the ear
    on offer, so she'll be happy at your approach.      160

## ADVICE FOR PAUPERS

I'm not making my way as a teacher of loving for the rich;
    whoever is willing to spend has no need for my art.
He who says "Take!" when he pleases has got all the genius he needs;
    I give up—he's got more charm than my inventions.
I'm a prophet for paupers, because I loved as a pauper;      165
    since I wasn't able to give gifts, I gave words.
The pauper must love with caution, the pauper must fear to give
    insults,
    must bear many things the rich don't have to put up with.
I remember how I messed up my mistress's hair in my anger:
    how many days that anger robbed from me!      170

166. **I gave words:** This phrase, in this context, is the translator's despair. Latin *dare verba*, literally "to give words," is also an idiomatic expression meaning "to trick." Elsewhere, I have generally translated it "to give the slip (to)"; the pun in the present line is thus roughly equivalent to something like "Since I couldn't give her the expensive dress, I gave her the slip."

169. **I remember:** Phrases like "I remember," in poets like Ovid, generally signal a reference to a previous text, a phenomenon modern scholars often call an "Alexandrian footnote" (after the similar practice in Callimachus and other Alexandrian poets). In this case, the *praeceptor* "remembers" the hair-tearing scene in *Amores* 1.7. Part of the joke is that the "I" of the *Amores* and the *Ars* is supposedly the same person (despite their different personae); see "When the *Praeceptor* Reads" in the introduction. "I remember" could equally

I don't think I tore her tunic—I didn't notice it—but she
 had said so, and it was paid for at my expense.
But you, if you're sensible—avoid the mistakes your teacher
 made, and fear the losses my fault incurred;
make war with Párthians, but make peace with a cultured
  girlfriend,                                                              175
 and jokes, and whatever provides the reasons for love.
If she's not flirting and flattering you enough as her lover,
 stay the course and hold firm: she'll soften up later.
Compliance will bend the branch and curve it away from the tree;
 you break it if you give it all your strength.                                 180
Compliance is what swims rivers, nor could you conquer the stream
 if you swam against the direction of the current.
Compliance is what breaks tigers and Numídian lions;
 the bull gradually submits to the farmer's plow.
What was pricklier than Nonácrian Atalánta?                                          185
 That bruiser still succumbed to the merits of a man.
They say for his own sad lot and the girl's ungentle deeds
 Milánion often wept out under the trees;
often at her command he bore treacherous nets on his neck;
 often he pierced fierce boars with his savage spear.                           190

---

well be used of a character "remembering" his or her behavior in a text by a
different author, as when, say, Ariadne in Ovid's *Fasti* "remembers" how she
called Theseus "traitor" back when she was a character in Catullus's poem 64.
175. **Parthians:** See on 1.179–80 "O buried Crassi and flag."
183. **Numidian:** Numidia, originally the country of African nomads, was an
ancient kingdom (then Roman province, then client kingdom) in North
Africa.
185. **Nonacrian Atalanta:** Nonacrian = Arcadian (from Mount Nonacris in
Arcadia, in the central Peloponnese). In the version of Atalanta's story fol-
lowed here, which is similar to that in Propertius 1.1 (who sees it as an exem-
plum of long-suffering love), Milanion won the beautiful virgin huntress's
love by protecting her from the would-be rapist centaur Hylaeus, as well as
by general subservience.

He often felt a wound from Hyláeus's outstretched bow
   (although he knew another bow better than this one).
I'm not commanding you to arm up and scale the Maenálian
   woods, or to carry hunting nets on your neck,
or commanding you to offer your breast to flying arrows;      195
   the commands my cautious art gives will be gentle.
Give in when she fights back: giving in, you'll walk away victor—
   just be sure to play the role she commands.
She's critical? Be critical. Whatever she approves, approve.
   What she says, say; what she denies, deny.      200
She's laughed? Laugh in response. If she weeps, remember to weep;
   she should set the terms for your expression.
Or if she's gambling and rolling ivory dice with her hand,
   roll badly, and let her win even if she rolls badly;
or if you play knucklebones, don't make her pay if she loses;      205
   make sure you often get the ruinous Dogs;
or if the counter will go forth in the guise of a bandit,
   make sure your soldier is killed by the glassy foe.
Hold out her parasol yourself with its ribs extended,
   yourself make room in the crowd for her when she comes.      210
Don't hesitate to produce a footstool for her trim couch;
   put on or take off the sandal on her tender foot.

192. **another bow:** Need I point out that this means Cupid's?
193–94. **Maenalian woods:** Maenalus is a mountain range in Arcadia, but also, in some versions, the name of Atalanta's father (in others he is Iasus or Schoeneus).
203. **ivory dice:** The reference here seems to be to the game of *tessera* (die), a kind of backgammon.
205. **knucklebones:** Knucklebones (*tali*) involved throwing four four-sided dice; the Dogs (all ones) was the worst throw, the Venus Throw (all different numbers) the best.
207. **bandit:** The reference is to a game called *ludus latrunculorum* (game of little bandits), a two-player military board game involving counters of different colors on a sort of checkerboard.
209. **Hold out her parasol yourself:** See on 1.139 "mistress."

Often, too, even if you're shivering yourself, you need to
  warm up your mistress's hand in your freezing bosom.
Don't think it's shameful for you (shameful, yes—but charming)       215
  to hold up her mirror with your well-bred hand.

## BE HUMILIATED (LIKE HERCULES AND APOLLO)

That man who earned heaven (which he himself had previously borne)
  when his stepmother got tired of supplying monsters
is said to have held a basket among the Iónian girls,
  and to have spun his unworked wool to perfection.                  220
The Tirýnthian hero obeyed his mistress's command:
  now go be shy about bearing what he bore!
She commands you to be in the Forum: always be sure you arrive
  before the commanded hour, and don't leave till late.
She's told you to go and meet someone? Put everything off:          225
  run! And don't let the crowd hold you back as you go!
She's done with her banquet and making her way back home at night?
  Then too, come if she calls, in place of her slave!
She's out in the country and tells you to come? Love hates the lazy:
  if you haven't got wheels, make your way on foot!                  230
The oppressive season and thirsty Dog Star must not delay you,
  or the road that's blinding white with heaps of snow.

217. **That man:** Hercules. During one of his labors (fetching the golden apples
of the Hesperides, nymphs who tended a mythical garden), he held up the
world for the Hesperides' father, Atlas, so Atlas could fetch the apples for
him. Atlas intended to leave Hercules with the burden permanently; Hercu-
les asked him to take it back for a minute so he could get his lion skin more
comfortably settled, then absconded with the apples.
219. **held a basket:** Hercules spent a year doing women's work for Omphale,
queen of Lydia (in Ionia, a region on the west coast of Asia Minor).
221. **Tirynthian:** Tiryns, a settlement in the Peloponnese near Argos, was
associated with Hercules either as his birthplace or as the kingdom he was
destined to rule.
231. **Dog Star:** Sirius, which rose in August and was seen as bringing destruc-
tive heat and disease.

Love is a military exercise. Withdraw, ye sluggish!
    These flags are not for timid men to guard.
Night, and winter, and long marches, and savage pains,        235
    and every labor belong to this soft camp.
Often you'll suffer a shower let loose from heavenly cloud,
    and often you'll lie there shivering on the bare ground.
Cýnthius is said to have pastured the cattle of Pheres's son
    Admétus and hidden out in a tiny hut.        240
What's fit for Phoebus is fit for anyone! Strip off your pride,
    whoever you are who care about love that will last.
If a path through safe and level ground is blocked for you,
    and the door barricaded by a stubborn bolt,
nevertheless, slip down head first through an open roof,        245
    and let a high window, too, give you secret passage.
She'll be happy in knowing that she's the cause of your danger:
    this will be a sure pledge of love to your mistress.
You could have often done without your girl, Leánder:
    you swam across so she might know your heart.        250

## TAMPERING WITH THE SERVANTS

You shouldn't blush to win over her maids, each in order
    of rank, and you shouldn't blush to win over slaves:
greet each one by his own name (it costs you nothing!),
    ambitious one, and shake their lowly hands!

233. **Love is a military exercise:** The following list of analogies between lovers and soldiers is abbreviated from the far more extensive one in *Amores* 1.9.
239. **Cynthius:** Phoebus Apollo (from Mount Cynthus on Delos), who fell in love with King Admetus and endured the indignities here described.
249. **Leander:** This brave soul proved his love to Hero, a priestess of Venus, by swimming the Hellespont (modern Dardanelles, a narrow—but not that narrow—strait between Greece and Asia Minor) every night to meet her, aided by the light she lit for him. One stormy winter night the light went out, he drowned, and she killed herself. *Heroides* 18 and 19 are love letters between the pair.

But still, when a slave solicits you (it's a minor expense!),                255
    give him some little gifts on the Day of Fortune;
give the maid some, too, on the day the Gallic band
    paid the penalty, deceived by the clothing of wives.
Trust me, make a crowd of your own; let the doorkeeper and
    the guard at her bedroom door always be among them.                     260
I'm not commanding you to give pricey gifts to your mistress;
    give little things, but little things cleverly chosen.
When the field is nice and rich, when the branches bend with their
        weight,
    the boy should bring her rustic gifts in a basket
(you can say they were sent you from your suburban property               265
    even if they were bought on the Sacred Way);
he should bring either grapes or the chestnuts that Amarýllis
    used to love, but now she loves no more.
Indeed, with a thrush, even, or by sending a garland,
    you can testify that you remember your mistress.                       270
(Using these to buy childless old people you hope will die soon
    is shameful; damn those who give presents a bad name!)

256. **Day of Fortune:** June 24. The cult of Fortune (Latin *Fortuna*) was established by Servius Tullius, the sixth king of Rome, who was thought to have had a slave mother; it was popular with slaves.

257–58. **day the Gallic band paid the penalty:** July 7. After the Gauls nearly took over Rome in 390 BC (see on 1.413 "tearful Allia"), the Romans' Latin neighbors demanded the surrender of the Romans' freeborn women and girls. Maidservants went in their place, then signaled the Romans to attack while their enemies were asleep. Ovid varies this by making the Gauls themselves, rather than the Latins, the victims of the deception.

266. **Sacred Way:** The Main Street of Rome.

267. **Amaryllis:** In Virgil's *Eclogue* 2.52, the shepherd Corydon refers to a gift of "chestnuts, which . . . Amaryllis used to like" (Amaryllis is a typical country-girl name); the implication there, which the *praeceptor* clarifies here, is that Amaryllis has developed more expensive tastes.

271. **childless old people:** The *praeceptor*'s outrage here only serves to underline the many parallels between courting a girl and courting an inheritance.

## Use Poetry

Why should I instruct you to send tender verses as well?
  Woe is me, song hasn't received much honor.
Songs are praised, but it's magnificent gifts that are sought:    275
  as long as he's rich, a total barbarian's charming.
Truly, we live in a Golden Age: the greatest honor's
  on sale for gold, and gold is what bargains for love.
Homer, you can arrive in person, flanked by the Muses,
  and if you bring nothing with you, out you go, Homer!    280
And yet there do exist—the rarest crowd—cultured girls;
  the other crowd isn't cultured, but wants to be.
Both of these should be praised through songs; the reciter should
  commend his songs, whatever they are, through sweet sounds.
Thus, for both groups, the song he spent all night on for them    285
  may possibly play the part of a tiny gift.

## Make Everything Her Idea

But what you're about to do on your own and you think is useful,
  always make sure your girlfriend asks you to do:
if freedom has been promised to some one of your slaves,
  be sure it's through your mistress that he seeks it.    290
If you're remitting a slave's punishment and savage fetters,
  make her owe you for what you were going to do.
The benefit should be yours, the glory should go to your girlfriend;
  no loss—let her play the part of the one in control.

## Be Wowed by Her Beauty

But whoever is concerned with holding onto a girl—    295
  be sure she thinks you're thunderstruck at her beauty.
If she's in Týrians, you'll praise the Týrian wraps;

297. **Tyrians:** Fabric dyed with the deep-purple dye from Tyre (a coastal city
in modern Lebanon) was a quintessential luxury item.

if she's in Cöans, think the Cöans are charming.
She's in gold? Let her be more precious to you than gold itself;
    if it's wool she's put on, applaud the wool she's put on.      300
She's standing there in her tunic? Shout, "You set me on fire!"—
    but beg her, with timid voice, to mind the cold.
Care's been taken in arranging her part? Praise her part.
    Her hair's been curled with fire? Curled hair, be charming.
Admire her arms while she's dancing, admire her voice while
      she's singing,      305
    and launch into a complaint because she's left off.
Even the sex itself—and the very best part—you're allowed
    to adore, and count off all the pleasures she's given.
Though she's been more violent than the gruesome Medúsa,
    to her own lover, she'll become gentle and kind.      310
Only make sure you're not obviously being fake in those words,
    and don't wreck what you've said by the look on your face.
If it stays hidden, art works; if it's found out, it brings shame
    and deservedly erases trust forever.

## When She's Sick

Often in autumn, when the year is most beautiful,      315
    and the grape begins to blush, full of purple wine,
when now we're shriveled with cold, and now relaxed with warmth,
    the dubious air brings a languor to our bodies.
Certainly, let her be well! But if she's lying there ill
    and has felt the evil of her climate in her sickness,      320
then should your love and devotion be made plain to the girl;
    sow, then, something to reap later on with full sickle.

298. **Cöans:** Silk clothing from the island of Cos (in the eastern Aegean) was formfitting and see-through.
309. **Medusa:** A snaky-haired monster whose glance turned men to stone. For more on this myth (and its Freudian implications), see on 3.504 "Gorgon's fire."

You shouldn't show any impatience with her fretful sickness,
    and whatever she'll allow should be done at your hands,
and she should see you weeping, and you should tirelessly kiss her,    325
    and she should drink in your tears with her parched mouth.
Make many prayers, but all in her presence—and as much as you want
    have happy dreams that you can tell her about.
An old woman should come to purify her bed and room,
    and to bring sulfur and eggs with trembling hand.    330
All these things will show evidence of pleasing concern;
    for many, this route has led to a spot in a will.
But don't go courting the patient's resentment by your services:
    your charming officiousness should know when to stop.
Don't keep her away from food or give her draughts of bitter    335
    medicine; let your rival mix *those* concoctions.

## BECOME HABITUAL

But don't keep using the wind to which you entrusted your sails
    near the shore, once you're out on the open sea.
While a new love toddles about, it gains strength through experience;
    it will grow strong with time if you feed it up well.    340
That bull you're scared of you used to pet when it was a calf;
    the tree you recline under now was once a sapling.
Tiny at birth, the river acquires wealth as it runs
    and picks up many waters wherever it goes.
Make her get used to you: there's no force greater than habit;    345
    until you achieve it, shy away from no boredom.
Let her always see you, always offer her ears to you;
    keep on showing your face, night and day.

330. **sulfur and eggs:** Two ingredients commonly used for ritual purification, though not necessarily in combination.
332. **a spot in a will:** See on 271 "childless old people."

## Then Make Yourself Scarce—But Not Too Long (with Mythological Examples)

Once you've got greater confidence that you could be missed,
    that she might actually care if you're far away,        350
give it a rest: the field that lies fallow repays investment,
    and arid land absorbs the waters from heaven.
Phyllis burned more moderately in Demóphoön's presence;
    as soon as he set sail, she really blazed up!
Wily Ulysses tortured Penélope with his absence;        355
    you missed your Son of Phýlacus, Laodamía.
But only short breaks are safe. With time, emotions wane;
    the absent love vanishes and a new one sneaks in.
While Meneláus was gone, so Helen wouldn't lie alone,
    she spent her night in the warm embrace of her guest.    360

353. **Phyllis:** This Thracian princess, married to the Athenian Demophoön, missed him so much when he had to go back to Athens that, fearing he would never return (though he did intend to), she killed herself. For her story, see *Rem.* 591–608.

355. **Wily Ulysses tortured Penelope:** His twenty years of war and wandering, reasons the *praeceptor*, were a clever means of sharpening his wife's passion (that man was wily indeed!).

356. **Son of Phylacus:** Protesilaus (grandson of Phylacus), the first Greek to die at Troy (a prophecy stated that the first Greek to set foot on Trojan soil would be killed, and he was that man). His new bride, Laodamia, unable to endure the separation, prayed to see his Shade, and her prayer was granted for a few hours. She then made a bronze statue of him, which she embraced like the real thing; when her father found out and had the image burned, she leapt on the flames and killed herself (thus joining her husband in the underworld).

360. **her guest:** Paris. Part of what makes this section so funny is the clash between the sacred obligations of hospitality in Homeric society, the violation of which resulted in a massive war, and the comparative triviality of entertaining in aristocratic Roman circles. See on 1.54 "Greek girl . . . Phrygian man."

How stupid was this, Meneláus? You went off by yourself,
    while your wife and your guest were under the same roof?
You're handing over timid doves to a hawk, you moron!
    Handing a pen full of sheep to a mountain wolf!
Helen's not the one sinning here, nor is the adulterer:                        365
    he's doing what you and anyone else would do.
You're forcing this adultery by giving them time and place:
    what did the girl do but take your suggestion?
What should she do? Man gone, guest here (no ignorant redneck!),
    and she's scared of sleeping alone in an empty bed.                       370
Átreus's son should deal with it. I declare Helen not guilty:
    she enjoyed the courtesies of a cultured man.

## HELL HATH NO FURY

But neither is the tawny boar so savage in wrath
    when it flings off rushing hounds with its lightning tusk,
nor the lioness when she's giving her teats to nursing cubs,                  375
    nor the little viper an unwitting foot has stepped on,
as a woman when she's caught a rival in her partner's bed:
    her blazing expression makes clear what's on her mind.
She rushes to fire and the sword, and is carried away, all decorum
    gone, like one struck by the horns of the Theban god.                    380
The barbarian woman of Colchis avenged her husband's fault
    and betrayal of marriage laws through her own sons;

363. **timid doves to a hawk:** The irony here is enhanced by the common use of such predator-prey animal similes in epic battle scenes, especially given Paris's conspicuous lack of prowess on the battlefield (as opposed to his superiority in the bedroom).
369. **ignorant redneck:** Latin *rusticus*; see on 1.607 "rustic."
380. **Theban god:** Bacchus (whose mother, Semele, was from Thebes and who often appeared with bull's horns).
381. **barbarian woman of Colchis:** Medea.

another baleful mother is this swallow you see here:
    look, she has a breast that's stained with blood!
This is what breaks down loves that are firmly established and
      strong:                                                                                    385
    prudent men had better fear such crimes!

## How to Cheat

Now, my ruling is not consigning you to just one girl—
    gods forbid! A new bride could scarcely get *that*!
Have fun, but let propriety in cheating conceal your fault;
    don't look to acquire glory from the sin.                              .               390
And don't give a gift the other woman could recognize,
    and don't always have your naughtiness at the same time;
and, lest the woman catch you in a hideout she knows,
    don't have just one place where you meet all your women;
and whenever you write, first carefully inspect the whole tablet      395
    yourself: many women read more than was meant for their eyes!
When wounded, Venus wages just war and hurls back the spear,
    giving *you* the same complaint she just complained.
While Átreus's son was content with one woman, she, too,
    was faithful; her man's sin was what made her wicked.                  400

---

383. **this swallow:** Procne. After the Thracian king Tereus, married to the Athenian princess Procne, raped her sister, Philomel (and locked her up in the woods and cut out her tongue), Procne found out when Philomel sent her a tapestry depicting the crime; Procne killed Itys, her son by Tereus, in vengeance. Tereus, Procne, and Philomel all turned into birds (he a hoopoe, the sisters a nightingale and a swallow—though which sister became which bird varies in different versions).

399. **Atreus's son:** This time, Agamemnon (though "Atreus's son" was Menelaus at 371). Ovid has fun juxtaposing the woman troubles of the two sons of Atreus with the two daughters of Tyndareus (Agamemnon and Menelaus were married to Clytemnestra and Helen, respectively). One of the payoffs for retaining patronymics in translation (e.g., translating *Atrides* as "Atreus's son" rather than substituting "Agamemnon") is that it highlights this irony.

She'd heard that, even with laurel in hand and fillet on brow,
    Chryses hadn't prevailed on behalf of his daughter;
she'd heard about your troubles, abducted Lyrnésian woman,
    and how disgraceful delays kept prolonging the war.
Yet these things, she'd heard: Priam's daughter, she'd seen herself:     405
    the victor was the shameful prize of his prize.
So Tyndáreus's daughter let Thyéstes's son in her heart and bedroom
    and took terrible revenge on her sinning man.
If things you've done a good job of concealing are somehow revealed,
    even if they're revealed, still, keep on denying them.     410
Don't be more submissive or more flattering than usual:
    that's a very clear sign of a guilty mind.
But don't go easy on the muscle; all peace depends on one thing:
    previous Venus must be refuted through sex.

## What to Eat (or Not)

There are women who'd instruct you take savory, noxious     415
    herb; in my opinion, that is poison.
Or they mix pepper in with the seeds of stinging nettle
    and golden chamomile ground up in old wine.
The goddess, however, can't stand to be forced to her joys like that
    (the one lofty Eryx holds on his shady hill).     420
White onion, from the Pelásgian city of Alcáthoüs,
    and the salacious herb that comes from the garden,

403. **Lyrnesian women:** Briseis; Achilles sacked Lyrnesos (near Troy).
405. **Priam's daughter:** Cassandra.
406. **prize:** See on 1.114 "prize."
420. **Eryx:** A mountain in western Sicily that housed a sanctuary of Venus.
421. **Pelasgian:** The Pelasgians were a mythical, pre-Greek tribe that lived in various Greek locations and colonized a lot; the term connotes something ancient and indigenous.
421. **Alcathoüs:** Son of Pelops (see on 8 "Hippodamia") and founder of the city of Megara (in Attica, near Corinth).
422. **salacious herb:** Arugula (Latin *eruca*), used as an aphrodisiac.

and eggs should be consumed, Hyméttian honey consumed,
   and nuts produced by the pine with its sharp leaves.

## AN OPPOSITE STRATEGY: JEALOUSY

Learned Érato, why are you veering into magic arts?         425
   My chariot should hug the post on the inside lane.
You who were just taking my advice to hide your crimes,
   change course, and take my advice to *reveal* your cheating.
My fickleness isn't to blame: the curved keel doesn't always
   make use of the same wind to carry its passengers.         430
Sometimes we sail with Thracian Bóreas, sometimes with Eurus;
   often the sails swell with Zephyr, often with Notus.
Observe how in the chariot the driver now lets the reins flow
   loose, now holds back the galloping horses by art.
With some women, timid indulgence gets no thanks for its slavery,   435
   and if there isn't a rival around, love wilts;
often when circumstances are favorable hearts get spoiled;
   benefits are hard to endure philosophically.
As a light flame whose strength is gradually wasting away
   lies hidden itself, with ash whitening on its surface,        440
but nevertheless, if you add some sulfur it finds its extinguished
   flame and the light that was there before returns:
so, when safety and stagnation make lazy hearts dull,
   it takes some stinging goads to draw love back out.
Make her afraid about you, reheat her lukewarm heart;        445
   let her grow pale at evidence of your crime.

---

423. **Hymettian:** Mount Hymettus, near Athens, was famous for its honey.
425. **Erato:** See on 16 "Erato."
426. **post:** The most dangerous part of a Roman chariot race was the tricky turn around the *meta* (turning-post) that marked its halfway point.
431–32. **Boreas . . . Eurus . . . Zephyr . . . Notus:** Roughly the North, East, West, and South winds.
435. **slavery:** See on 1.139 "mistress."

O four times and—as many times as I can't even count—
  happy, the man over whom an injured girl grieves!
A girl who, as soon as the crime has reached her unwilling ears,
  collapses, and speech and color desert the poor thing!          450
I want to be the man whose hair she tears out in her fury,
  the man whose soft cheeks she goes after with her nails,
the one she looks at through tears, and glares at with savage eyes,
  the one she wants to live without—but can't.
How long, you ask? She should complain of her wound only
    briefly,                                                        455
  so wrath doesn't gather strength from protracted delay.
Long before that, your arms should encircle her snowy neck,
  and you should receive her weeping into your bosom;
give kisses as she weeps, give Venus's joys as she weeps:
  peace will reign! That's the only way to cure wrath.             460
When she's got up a good rage, when she seems your determined foe,
  then, go after the pact of sex: she'll be tame.
That is where Concord lives, with weapons laid aside;
  that's the place—believe me—where Grace is born.
The doves that fought just now—they're nuzzling beaks together;   465
  their murmuring is full of words and sweet nothings.

## THE ORIGIN OF THE WORLD AND HUMAN SOCIETY

The universe at first was a confused, jumbled mass,
  and the face of stars and earth and sea was the same;

447. **four times and:** The *praeceptor* takes the epic formula "three and four times" to the next level.
463. **Concord:** Latin *Concordia*. The *OCD* remarks, "The cult of personified harmonious agreement . . . within the body politic at Rome . . . is an effective diagnostic of its absence." As so often, a political concept has been mischievously eroticized.
464. **Grace:** Latin *Gratia*—one of the hardest words to translate, as it embraces the whole range of its English cognates ("grace," "gracefulness," "gratitude," "graciousness").

soon sky was imposed on earth, the ground was encircled by sea,
    and empty void retreated to its own place;                             470
the forest received beasts, the air received birds to hold,
    and you, fish, kept hidden in yielding water.
Then the human race used to wander in lonely fields—
    it consisted of pure strength and a rough body;
the forest had been its home, grass its food, leaves its bed,              475
    and for a long time no one recognized anyone else.
They say seductive pleasure softened those fierce spirits:
    woman and man had come to a stop in one place.
All by themselves, without a teacher, they learned what do to:
    Venus did her delicious work without art.                              480
The bird has something to love; something to join her joys with
    is found by the female fish in the middle of the water;
the deer follows her mate, serpent is captured by serpent;
    the dog clings in adultery with the dog;
the ewe is happily mounted, the cow is happy with a bull;                  485
    the snub-nosed she-goat holds up the smelly male.
Mares are driven to frenzy, and follow stallions through places
    far distant, even with rivers in between.
Therefore, for a wrathful woman, go get strong medicines;
    those are the only things to calm her fierce pain.                     490
Those medicines are better than Macháon's potions;
    when you've sinned, it's by these you'll be reinstated.

484. **adultery:** Latin *adulterium*, which implies the "contamination" or "coun-
terfeiting" that would result from an illicit affair with a woman whose chil-
dren *should* be legitimate heirs to their father's property. "Adultery" seems a
strange word to apply to sex between animals (and dogs no less, proverbial
for their sexual shamelessness), but it is the word the *praeceptor* chooses.
491. **Machaon's potions:** In Homer, Machaon is a son of the healing god
Asclepius and a skilled doctor himself.

## AN APOLLONIAN INTERVENTION

As I was singing this, suddenly Apollo appeared at hand
    and moved the strings of his gilded lyre with his thumb.
Laurel was in his hands, his sacred hair was woven          495
    with laurel: he was a prophet to see as he came!
He said to me, "O tutor of lascivious Love,
    go on and bring your students to my temple,
where there is an inscription, famous throughout the whole world,
    that orders each person to be known to himself.        500
He who is known to himself is the only one who'll love wisely
    and finish every job according to his strength.
He whom Nature has given beauty, the woman should watch;
    one with good color, lie down and keep showing some shoulder;
one who's charming in conversation, avoid sulky silence;     505
    one who sings artfully, sing; who drinks artfully, drink.
But orators mustn't declaim in the middle of a conversation,
    or a crazy poet read his own songs out loud."

493. **As I was singing . . . at hand:** The sudden appearance of Apollo leads the reader to expect a *revocatio* (calling back), a formulaic scene (with pedigree harking back to Callimachus) in which a god appears and tells a poet to sing a different kind of poetry. For instance, as Virgil's alter ego Tityrus was singing of kings and battles (i.e., epic poetry), Apollo plucked his ear and told him to sing of pastoral themes instead (*Eclogue* 6.3–5). Such is not quite the intervention in store here.

495. **Laurel:** In *Metamorphoses* 1, Ovid relates how the laurel became Apollo's sacred tree: to save herself from Apollo's attempts to woo/catch/rape her, Daphne (Greek "laurel") metamorphosed into that tree in the nick of time. All of Apollo's attempts to find love in the *Metamorphoses*, in fact, end in frustration or disaster (he made the mistake of taunting Cupid early on, not entirely unlike a certain poet: see on 1.24 "the wound he's made").

500. **to be known to himself:** The famous inscription on Apollo's temple at Delphi, "Know Thyself," is applied (naturally) to erotic pursuits.

508. **a crazy poet read his own songs out loud:** Wouldn't it have been wonderful to be at the dinner party where Ovid read this line out loud?

That's what Phoebus advised; when Phoebus advises, listen!
    Faith in this god's sacred mouth is solid.                              510

## Back to the Sufferings of Love

I'm called back to the topic. Whoever will love wisely
    will prevail and get what he's after through my art.
Furrows don't always return what's invested in them with interest,
    nor does the breeze always help out wavering ships.
As for lovers, there's little that helps them and more to hurt them:   515
    they need to accept that their spirits must bear a great deal.
As many rabbits as graze on Mount Athos, or bees in Hybla,
    as many berries as Pallas's blue-green tree bears,
as many shells on the shore—that's how many pains are in Love!
    The arrows we suffer are dripping with plenty of poison.            520
They'll say she's gone out—but perhaps you'll see her there inside:
    believe that she's gone out and your eyes deceive you.
Her door is locked to you, even though she promised you a night:
    put up even with lying on the dirty ground.
Perhaps that perfidious maid will even say with a haughty              525
    expression, "What's *that* man doing besieging our door?"
Get on your knees and sweet-talk the doorpost and the harsh girl
    and hang on her door some roses you've swiped from your head.
When she wants, be there; when she's avoiding you, go away;
    it's boorish for men of breeding to become bores.                 530
Why should your girlfriend be able to say, "There's no escaping
    this man!"? Common sense isn't always a bad thing.
And don't think there's any disgrace in putting up with the girl's
    curses and lashes, or kissing her tender feet.

517. **Mount Athos:** A mountain in Macedonia.
517. **Hybla:** A town in Sicily that made great honey.
518. **Pallas's blue-green tree:** The olive.

## Dealing with Rivals

Why get hung up on small stuff? My soul urges greater things:          535
  great things I sing! People, give me your whole attention.
My labor is arduous—but virtue is nothing if not
  arduous. My art demands difficult toil!
Endure a rival with patience: victory will be on your side,
  and you'll be the victor in great Jupiter's Citadel.                 540
Believe that no mere man, but the Pelásgian Oak
  is telling you this: it's the greatest thing my art has.
She's flirting? Deal with it. Writing to him? Don't touch the tablets.
  Let her come and go wherever she pleases.
Husbands afford this freedom to lawfully wedded wives                  545
  (when you, soft Sleep, are also assisting their cause).
In this art, I confess, I'm not exactly perfect;
  what can I do? I fall short of my own advice.
Some guy gives my girl a secret sign in my presence,
  I live with it? Don't let rage take me for a ride?                   550
I remember, her own man had kissed her; I complained
  about the kiss: my love's overflowing with savagery!
More than once this flaw has hurt me: that man is more skillful
  who politely invites other men to come in.

540. **Jupiter's Citadel:** The temple of Jupiter Optimus Maximus ("Best and Greatest") on the Capitoline Hill (the source of that baffling "o" in our word "capitol"—i.e., "building that houses a legislature") held the Romans' greatest war trophies, such as the *spolia opima* (finest spoils), armor taken directly by a victorious general from a conquered general.
541. **Pelasgian Oak:** See on 150 "Chaonian bird" and 421 "Pelasgian."
545. **lawfully wedded wives:** But of course, the *praeceptor* is not teaching adultery! He means only freedwomen (*libertinae*), who don't count! See on 3.615 "freedom has . . . been claimed."
551. **I remember:** An "Alexandrian footnote" (see on 169 "I remember") to *Amores* 1.4.
554. **politely invites:** Latin *conciliare*, sometimes used as a euphemism for "to act as a pander" (as in *Rem.* 524). For a husband to collude in his wife's

But it's better not to know. Let her cheating be covered up,                555
    so shame doesn't flee in defeat from a face that's told all.
All the more then, young men, don't try to catch out your women:
    let them sin and think they've fooled you in sinning.
Love grows for those who are caught: when two share the same
      fortune,
    both persist in whatever caused their downfall.                560

## MARS AND VENUS

A story is told—the best-known one in all of heaven—
    of Mars and Venus captured by Múlciber's tricks.
Father Mars, driven crazy by his insane love of Venus,
    had turned from a frightening captain into a lover.
When he asked her, Venus (no goddess is more tender than she),     565
    no farm girl, didn't play hard to get with Gradívus.
Ah, how often that minx is said to have laughed at her husband's
    feet, and his hands, hardened by fire or art!
Whenever she mimicked Vulcan in front of Mars, it was charming;
    with her beauty was mixed an abundance of grace.               570
But at first, they'd take great pains to keep their sex a secret;
    their misbehavior was full of bashful shame.
On evidence from the Sun (who could deceive the Sun?),
    the actions of his wife were made known to Vulcan.
(Sun, what a bad example you're setting! Ask her for a gift:        575
    if you'll shut up she's got something to give you, too!)

---

adultery, let alone to arrange it, was a serious and punishable offense (*leno-cinium*, "pimping") under Augustus's adultery legislation.
562. **Mulciber's:** Vulcan (Mulciber), the god of blacksmiths and technology, was great with his hands but lame in his feet—not the most attractive choice for the goddess of sex. The epithet "Mulciber" seems to have been derived from Latin *mulcere*, "to soothe" (he "soothed" destructive fire so it could be used).
566. **farm girl:** Latin *rustica*; see on 1.607 "rustic."
566. **Gradivus:** A title of Mars, from the word for "stride" or "march" (*gradi*).

Múlciber arranges invisible nets around
    and above the bed: his work deceives the eyes.
He pretends he's going to Lemnos. The lovers come to their pact:
    they get tangled in the nets and both lie there naked!       580
He summons the gods. The captives make quite a spectacle;
    it's thought that Venus could scarcely contain her tears.
Not only can't they cover their faces, they can't even make
    a screen for their obscene parts with their hands!
Some joker said with a laugh, "O bravest Mars, if they're a    585
    burden for you, transfer those chains to *me*!"
Scarcely did he free those captive bodies, Neptune,
    by your prayers: Mars heads to Thrace, she to Paphos.
Now you've done it, Vulcan! What they did in secret before
    they do quite openly now, and all shame has vanished!    590
But you keep confessing you acted like a fool, you dolt,
    and they say that you are sorry about your art.
You all must be forbidden this: Dióne, captured, forbids
    the setting of that trap which caught herself.
Don't you all go setting out nets for your rival, and don't go    595
    tracking down words a secretive hand has written;
men should go after those things (if they think they're worth going
    after)
    whom fire and water has turned into lawful men.

---

579. **Lemnos:** An island sacred to him in the northern Aegean.
585. **Some joker:** In Homer, it is Mercury (a notorious prankster; he too has an affair with Venus later on).
587. **Neptune:** Neither Homer nor Ovid explains why the god of the sea should be the one to intervene here.
588. **Paphos:** A city sacred to her on the coast of Cyprus.
593. **Dione:** In some versions she's the mother of Venus, but she comes to be associated with Venus herself.
598. **fire and water:** The groom would offer these, as key ingredients of life, to his bride; the singular verb "has" emphasizes the formulaic nature of the phrase (which signifies not "fire" and "water" individually but "the ceremonial

See, I'm testifying once more: my fun here is only
    with things outside of the law: there's no hem in my jokes!    600

## KEEP IT SECRET

Who'd dare to broadcast to the profane the rites of Ceres,
    or the great rituals founded in Sámothrace?
It's a minor virtue to keep things quiet; on the other hand,
    to blab things that should be kept quiet is a major vice.
It's right that tattletale Tántalus keeps on grabbing in vain    605
    at apples on the tree and thirsts in the middle of the water!
Cytheréa expressly commands that her rites be kept quiet:
    I'm warning you—no chatterbox should approach them.
Even if Venus's mysteries aren't hidden in caskets
    and tambourines don't clatter out frenzied warnings,    610
still, every day, they're practiced in such a way between us
    that they're meant to remain just that: between us.
Venus herself, when she's taken her clothes off, stoops a bit
    to cover her private parts with her left hand.

---

offering of fire and water"). Exiles were forbidden fire and water in the land
from which they were banished. The two uses of "men" in this couplet play
on the senses of *vir* as "male" and "husband"; see on 1.310 "your man . . .
with a man."

600. **hem:** See on 1.31–32 "Get ye . . . foot."

601. **rites of Ceres:** The Eleusinian Mysteries (Eleusis was near Athens). In
the Christian era, someone did in fact blab that these rites, which suppos-
edly led to a blessed afterlife, culminated in the revelation of an ear of grain.

602. **Samothrace:** A Greek island in the northern Aegean, home of the Sanc-
tuary of the Great Gods, which hosted another famous mystery cult.

605. **tattletale Tantalus:** A legendary king of Sipylus (in Asia Minor) who
was invited to dine with the gods and betrayed their hospitality by sharing
their secrets; he also did some unpleasant things like pilfering their nectar
and ambrosia and serving up his son Pelops in a stew. His punishment was
to be eternally "tantalized" in the underworld.

607. **Cytherea:** See on 15 "Cytherea."

613–14. **Venus . . . left hand:** In works of art, at any rate.

Cattle do it everywhere, out in the open: naturally,                     615
    at this sight, a girl averts her eyes.
For our affairs, bedrooms and locked doors are appropriate;
    embarrassing parts are hidden under clothing;
we look, if not for darkness, at least for a bit of shadowy
    cloud, and something less than open daylight.                 620

## THE EVILS OF SHOWING OFF

Even back when no roof yet kept out the sun and rain,
    and the oak tree used to provide both shelter and food,
they took their pleasure in groves and caves, not under Jove:
    primitive people had such concern for modesty.
But now, we put up posters about our nocturnal business,                 625
    and pay big money just for the right to brag!
Of course, you'll test out all the girls—whoever, wherever—
    so you can tell any man, "This one was mine too"?
So you'll never be lacking ones you can point to with your finger?
    So whichever you touch will turn into an ugly story?           630
That's a small complaint! Some make things up they'd deny if true,
    and say there's no one with whom they haven't had sex.
If they can't touch their bodies, they touch what they can—their
      names!
    Rumor makes for a crime with the body untouched.
Now go lock the door, you loathed guardian of the girl,                  635
    and stick a hundred bolts in the sturdy post:

622. **oak tree . . . food:** Acorns were considered the standard fare for Primitive Man.
623. **under Jove:** A stock phrase for "under the open sky," though in the *Metamorphoses* (3.363) Ovid re-activates the literal meaning when Juno finds nymphs in this compromising position.
625. **posters:** Latin *tituli*, "posters" or "placards," like the *VENI VIDI VICI* ("I came, I saw, I conquered") carried in Julius Caesar's triumphal procession (interesting anecdotal evidence for the basic literacy of the Roman populace).

what's safe, when the adulterer of her *name* is around,
   wanting people to think he got something he didn't?
*I'm* stingy about confessing even loves that have happened,
   and cover clandestine intrigues with solid good faith.      640

## NEVER CRITICIZE

Whatever you do, don't criticize any faults in girls
   which many have found it useful to cover up.
Andrómeda's complexion was never brought up with her
   by the one with lively feathers on both his feet.
Andrómache seemed a bit too tall to everyone else:      645
   Hector alone declared she was just the right size.
What you can hardly stand, get used to—you'll stand it fine;
   time will soften all; a new love is too sensitive.
While a new grafted branch is growing inside the green bark,
   if any breeze rustles the tender thing, it'll fall;      650
but soon, hardened by time, it will resist even gales,
   and the firm tree will possess adopted wealth.
Time itself removes all blemishes from the body,
   and what was a fault ceases to be an impediment.
Tender nostrils refuse to endure the hides of bulls;      655
   the smell goes unnoticed after persistent time tames them.

---

644. **the one . . . his feet:** See on 1.53 "Perseus . . . Indians."

645. **Andromache:** The epic and tragic heroine par excellence. The *praeceptor* takes particular delight in imagining her sexual behavior: see 709–10, 3.519–22, and 3.777–78.

654. **an impediment:** Latin *mora*, "delay," can mean either "lapse of time" or "impediment." It is unclear whether this is nominative *moră* (the translation I've chosen), which emphasizes the man's subjective experience ("an impediment to your finding her attractive"), or ablative *morā*, "what *was* a fault ceases to be (a fault) through lapse of time," which restates the point "time removes all blemishes" from the hexameter.

656. **tames them:** Usually, of course, it is bulls that need to be "tamed," not nostrils unaccustomed to the scent of leather.

Evils can be softened by names: have her called "dusky"
  whose blood is blacker than Illýrian pitch;
if she's got a squint, "like Venus"; grey hair, "like Minérva";
  "slender," if she's so skinny she's barely alive;                    660
whoever's short, call "handy"; whoever's obese, "full-breasted";
  let vice be concealed by proximity to virtue.
Don't go asking what year she's in, or under what consul
  she was born (the rigid censor has got *that* job),
especially if she's a little short on bloom, and her better        665
  years have gone by, and she's already plucking white hairs.
Young men, both this age and the later one are useful:
  one field will bear crops, the other needs sowing.
[While your strength and years allow, put up with labors:
  soon stooping old age will creep in on silent feet.             670
Cleave either the sea with oars or the earth with a plow,
  or give your warrior hands to savage battle—
or else exert your muscle and strength and toil on girls:
  this too is military, this too takes resources.]

## MATURE WOMEN ARE BEST

Moreover, they've got superior insight into the work,           675
  and that which alone can make a true artist: experience.

657. **names:** The following section parodies the "lovers' euphemisms" theme, commonplace in satirical and philosophical discourse, which points out besotted lovers' folly in covering flaws with pet names (calling a gangly girl "gazelle," etc.). Naturally, the *praeceptor* turns the diatribe into prescriptive advice.
658. **Illyrian:** Illyricum, a territory in the western Balkan Peninsula that became a Roman province, was an exporter of *pix fossilis* (pitch dug out of the ground).
664. **rigid censor:** The censor's job was to keep lists of Roman citizens, including their birth dates. Censors also exercised control over morals by putting black marks by the names of citizens who had disgraced themselves in various ways, which would debar them from political privileges (such as voting or holding office).

The losses brought on by years they make up for by cultivation,
    and their care ensures they won't appear to be old:
and—just what you'd want!—they'll take their Venus a thousand
        ways:
    no manual has discovered more positions!                      680
It's doesn't take much prompting for them to experience pleasure;
    woman and man should equally find it rewarding.
I hate that sex which doesn't give both a good conclusion;
    that's why I find the love for boys less appealing.
I hate a woman who puts out because she has to put out,           685
    but she's totally dry and thinking about her weaving.
For me, pleasure that's given out of duty holds no charm;
    I want no girl to perform a duty for me.
I like to hear a voice that's confessing its own delight
    and begging me to go slow and hold myself back!               690
I want to look into the conquered eyes of my mistress frenzied,
    languid, not letting herself be touched for a while!
Nature has not bestowed these goods on early youth;
    they usually take three-and-a-half decades plus.
Those who are in a hurry can have the new wine; I'll take          695
    my grandfather's bottle, laid up under ancient consuls.
A plane tree, unless it's mature, isn't able to screen out Phoebus,
    and a meadow just sprouted is hard on the bare feet.
As if you could put Hermíone ahead of Helen,
    and Gorgë was superior to her mother!                          700

696. **under ancient consuls:** Romans generally marked years by the names of
the two consuls (leaders of the senate, like joint presidents) for that year.
699. **Hermione:** Helen's daughter; pretty enough, but no competition for her
mother.
700. **Gorgë . . . her mother:** This example is complicated, because Oeneus,
father of Gorgë by Althaea, did in fact sleep with his daughter. It is possible
that instead of *Gorgë* the text read *Gorgo*, "The Gorgon" (see on 309 "Medusa"
and on 3.504 "Gorgon's fire"), who would not have been difficult to beat in
a beauty contest.

Whoever you are who want to attain a mature Venus,
  if you can hold out, you'll get a fitting reward.

## In Bed at Last
## (with Examples from Mythology)

Look! The bed's an accomplice, harboring a pair of lovers!
  Muse, stand back—wait outside the locked door.
All by themselves, without you, they'll find a flood of words;        705
  their left hands won't be lying useless on the bed.
Fingers will discover something to do in those regions
  in which Love dips his arrows secretively.
Most valiant Hector did this formerly with Andrómache,
  nor was it only in war that he came in handy;                       710
great Achilles did it too with the Lyrnésian captive,
  flopping into his soft bed, worn out by the foe.
Briséis, you allowed yourself to be touched by those hands,
  the ones that were always dyed with Phrygian blood?
Or was this the very thing that turned you on, you minx—             715
  that the hands of a conqueror were touching your limbs?

## Advice on Technique

Believe me, the pleasure of Venus is not to be hurried along,
  but drawn out, gradually, with slow delay.
When you've discovered the place the woman loves to be touched,
  don't let modesty stand in the way of your touching it:            720
you'll see her eyes gleam, sending tremulous bursts of lightning,
  as sunlight often flashes back from clear water;
there will also be moans, there will be a loving murmur,
  sweet groans, and words appropriate to the game.

709. **Andromache:** See on 645 "Andromache."
711. **Lyrnesian captive:** Briseis; see on 403 "Lyrnesian women."
713. **those hands:** See on 1.15 "hands that Hector was to feel."
714. **Phrygian:** See on 1.54 "Greek girl . . . Phrygian man."

But don't either spread your sails too big and leave your mistress     725
    behind, or let her pass you in the race:
reach the finish line together! Then pleasure is complete,
    when woman and man lie there equally beaten.
That's the course you should stick to when there's lots of free time,
    and fear isn't urging on a secretive work;     730
when taking your time isn't safe, it's best to bear down with all your
    oars, and give free rein—and spurs—to your horse.

## WHO'S THE GREATEST LOVE POET NOW?

The end of the work is at hand: give me the prize, grateful youth,
    and bring a myrtle wreath for my perfumed hair!
As great as Podalírius with healing art for the Dánaans,     735
    Achilles with right hand, and Nestor with brain,
as great as Calchas with entrails, Télamon's son with weapons,
    Autómedon with chariot: so great a lover am I!
Celebrate me as a prophet, men, to me sing praises:
    let my name be chanted throughout the whole world!     740

---

734. **myrtle:** Venus's favorite tree, lush and abundant in the Mediterranean world.
735. **Podalirius:** Brother of Machaon (see on 491 "Machaon's potions") and another skilled practitioner of the family art of healing.
735. **Danaans:** A name for the Greeks in the *Iliad* (Danaus was a mythical progenitor of the Greeks; see on 1.73 "daughters of Belus").
736. **Achilles with right hand:** See on 1.15 "hands that Hector was to feel."
736. **Nestor:** The proverbial wise (if somewhat long-winded) old man who counsels the Greeks in the *Iliad*.
737. **Calchas:** The seer whose advice helped the Greeks win the Trojan War—though an oracle predicted that he would die when he met a prophet better than himself, which happened when he met Tiresias's grandson Mopsus. Prophecy through observation of animal entrails ("haruspicy") was a well-established pseudoscience in the ancient world.
737. **Telamon's son:** Ajax.
738. **Automedon:** See on 1.5 "Automedon."

I've given you arms! Vulcan had given arms to Achilles:
  conquer, as he conquered, with the presents given.
But whoever has overcome an Amazon with my sword
  should inscribe on the spoils, "NASO WAS MY TEACHER"!

Look! Tender girls are begging me to give *them* instructions!     745
  You all will be the next concern of my pages.


741. **Vulcan had given arms to Achilles:** After Achilles lost his armor by lend-ing it to Patroclus (who was killed), his mother, Thetis, solicited spectacular new armor from Vulcan, including the world's most famous shield (described at length in *Iliad* 18).

743. **Amazon:** The most famous group of mythical female warriors; in the final metaphor of this book, the *praeceptor* takes the "battle of the sexes" quite literally.

744. **NASO:** Literally, "the Nose"; Ovid calls himself this fifty-two times in his poetry. Roman *cognomina* (sg. *cognomen*) or "official nicknames" were often (apparently) silly or insulting: e.g., Brutus = "Stupid," Strabo = "Cross-eyed," Cicero = "Chick Pea," etc.

# *Ars Amatoria*

BOOK 3

I've given Dánaans arms against Amazons! Arms remain
    for me to give you and your troops, Penthesiléa.
Go to war equally armed; let them win whom kind Dióne
    favors, and the boy who flies all over the world.
It wasn't fair for armed men to do battle with naked women;        5
    for you too, men, to win that way's a disgrace.
One in the crowd may say, "Why are you giving serpents
    venom and handing sheep to the ravenous she-wolf?"
Refrain from tarring all women with the crime of a few;
    each girl should be judged on her own merits.        10
If Átreus's younger son has a valid complaint against Helen,
    and his elder son a complaint against Helen's sister,

1. **Danaans:** See on 2.735 "Danaans."
2. **Penthesilea:** The leader of the Amazons (see on 2.743 "Amazon"). Achilles fell in love with her moments after he had delivered a mortal wound to her.
3. **Dione:** Venus; see on 2.593 "Dione."
4. **the boy:** Cupid.
5. **naked women:** Latin *nudae*, a mischievous play on the word's double sense of "unarmed" and "unclothed."
8. **she-wolf:** Latin *lupa*, which has a secondary meaning of "prostitute" (a brothel was called a *lupanar*, "wolf-house").
11. **Atreus's younger son:** Menelaus; see on 2.399 "Atreus's son."

if Oecles's son through the crime of Eriphýle daughter of Tálaus
    went to the Styx alive and on living horses,
Penélope was faithful for twice five years while her man        15
    wandered, and equally many while he was at war;
look at Phýlacus's son and her who was said to have gone
    as her husband's comrade, and die before her time;
the wife from Págasae bought off the fate of Pheres's son:
    the wife, for her man, was borne in her man's funeral.      20
"Take me, Capáneus! We'll mingle as ashes!" said the daughter
    of Iphis, and leapt on the middle of the pyre.
Even Virtue herself, by cult and by name, is a woman:
    no wonder if she's charming to her people.
(And yet, it isn't minds like these that are sought by my art;    25

13. **Oecles's son:** Amphiaraus, a seer who foresaw his own death if he joined the expedition of the Seven against Thebes, the war between Oedipus's sons (both of whom wanted to rule Thebes solo). His wife Eriphyle, bribed with a necklace, persuaded him to go anyway (and was later killed for her crime by her son Alcmaeon, in some versions with his brother Amphilochus). Before he could die, however, Jupiter opened the earth so he could enter the underworld alive and in style.

14. **Styx:** See on 1.635–36 "Jupiter . . . Styx."

15–16. **her man wandered:** A cynic might note that Ulysses's "wanderings" included some lengthy stopovers with Circe and Calypso.

17. **Phylacus's son:** Protesilaus; see on 2.356 "Son of Phylacus."

19. **wife from Pagasae:** Alcestis (from Pagasa or Pagasae, the town in Thessaly where the Argo was built), who chose to die in place of her husband, Admetus (Pheres's son; see on 2.239 "Cynthius").

21–22. **daughter of Iphis:** Evadne, who threw herself on her husband Capaneus's funeral pyre after he died during the attack of the Seven against Thebes.

23. **Virtue:** Latin *Virtus* literally means something like "manliness" (*vir* = "man/adult male"). Since the noun-ending *-tūs* (English "-tude," an ending like "-ness" that creates an abstraction) is always feminine, however, *virtus* was (ironically) a feminine noun, and hence personified as a female goddess.

25. **minds like these:** That is, the *praeceptor* is not in the business of epic and tragedy (which starred women like the ones he has just enumerated); his aesthetics, like his morality, aims at smaller game.

smaller sails are the right size for my skiff.
Nothing but promiscuous loves are learned through me;
    I shall teach how a woman ought to be loved.)

## WOMEN TAKE LOVE HARD
## (AND A CAMEO FROM VENUS)

A woman can shake off neither flames nor savage bows;
    I see these weapons do less harm to men.                                    30
Men are often deceivers, tender girls not so often;
    they're rarely guilty of fraud, if you really investigate.
That weasel Jason jilted the Phasian when she was a mother;
    a second bride came into Aeson's son's bosom.
For all you cared, Theseus, Ariádne could tremble at sea birds,          35
    left behind alone in an unknown place!
Ask why one road is called Nine Roads, and hear how the forests
    wept for Phyllis, casting down their hair.
He even had a reputation for loyalty—and yet
    the guest gave a sword and a cause for your death, Elíssa.          40
Let me tell you what ruined you: you don't know how to love!
    Art was what you were missing: love lasts through art.

28. **I shall teach how a woman ought to be loved:** Something is fishy about this line, since the sense seems to require "a certain class of woman" rather than "woman" in general. But no convincing alternatives have been offered.
32. **they're rarely guilty of fraud:** The *praeceptor* has changed his tune (or at least his putative audience) since 1.645–46.
33. **the Phasian:** Medea.
35. **Ariadne:** For the story of her abandonment (and its happy sequel), see 1.525–64.
38. **Phyllis:** See on 2.353 "Phyllis."
39–40. **He even . . . Elissa:** Despite his trademark *pietas* (loyalty, dutifulness), Aeneas abandoned Dido (Elissa, the name Aeneas calls her during his desertion speech), who killed herself with the sword he had given her as a gift. Dido bitterly calls him "guest (*hospes*), since this name is all that remains of 'husband'" (*Aen.* 4.323–24).

They still wouldn't know even now! But Cytheréa commanded me
   to teach, and stood there herself before my eyes.
Then she said to me, "What have wretched girls done to deserve
   this?                                                                         45
   The crowd is handed over unarmed to armed men.
A pair of books has made them practitioners of art;
   your instructions must train the other side, too.
He who had sung the reproaches of the Therápnean wife
   soon hymned her praises with a more fortunate lyre.                  50
If I know you—do no harm to cultured girls:
   you'll be seeking their favor(s) as long as you live!"
She spoke, and from her myrtle (for she'd appeared with her hair
   wreathed in myrtle) she gave me a leaf and a few berries;
when I'd received them, I felt divine power too: the air                        55
   shone brighter, and a weight was lifted from my whole heart.
As long as my genius is working, seek instruction from here, girls
   (the ones allowed by modesty, law, and their rights).

43. **Cytherea:** Venus; see on 2.15 "Cytherea."
49. **the reproaches of the Therapnean wife:** Helen was born in Therapne,
part of Sparta; the bard Stesichorus was struck blind after singing of her
infidelity, but his sight was restored when he sang a famous palinode claim-
ing that only a phantom of Helen went to Troy. Latin *probra*, like our "re-
proach," can mean either "blame" or "that which causes blame," and "wife"
(*maritae*) could be either dative, yielding "insults against the wife," or geni-
tive, yielding "the wife's misdeeds." The ambiguity allows the prudent *prae-
ceptor* to sidestep the issue of whether Helen was justly or unjustly accused.
See on 1.54 "Greek girl . . . Phrygian man."
51. **do no harm:** As the Love Doctor (a metaphor developed ad nauseam in
the *Remedia*), the poet is right to obey this dictate of the Hippocratic Oath.
52. **favor(s):** Latin *gratia*, an extremely slippery and ambiguous word; see on
2.464 "Grace." The translator has sneaked in a little pun that plays on the
innocent singular vs. the erotic plural of "favor."
53. **myrtle:** See on 2.734 "myrtle."
58. **the ones allowed by modesty, law, and their rights:** See on 1.33 "safe
Venus."

GATHER YE ROSEBUDS WHILE YE MAY

Even now, be mindful of old age to come:
    that way none of your time will be spent without profit.       60
While you can, and can even disclose what your age really is,
    have fun: the years slip by like flowing water.
A wave, once it has passed, cannot be called back again,
    nor can an hour, once it has passed, return.
Youth must be used: with speedy foot, youth slips away,       65
    and what follows is never as good as it was at first.
These stalks getting withered and grey I once saw as beds of violets;
    a lovely garland was given me once from these thorns.
The time will come when you, who are currently locking out lovers,
    will lie there a chilly old woman in the lonely night,       70
nor will your door be broken down by nocturnal brawls,
    and you won't find roses strewn on your threshold at dawn.
How quickly—woe is me!—are bodies slackened with wrinkles,
    and the color dies that was once on a radiant face,
and those grey hairs you swear you've had since you were a girl    75
    are suddenly sprinkled all over your whole head!
For serpents, old age is shed along with their slender skin,
    and casting their horns keeps stags from becoming old men;

59. **be mindful of old age to come:** Roman erotic poets constantly hold over women's heads the threat of old age, with its consequent unattractiveness (a state more frightening than death). As often in this poem, the reader is caused to wonder whose best interests the *praeceptor* actually has in mind here. (Hint: middle-aged poets.) "Gather ye rosebuds while ye may" is the opening line of a poem ("To the Virgins, to Make Much of Time") by Robert Herrick (1591–1674) whose message and imagery track Ovid's closely—except that Herrick's target market is "virgins" and his conclusion is to "go marry."

69. **locking out lovers:** The *exclusus amator* (locked-out lover), assaulting his beloved's door with everything from songs to crowbars, is a stock figure in Roman love poetry—and he often includes threats about the ravages of age on female beauty.

*our* assets fly the coop, there's no help for it; pluck that flower
    which, if not plucked, will fall in disgrace on its own.    80
Furthermore, childbearing, too, makes the season of youth
    even shorter; the field wears out through continual harvests.
Látmian Endýmion, Luna, isn't making you blush,
    nor the rosy goddess reddening for Céphalus, her prey;
even if Venus is granted Adónis, whom she's still mourning,    85
    where did she get her Aenéas and her Harmónia?
Follow the example, O mortal race, of the goddesses,
    and don't refuse your pleasures to longing men.
Though they jilt you soon, what do you lose? It all remains.
    They can take a thousand; nothing is lost from there.    90
Iron gets worn down, flint gets thin and brittle through use;
    *that* part is sturdy and free from fear of loss.
Who would refuse for a torch to be lit from a torch close by,
    or who would hoard the cavernous sea's vast waters?
And still, some woman will tell the man, "It's not advantageous"?    95
    Tell me, what do you lose but the water you wash with?
My speech isn't prostituting you, it's just forbidding you
    to fear illusory costs: your gifts have no costs.
But since I'm about to encounter the gales of a greater wind,
    may a light breeze carry me forth while I'm still in harbor.    100

83. **Latmian Endymion:** Actually, rumor has it that this mortal, enjoying a lifetime of unending beauty rest, is sleeping still in a cave on Mount Latmus (in Asia Minor), visited by Luna (the Moon) on her nights off.
84. **rosy goddess:** Aurora, goddess of the dawn, had a thing for hunters (one of the hazards—or benefits?—of being a morning person).
84. **prey:** Latin *praeda*; see on 1.114 "prize." I have chosen the hunting term here because Cephalus was a hunter.
85. **Adonis:** See on 1.75 "Adonis."
86. **her Aeneas and her Harmonia:** From Anchises (see on *Tr.* 2.299–300 "Anchises . . . Iasion") and Mars (for the story, see 2.561–92), respectively.
89–98. **Though . . . costs:** This whole outrageous passage is a brilliant send-up of both scientific and legal reasoning (see Gibson 2003:122–23).

GROOMING

I'll start with grooming. Liber comes forth nicely from well-groomed
    grapes, and the crops stand tall in well-groomed soil.
Beauty is the god's gift; how few can be proud of their beauty!
    Most of you are deficient in that sort of gift.
Care will produce good looks; good looks neglected will perish,    105
    even if they're like the Idálian goddess.
If girls in the old days didn't groom their bodies like that,
    they didn't have men in the old days groomed like that.
If Andrómache used to clothe herself in sturdy tunics,
    no wonder—she was the wife of a hardened soldier.    110
Sure, wife of Ajax, you'd get all dolled up to meet the man
    whose shield was covered with seven hides of cattle!
Before, there was rough simplicity; now, Rome is golden,
    possessing the great wealth of the conquered world.
Look at the Capitol that's there now, and what used to be there:    115
    you'll say the first one belonged to different Jupiter!
The Cúria that's there now is most worthy of such a council;
    the one under Tatius's reign was made of straw.


101. **grooming:** Latin *cultus*, "cultivation" (related also to "culture" and "cult"),
a word with aesthetic, agricultural, and even religious resonances. Compare
this with the advice given to men in 1.505–24.
101. **Liber:** Bacchus; see on 1.525 "Liber."
106. **Idalian goddess:** Venus, from her cult center Idalium (on Cyprus).
109. **Andromache:** See on 2.645 "Andromache."
115. **Capitol:** See on 2.540 "Jupiter's Citadel."
117–18. **Curia . . . straw:** The Roman senate house begun by Julius Caesar in
44 BC and inaugurated by Augustus in 29 (the Curia Iulia) replaced the
original senate house supposedly built by Tullus Hostilius (the third king of
Rome, ca. 672–641 BC), which itself had been rebuilt several times. Ovid
fantasizes about an even earlier structure built by Romulus (the first king of
Rome, traditionally founded in 753 BC), who shared his rule with Tatius,
king of the neighboring Sabine community that supplied Rome with women
(for that story, see 1.101–32).

The Pálatine that now gleams under Phoebus and the leaders—
    what was it but pasture for plowing oxen?                                    120
Others can like the old days; I congratulate myself
    that I was born only now. This age suits my character,
not because pliant gold is now drawn out of the earth
    and pearls flood in, gathered from a distant shore,
nor because the mountains are shrinking from quarrying marble                                    125
    or dark-blue waters are put to flight by jetties,
but because *grooming* is here, and that famous rusticity hasn't
    made it past our old grandfathers into our times.
You, too—don't burden your ears with expensive gems
    the colored Indian gathers from green water,                                    130
nor strut weighed down by clothing heavy with in-sewn gold:
    you drive us away with the wealth you use to lure us.
We're captivated by neatness: your hair should not be lawless;
    the touch of your hands is what gives or refuses beauty.

## CHOOSING THE RIGHT HAIRSTYLE FOR YOU

There's not just a single type of adornment; each should choose                                    135
    what will suit her best, and take the advice of her mirror.
An oval face likes a part down the center of hair simply worn;
    that's how Laodamía did her hair.

119. **Palatine . . . leaders:** Augustus's dwelling on the Palatine Hill (whence our word "palace") adjoined the temple of Phoebus Apollo, his patron deity.
125. **marble:** Marble used for private dwellings (for statues, columns, siding, etc.), as opposed to the public buildings where it belonged, was considered an extravagance.
126. **jetties:** Wealthy Romans liked to show off by building houses out into the sea and by creating calm waters for fish ponds—two activities that were frequently held up as examples of violence against nature for the purpose of useless luxury.
127. **rusticity:** See on 1.607 "rustic."
138. **Laodamia:** See on 2.356 "Son of Phylacus." Such a simple style (the *praeceptor* reasons) would be appropriate for a bride who missed her husband (and

A little knot to be left for them at the tip of the brow,
    so the ears will show—that's what round faces want.      140
Another's hair should be tossed freely over both shoulders:
    tuneful Phoebus, that's you when you play your lyre.
Another should wear it tied back in the manner of girt Diana,
    the way she does it when hunting astonished beasts.
This one looks good with her floating tresses lying loose;      145
    that one should be bound up with her hair tied tight.
This one is charming adorned with Cyllénian tortoise shell;
    that one should keep her curls like billowing waves.
But you cannot count the acorns on the branching oak
    or the number of bees in Hybla or beasts in the Alps,      150
nor is it right for me to hold so many styles to a number:
    each successive day adds some new adornment.
Even neglected hair suits many: often you'd think
    yesterday's hair is lying there—it was just combed!
Art should simulate chance: thus, when her city was captured      155
    and Alcídes saw Íole, he said, "*Her* I love!"

---

in *Heroides* 13.31–42, Laodamia asserts her refusal to dress up in her husband's absence).

142. **tuneful Phoebus:** Apollo's famously unshorn locks were pretty enough to be imitated even by females.

143. **girt Diana:** The huntress goddess would, naturally, need her hair tied back and her dress hitched up.

147. **Cyllenian tortoise shell:** Mercury, born on Mount Cyllene (in Arcadia), made the first lyre out of a tortoise shell. It is not clear whether the reference here is to a tortoise-shell comb (or barrette or other hair jewelry) or to a hairstyle that resembles a tortoise shell, though the former seems more likely.

150. **Hybla:** See on 2.517 "Hybla."

156. **Alcides:** Hercules ("son of Alcaeus"; actually he was the son of Jupiter and Alcmena, and his foster-father Amphitryon, Alcmena's husband, was the son of Alcaeus), who took Iole captive after sacking her town.

That was how Bacchus took you into his chariot, abandoned
   Cnossian, while the satyrs all shouted "Euhoe!"
Oh, how indulgent Nature is to your beauty, you whose
   losses can be recovered in so many ways!            160
*We* are just stripped clean, and our hair, ravaged by age,
   falls like leaves at the onslaught of wintry Bóreas.
The woman dyes her grey hair with herbs from Germany,
   and color better than real is sought by art;
the woman sallies forth all lush with purchased locks,      165
   and turns another's into her own through cash.
Nor do they blush to have bought them—we see the sales take place
   under Hercules's very eyes, and the maiden chorus!

## CLOTHES

What should I say about clothes? I've got no need for you, flounces,
   nor you, wool, who blush purple with Týrian dye.     170
When so many colors have come out more modestly priced,
   what madness it is to wear bank accounts on the body!
Look! There's the color of the sky when the sky is cloudless
   and balmy Auster's not shaking out drops of rain.
Look! There's one like you, who they say once rescued Phrixus   175

157–58. **abandoned Cnossian:** For the story of Ariadne and Bacchus, see 1.525–64.
162. **Boreas:** The North Wind.
168. **Hercules's very eyes, and the maiden chorus:** The temple of Hercules and the Muses (with statues of the nine Muses and of Hercules playing the lyre), in the Circus Flaminius (see on 1.407–8 "Circus . . . statues"), was surrounded by shops.
169. **flounces:** Latin *segmenta*, pieces of fabric (usually purple or gold) sewn on the outside of a garment for decoration.
170. **Tyrian dye:** See on 2.297 "Tyrians."
174. **Auster:** The South Wind.
175. **you:** It is not clear whether this refers to the golden ram or to the cloud goddess Nephele (the twins' mother), though the cloud would make a nice contrast with the blue sky of the previous couplet (and "yellow" is in line 180).

and Helle from the treachery of Ino.
This one imitates waves, it has its name from waves too:
    I could believe this cloth is what nymphs wear;
that one simulates saffron (clothed in a saffron dress,
    the dewy goddess of dawn yokes her light-bringing horses),         180
this one Páphian myrtles, that one purple amethysts,
    or cream-colored roses, or the Thracian crane;
nor are your acorns missing, Amarýllis, nor your almonds,
    and wax has also given its name to wools.
As many flowers as fresh earth bears, when in balmy spring         185
    she sprouts vine buds and sluggish winter flees,
wool slurps that many juices—or more! Pick the right ones,
    for every kind will not be the thing for everyone.
Dark's right for snowy skin; dark was right for Briséis;
    when she was seized, she was wearing a dark dress.              190
White's right for olive skin: Cépheus's daughter, you were hot in
        white—
    that's what you wore when you'd gone for a walk on Seríphos.

177. **it has its name from waves too:** The reference is to *cumatilis vestis*, "wave-colored clothing" (from Greek *kūma*, "wave"), though Ovid does not use the word *cumatilis* here (he expects his learned readers to figure it out).
181. **Paphian myrtles:** Venus's haunt and tree: see on 2.588 "Paphos" and 2.734 "myrtle."
182. **Thracian crane:** These birds were whitish gray.
183. **Amaryllis:** See on 2.267 "Amaryllis."
189. **Briseis:** She would have been in mourning (the *praeceptor* reasons) over the sack of her town.
191. **Cepheus's daughter:** Andromeda; see on 1.53 "Perseus . . . Indians."
192. **Seriphos:** An island in the Cyclades where Perseus went to deal with his stepfather, Polydectes—an obscure mythological detail to which Andromeda's color of dress has no discernible relevance.

## HYGIENE AND MAKEUP

How close I came to warning lest the foul goat enter
    your armpits, or your calves be rough with tough hairs!
But I'm not instructing girls from the crags of Mount Caúcasus    195
    nor such as slurp your waters, Mysian Caícus.
What if I taught you not to let laziness darken your teeth,
    or to rinse your face with water in the morning?
You also know to strive for whiteness by rubbing on chalk;
    she who won't blush with real blood blushes by art;    200
by art, you fill out the bare common borders of the eyebrows,
    and a little patch of leather makes flawless cheeks.
Don't be ashamed to outline your eyes with slender charcoal
    or saffron, crystal Cydnus, born near you.

193. **How close I came:** A classic *praeteritio* (passing by), the rhetorical device in which one emphasizes something by saying one won't mention it.

193. **the foul goat:** The *praeceptor* has no qualms about giving such advice to *men*; see on 1.522 "man and father of the herd."

195. **Mount Caucasus:** A mountain range from the Black Sea to the Caspian Sea, known for its wild beasts and as the site of Prometheus's punishment. The implication is that such girls would be not only hicks but hard-hearted and even bestial ones.

196. **Mysian Caicus:** The Caicus river was in Mysia in northwest Asia Minor—a place proverbially barbaric and far away. (The phrase Mysian Caicus hails from Virgil's *Georgics* [4.370], allusions to which pepper all of the "grooming" advice.)

200. **by art:** This whole passage on female cosmetics flies in the face of a longstanding moralizing tradition that viewed such artifices as deceitful and "unnatural." By implicitly aligning his own "art" with that of the females he instructs, the poet is thus making a daring statement with both aesthetic and moral implications. See "Fifty Shades of Metaphor" in the introduction.

201. **fill out . . . eyebrows:** The unibrow was admired in antiquity.

202. **little patch of leather:** A beauty patch, used to cover blemishes.

204. **crystal Cydnus:** A river in Cilicia, the south coastal region of Asia Minor, famous for saffron production.

I've got that work in which I spoke of concoctions for your          205
    beauty—a little book, but through care, a great work:
seek hence, too, a refuge for your wounded looks;
    my art is not sluggish on behalf of your interests.
Yet lovers must not discover upon your table exposed
    jars: it's through concealment that art makes beauty.          210
Who wouldn't be disgusted by scum smeared all over your face,
    so heavy it slithers down into your warm bosom?
What a stink lanolin makes, even imported from Athens—
    juice squeezed out of the dirty fleece of a sheep!
I could not give my approval to publicly using a mixture          215
    of doe marrow, or to publicly brushing the teeth.
Such things will produce beauty, but will be hideous to see;
    many things ugly in the doing are charming when done.
Those statues which now bear the name of painstaking Myron
    were once an inert weight and a solid mass;          220
gold, to become a ring, must first be hammered out;
    the clothing that you're wearing was filthy wool.
In process, it was rough stone: now, as a noble statue
    nude Venus wrings the water from her wet hair.

205. **that work:** *Medicamina Faciei Femineae* (Concoctions for the Female Face).

213. **even imported from Athens:** Athens produced the best lanolin (but it still stank).

216. **doe marrow:** This substance could be used to help skin discoloration and sores; either sex of deer would work, but the *praeceptor* specifies the female (presumably) for his female pupils.

219. **Myron:** A Greek sculptor (fifth century BC), now most famous for his statue the *Discobolus* (Discus Thrower).

224. **nude Venus:** Gibson 2003:188: "Since the beauty of the naked Anadyomene [Rising from the Sea] may have been a standard paradigm in the anti-cosmetic tradition (see McKeown on *Am.* 1.14.33f.), there is typical Ovidian cheek in using her to make a point in favour of cosmetics. *nuda* also specifies a reference to a particular type of the Anadyomene, as she came in both a naked and a half-clothed version."

You, too, while you're preening—we should think you're asleep:          225
    after the finishing touch, you'll be better for viewing.
How come I know where your face picked up that radiant glow?
    Keep your door shut! Why publish a rough draft?
There's lots it's better for men not to know; most things would be
    disgusting if you didn't hide their insides.          230
Those golden statues that glitter in the lavish theater?
    Look hard and you'll scorn them: gold foil over wood!
But the people aren't allowed to come close to them till they're done;
    nor should beauty be prepped unless men are cleared out.

## More Hair Advice

Yet presenting in public hair that needs combing, so that it falls          235
    loosely down your back—that I *don't* forbid.
Make sure, especially, at that time, that you're not grumpy,
    and don't keep unbinding tresses that have slipped.
Your hairdresser should be in no danger: I hate her who scratches
    faces with nails and grabs hairpins to jab into arms;          240
that maid will curse her mistress's head when she touches it, weeping
    over the hateful tresses while streaming with blood!
She with a bad head of hair should place a guard at her threshold
    or always get styled in the temple of the Good Goddess.
My sudden arrival had been announced to a certain girl:          245
    she got all confused and put her hair on backward.
May such a cause of loathsome shame befall my enemies,
    may that blot strike the daughters-in-law of Párthia!
Shameful are sheep without horns, shameful a field without grass,
    a shrub without foliage, and a head without hair.          250

244. **Good Goddess:** Latin *Bona Dea*, whose rites men were forbidden to see.
248. **daughters-in-law of Parthia:** See on 1.179–80 "O buried Crassi and flag"
and 1.210 "shoots . . . in retreat." Backward wigs would be condign punish-
ment for the female relations of this treacherous backward-shooting people.

## HIDING FLAWS

You haven't come to me to be taught, Sémele, or Leda,
   or Sidónian whom a fake bull carried over the sea,
or Helen, whom you're no fool for demanding back, Meneláus,
   and you're also no fool for keeping, Trojan abductor.
The crowd that comes to be taught is girls both lovely and ugly.       255
   (Inferior things always outnumber good ones.)
The beautiful aren't looking for help from art, or instruction.
   They've got their endowment: artlessly powerful beauty.
The sailor relaxes, free from care, when the sea is calm;
   he takes stock of his resources when it swells.                     260
Yet rare is that face which is without blemish: cover your blemishes,
   hide your body's flaws as best you can.
If you're short, sit, so you don't appear to be sitting when standing;
   however small you are, you should lie on your couch
(here too, so your measure can't be taken while you lie there,         265
   make sure to throw on a robe to hide your feet).
One who's too skinny should put on coverings made of thick yarn,
   and her cloak should fall down loosely from her shoulders.
The pale one should touch up her body with some reddening sticks.
   Darker one, fly to the help of the Phárian fish.                    270
An ill-formed foot should always be covered in snowy leather,
   and don't release spindly ankles from their fetters.

251. **Semele:** A Theban princess who, in the course of her affair with Jupiter, was tricked by Juno into asking him to make love to her as he did to his wife. She was incinerated immediately by his thunderbolts, but Jupiter rescued her unborn child Bacchus and gestated and gave birth to him himself.
251. **Leda:** Woman from Sparta whom Jupiter seduced in the form of a swan; she was the mother of Helen, Clytemnestra, Castor, and Pollux.
252. **Sidonian:** Europa (from Sidon, a town on the coastline of modern Lebanon); see on 1.323 "Europa."
270. **Pharian fish:** Apparently an erudite reference to the crocodile (Pharos was an island off Alexandria used poetically for "Egypt"), whose dung was used as a facial whitener.

Slender pads are appropriate for prominent shoulders,
    and a bra should go around the narrow chest.
She should mark what she's saying with but a tiny gesture    275
    whose fingers are fat and fingernails are ratty.
She who has bad breath should never speak after fasting,
    and always stand at a distance from the man's face.
If some tooth that's black, or enormous, or in the wrong place
    has popped up for you, laughing will do you great damage.    280

## LAUGHTER, TEARS, SPEECH, AND GAIT

Who could believe it? Girls learn even the way to laugh,
    and search for decorum even in this quarter.
Grins should be moderate, with small dimples on either side,
    and the bottom lip should cover the tips of the teeth;
nor should they distend their guts with perpetual cackles,    285
    but sound forth something or other light and feminine.
There's one who distorts her face with a crazy guffaw;
    another is shaking with cackles—you'd think she's crying;
that one sounds forth something unlovely and raucous; she laughs
    as the ugly she-ass at the rough millstone brays.    290
Where does art not reach? They learn to cry attractively
    and weep however and whenever they please.
What about when a letter is cheated of its proper sound
    and the tongue is forced to stammer its sounds on command?
There's beauty in faults: some learn how to say words badly,    295
    to be able to speak less well than they were able.
Take good care on all these things, since they're advantageous.
    Learn how to carry your body with feminine stride:
even the way you walk is no small part of beauty—
    it lures in unknown men (or chases them off).    300

293. **letter is cheated of its proper sound:** This seems to be a reference to a (charming) lisp.

294. **stammer:** Like a lisp, a stammer seems to have been considered attractive.

This one moves her flank artfully, letting in breezes with flowing
   tunic and haughtily placing her measured steps;
that one walks like the redneck wife of an Úmbrian husband,
   taking enormous strides with her legs spread wide.
But—as in many things—there should be moderation here too:     305
   one motion's rustic, the other softer than allowed.
Yet the lower part of your shoulder, the upper part of your arm
   should be bare, fit for viewing from the left-hand side.
This suits you especially, snowy-complexioned; when I've seen it
   I always want to kiss where the shoulder's exposed.     310

## MUSIC

Sirens were sea monsters who, with their melodious voices,
   held ships back, no matter how fast they were going;
the son of Sisyphus, when he heard them, almost cut loose his own
   body (for wax had been smeared in his comrades' ears).
Singing is a sexy thing: girls should learn to sing     315
   (many have made voice—not face—their procuress),
and now sing back the things they've heard in the marble theater,

303. **redneck wife of an Umbrian husband:** Here "redneck" is *rubicunda*,
literally "ruddy-complexioned" (from the sun). Umbria was a region in cen-
tral Italy known for its agriculture. Unlike girlfriends, wives have no reason
to walk sexy.
306. **rustic:** See on 1.607 "rustic."
313. **son of Sisyphus:** Ulysses, who in some (negative) versions is the son of
Sisyphus, not of Laertes. Sisyphus, founder of Corinth, was of legendary
cunning; he is punished eternally in the underworld (by pushing a rock up
a hill, then having it roll down again) for trying to cheat Death. Perhaps the
implication here is that great singing can lure in even hereditary tricksters.
317. **marble theater:** See on 125 "marble." Though proud of the marble on
his public buildings, Augustus may have been less than pleased to hear of
them used to teach seductive singing (Ovid has a way of being complimen-
tary and subversive at the same time).

now songs turned lightly in measures of the Nile.
No woman taught under my supervision should be unschooled about
    holding the pick in her right, the harp in her left.                                    320
Rhodopéan Órpheus moved stones and beasts with his lyre,
    and the pools of Tártarus, and the three-headed dog;
at your singing, most just avenger of your mother, stones
    dutifully arranged themselves into new walls;
though he was mute, the fish is thought to have shown
    admiration                                                                              325
    for the lyre of Aríon, a well-known tale.
Also learn how to strum the cheerful harp with both hands:
    those are appropriate for pleasant games.

318. **measures of the Nile:** Egyptian music had a reputation for lasciviousness.
321. **Rhodopean Orpheus:** Orpheus, a mythical singer considered the great-
est of them all, was from Mount Rhodope in western Thrace.
322. **Tartarus:** A name for the underworld.
322. **three-headed dog:** Cerberus ("Fluffy," to Harry Potter fans), guardian
of the underworld.
323. **most just avenger of your mother:** Amphion, who (along with his
brother Zethus) killed Dirce; she had mistreated his mother, Antiope (preg-
nant by Jupiter, but Dirce thought her own husband had cheated with her
maid). Amphion's singing inspired stones to form themselves into the walls
of Thebes.
326. **Arion:** An actual musician (in the court of the tyrant Periander at
Corinth around 600 BC) who was thrown overboard while returning from
Sicily to Greece; a dolphin, impressed by his music, carried him on its back
to Corinth. Though the story was proverbial as something that beggars belief,
the *praeceptor* relates it here as a fact supporting his point.
327. **harp:** Latin *nablia*, an exotic stringed instrument of Phoenician (Semitic)
origin about which little is known.

## Know Your Poetry

Callímachus's Muse, and the Cöan poet's, should be well known
    to you, and the Tëan one of the boozy old man;          330
Sappho should also be well known (for what's sexier than she?),
    or the one whose Father is duped by sly Geta's art.
You should be able to read the song of tender Propértius,
    or something of Gallus, or something of yours, Tibúllus,
and the fleece, described by Varro, conspicuous with its golden    335
    tufts, a source of complaint to your sister, Phrixus,
and fugitive Aenéas, the origin of high Rome;
    Latium has no more brilliant work than him.
It's possible that my name, too, will be mingled with these,

329. **Cöan poet:** Philetas/Philitas (from the island of Cos in the eastern Aegean), an older contemporary of Callimachus; at least some of his poetry dealt with erotic themes (only fragments survive).

330. **Tëan . . . old man:** Anacreon (ca. 575–490 BC), a Greek lyric poet from Teos (a city on the coast of Asia Minor), was known for his poems about wine and love as well as for his longevity.

331. **Sappho:** Greek poetess (late seventh century BC) from the island of Lesbos (in the northeastern Aegean), famous for her poetic skill—she was called "the tenth Muse"—and for her love poems to women and girls (whence our word "lesbian").

332. **the one . . . Geta's art:** Menander, the Greek playwright (ca. 343–290 BC) who pioneered "New Comedy," the ancient ancestor of our romantic comedies. The "Father" is a stock character in his plays, the foolish miser tricked by another stock character, the clever slave (Geta was a common slave name).

335–36. **fleece . . . Phrixus:** Publius Terentius Varro Atacinus (b. 82 BC) wrote an epic on the Argonauts.

337. **origin:** Every word in this line belongs to the proem (opening lines) of Virgil's *Aeneid* except for "origin," Latin *primordia*, which hails instead from Lucretius and generally refers to atoms—a fascinating conflation (especially for those of us who see deep Lucretian resonances in the *Aeneid*).

338. **Latium has no more brilliant work than him:** Such is the fame of Virgil that Ovid does not need to name him, and such is the power of poetry that Aeneas has turned into the "work" about himself. Latium (see on 1.202 "Latium") stands for all of Italy, but is also the site of half of the *Aeneid*'s action.

and my writings won't be given to Lethe's waters,                    340
and someone will declare, "Read the cultured songs
    of our master, the ones in which he equips both sides,
and from the books he marks with the tender title of *Loves*
    choose something to read out, softly, with practiced voice,
or let a *Letter* be sung by you, with studied diction;                    345
    he invented this work, unknown to others."
O Phoebus, may such be your will, and yours, righteous gods of poets,
    Bacchus of glorious horns and goddesses nine!


## DANCING AND GAMES

Who could doubt that I'd want a girl to know how to dance,
    to move her arms on command when it's time for the wine?                    350
Artists of the flank, spectacles of the stage, are loved:
    that sinuosity is very sexy!
I'm ashamed to give advice about trivia—that she should know

340. **Lethe's waters:** Drinking from this underworld river erased all memories.
341. **cultured:** Latin *culta*; see on 101 "grooming." The poems referred to here are, of course, the ones the reader is currently reading, making this an extraordinary example of product placement.
346. **he invented this work:** Though Ovid's *Heroides* was the first *collection* of poetic love letters, he is exaggerating a bit to say that he invented the genre; Propertius 4.3, a letter from Arethusa (pseudonym of a young Roman bride) to her husband, is a notable forerunner.
348. **goddesses nine:** By invoking the Muses *and* the two gods most closely associated with poetry, the *praeceptor* covers all his bases.
350. **arms:** See on 1.595 "supple arms, dance."
351. **Artists of the flank, spectacles of the stage:** Pantomimes, actors/dancers who would portray famous scenes from myth or drama. Like modern rock stars, they were sources of fascination, but not the sort of people you would wish your children to bring home.
353. **trivia:** The details of some of the various dice and board games referred to here elude us; see Gibson 2003 for a fuller discussion and bibliography. The first three, *tali* (knucklebones), *tessera* (die), and *ludus latrunculorum* (game of little bandits), are listed in 2.203–8 as games the lover must allow the woman to win.

how to call the knucklebone throws, and your value, thrown die,
and that she should now throw three numbers, now ponder
    cleverly                                                                                     355
    which part is best to enter and which to call back,
and that she play prudently, not foolishly, Battles of Bandits
    when one counter perishes, vanquished by a twin foe,
and the warrior, caught without his companion, wages war
    and the rival keeps retracing the path he's begun;                                  360
and that the smooth balls be poured out from the open mesh bag
    and no ball be stirred except the one you'll remove.
There's a kind of game board divided by slender proportioning
    as many times as the gliding year has months;
a little board receives three pebbles on either side,                                           365
    on which to have joined your pieces is to have won.
Perform a thousand games! For a girl not to know how to play
    is shameful: love is often obtained through playing.
But it's a minuscule task to make clever use of throws;
    the greater work is to have composed one's character.                            370

354. **knucklebone throws:** See on 2.205 "knucklebones."

354–56. **thrown die . . . call back:** See on 2.203 "ivory dice."

357. **Battles of Bandits:** See on 2.207 "bandit."

361. **balls:** This game seems to have been a sort of "pick-up sticks" with balls, in which balls are poured into a pile and players take turns removing them without disturbing the others. But since no other author refers to this game, some have doubted the authenticity of this couplet.

363. **kind of game board:** This may be the game *duodecim scripta* (twelve marks), which involved three rows of twelve marks (or letters) arranged in two columns.

365. **three pebbles:** This game (for which no Latin name survives) seems to have been a sort of tic-tac-toe. The board looked like a flattened cootie catcher (four squares crisscrossed with diagonal lines), on which the players would alternately place each of their three counters at a point of intersection, then move them until all three were in a row.

370. **the greater work:** Virgil famously refers to the second half of the *Aeneid* (which deals with the war in Italy) as his "greater work" (*maius opus, Aen.*

It's then that we're imprudent, and we're revealed in the heat
   of the contest, and our hearts lie bare through games;
wrath flares up, a hideous evil, and lust for gain
   and tantrums and brawls and overanxious grief;
accusations are made, the heavens resound with shouts,      375
   and each invokes the wrathful gods for his cause.
There's no trust in the game board (what is not sought through
     prayers!).
   Quite often, I've even seen cheeks grow wet with tears.
May Jupiter drive far from you such shameful reproaches,
   you who care about charming any man!      380

## You Need to Get Out More

Lazy Nature has bestowed these games upon girls;
   men have richer material to play with.
They've got swift-flying balls, and javelins, and hoops,
   and arms, and horses trained to go round in circles;
the Campus doesn't know you, nor the iciest Virgin;     385
   the Tuscan river's placid waters don't carry you.
But it's allowed, and helpful, to go through Pompey's shade
   when the head is scorched by the Virgin's heavenly horses;

---

7.45), because martial epic is considered the highest of genres. Ovid's next
eight lines show what can happen when people allow games to become too
epic (through failure to "compose" themselves properly).
385. **Campus:** See on 1.513 "Campus."
385. **iciest Virgin:** The Aqua Virgo ("Virgin/Girl Water," allegedly named
for a girl who showed thirsty Roman soldiers the spring that would come to
supply its water), an aqueduct that fed Rome's first public baths. It was very
cold.
386. **Tuscan river:** The Tiber (see on 1.111 "Tuscan flautist"); swimming there
was a prototypical manly activity.
387. **Pompey's shade:** See on 1.67 "Pompey's shade."
388. **the Virgin's heavenly horses:** The horses of the chariot of the Sun, which
was in the constellation Virgo ("The Virgin") in August. This "hot" virgin

visit the sacred Pálatine of laurelled Phoebus
  (he drowned the Paraetónian ships in the deep)                390
and the monuments that the sister and wife of the leader prepared,
  and the son-in-law, girding his head with naval honor;
visit the Memphític cow's incense-burning altars,
  visit the triple theaters in prominent seats;
the sands, stained with warm blood, should be something to see,    395
  and the turning-post circled round with burning wheel.
What's hidden is unknown; no desire for the unknown.

---

(in a place frequented by both sexes) contrasts suggestively with the afore-
mentioned "cold" virgin (in a place for men only).

389. **Palatine:** See on 119 "Palatine . . . leaders."

389. **laurelled Phoebus:** See on 2.495 "Laurel."

390. **Paraetonian ships:** Paraetonian = Egyptian (Paraetonium is on the west
coast of Alexandria). Apollo was Augustus's divine patron during the Battle
of Actium (31 BC), a naval battle off the western coast of Greece in which the
forces of Mark Antony and Cleopatra were finally defeated. Even though
Antony was Roman and had many Roman followers, Augustan propaganda
portrayed the civil war as a foreign war against Cleopatra and her degenerate
Egyptians.

391. **sister and wife:** That is, the sister (Octavia) and the wife (Livia), though
the phrase "sister and wife" initially calls to mind Juno, the "sister and wife
of Jupiter," as well as the incestuous brother-sister marriages of the Egyptian
Ptolemies (since the royal family was considered divine, it mimicked the
behavior of the divine siblings Isis and Osiris). On the monuments, see on
1.69–70 "mother . . . marble" and 1.72 "Livia."

392. **son-in-law . . . naval honor:** Agrippa (who married Augustus's daugh-
ter, Julia, in 21 BC and died in 12 BC) was awarded the *corona rostrata* (crown
with ships' beaks) after the battle of Naulochus (a promontory in Sicily) in
36 BC, which marked the defeat of Sextus Pompey, son of Pompey the Great
and one of Augustus's chief rivals.

393. **Memphitic cow:** See on 1.77 "Memphitic . . . heifer."

394. **triple theaters:** See on 1.89 "theater."

395. **sands:** See on 1.164 "grim sand . . . Forum."

396. **turning-post:** See on 1.136 "Circus" and 2.426 "post."

There's no reward when a pretty face has no witness.
You could surpass Thámyras and Amoébeus in singing—
    there will be no delight in an unknown lyre.                      400
If Venus had never been painted by Apélles of Cos,
    she'd have lain hidden, submerged by the waters of the sea.

## ON FAME

What is sought by sacred poets but Fame alone?
    The whole of our labor has this as its desire.
In the old days, poets were the care of gods and of kings,            405
    and ancient choruses won great rewards:
the dignity of poets was sacrosanct, and their name
    was revered, and they used to be given piles of money.
Énnius, born in the mountains of Calábria, earned
    the right to be placed next to you, great Scípio;                 410
now ivy lies without honor, and wakeful care devoted
    to the learned Muses has the name of "sloth."
But Fame is worth staying up for: who would have heard of Homer
    if the *Iliad*, that eternal work, had lain hidden?

399. **Thamyras:** A mythical singer struck blind by the Muses.
399. **Amoebeus:** A famous lyre player of the third century BC.
401. **Venus . . . Apelles of Cos:** See on 224 "nude Venus." The depiction by
Apelles (fourth century BC; Cos is an island in the eastern Aegean) of Venus
Anadyomene was the most famous painting in antiquity. Ovid does some-
times go so far as to say that gods are created by art.
409. **Ennius:** Quintus Ennius (239–169 BC), a great poet of both drama and
epic, born in Calabria (an arid backwoods peninsula in southeastern Italy)
and brought to Rome in 204 BC.
410. **Scipio:** Publius Cornelius Scipio Africanus (236–183 BC), a great hero
of the Second Punic War against Hannibal (218–202 BC). Ovid maintains
that the statue of Ennius (here identified with the poet himself) stands next
to the tomb of the Scipios on the Appian Way, though other writers express
less certainty about the statue's identity.
411. **ivy:** A plant associated with Bacchus in his capacity as god of poetry.

Who would have heard of Dánaë, if she'd always stayed locked      415
    in her tower, and kept lying hidden there as an old woman?
Beautiful girls, a crowd is a useful thing for you:
    keep bearing your wandering footsteps beyond your threshold.
The she-wolf heads for many sheep to carry off one,
    and Jupiter's eagle swoops down on many birds.                   420
A pretty woman should present herself too for public viewing;
    perhaps there'll be one in the crowd for her to draw in.
She should remain in all locations, eager to please,
    and direct her entire mind to care for her beauty.
Chance prevails everywhere: your hook should always be dangling;   425
    a fish will be in the pool where you least expect it.
Often the hounds wander in vain on the wooded mountains,
    while the stag falls into the net with no one driving him!
What could Andrómeda, in chains, have had less to hope for
    than that her tears could work their charms on anyone?           430
Often at a man's funeral a man is sought: to go
    with your hair down and not restrain your tears is attractive.

## Beware of Well-Groomed Men (and Others Too)

But stay away from men with pretensions to grooming and beauty,
    and those who carefully put their hair in order:

415. **Danaë:** See on 1.225 "descended from Danaë."
419. **she-wolf:** See on 8 "she-wolf."
420. **Jupiter's eagle swoops down on many birds:** And occasionally on other species: see on *Tr.* 2.406 "Ilian boy."
425–28. **your hook . . . driving him:** Compare 1.45–48: the prey has become the hunter.
429. **Andromeda:** See on 1.53 "Perseus . . . Indians." The enforced passivity of Andromeda chained to a rock contrasts ironically with the active role the *praeceptor* is allegedly urging women to take in the seduction process.
431. **a man's . . . a man:** See on 1.579 "the man."
433. **grooming:** See on 101 "grooming."

the things they're saying to you they've said to a thousand girls.      435
    Love is a vagrant and never stays put for long.
What's a woman to do when the man is smoother than she
    and, perhaps, could have had a greater number of men?
You'll hardly believe me, but—believe me (Troy would be standing
    if she'd followed the instructions of her Priam).      440
There are some who prowl around under false cover of love
    and seek shameful lucre using such an approach.
Don't let their hair deceive you, slick and gleaming with perfume,
    or the short shoe-strap folded into its creases;
don't let the toga of finest thread take you in, or if      445
    there's one ring after another upon their fingers:
it may be that the most refined of all from that crowd
    is a thief, and is burning with passion—for your clothes!
"GIVE MINE BACK!" That's what girls often shout when they're
    robbed.
"GIVE MINE BACK!" Their cries bellow through the
    whole Forum.      450
Venus, from temples gleaming with gold, you look unmoved
    upon such quarrels, and so do your Áppian nymphs.

437. **smoother:** See on 1.506 "smooth your calves with biting pumice-stone."
438. **a greater number of men:** See on 1.524 "scarcely a man, is looking for a man."
440. **instructions of her Priam:** The text here is a bit uncertain, and some editors emend it to read "Priam's daughter"—i.e., Cassandra. In any case, both Priam and Cassandra (according to some traditions) advised the Trojans to give back Helen; instead, the Trojans bowed to the will of the seducer Paris (a dandy rather like the men the *praeceptor* advises women to avoid in this passage).
450. **bellow through the whole Forum:** There seems to be a pun here on the Forum Boarium ("Cattle Forum"), a commercial area named after the city's cattle market; the words for "cow" (*bos*) and "bellow" (*bovo*) are obviously related.
452. **Appian nymphs:** See on 1.81–82 "temple of Venus . . . water."

There are certain evil names, too, that have clear reputations:
  many men bear the charge of deceiving a lover.
Learn from the laments of others to fear for your own,      455
  so you don't open the door to a scheming man.
Daughters of Cecrops, beware of trusting in Theseus's oath:
  the gods he'll call to witness he called before, too.
Demóphoön, heir of Theseus's crime, you too have no
  credibility left after playing that trick on Phyllis.      460
If they make good promises, promise with as many words;
  if they give, you, too, give the pleasures agreed on.
That woman could extinguish the watchful flames of Vesta
  and snatch holy things from your temple, Ínachus's daughter,
and feed a man aconite with a dash of pounded hemlock,      465
  who gets a gift and then says no to Venus.

## LETTERS

The spirit moves me to take my stand closer; pull the reins,
  Muse, and don't be hurled out by speeding wheels.

457. **Daughters of Cecrops:** See on 1.172 "Cecropian." Theseus was Athenian, so the *praeceptor* gives a special warning to the women of his native city.
457. **Theseus's oath:** For the story of Theseus's abandonment of Ariadne, see 1.525–64.
459. **Demophoön:** See on 2.353 "Phyllis."
463. **Vesta:** The goddess of the hearth, whose sacred flame in her shrine in the Roman Forum was tended by the sacrosanct Vestal Virgins. The flame was the symbolic heart of the city; if it went out (a very bad omen for Rome), the assumption was that a Vestal had lost her virginity, and she was punished by being buried alive. Needless to say, the use of this particular example to illustrate the wickedness of a woman who *refuses* to have sex is a tad ironic.
464. **snatch:** Latin *rapere*, often used of what we would call "rape" (e.g., what Jupiter did to Io)—again, rather ironic in this context.
464. **Inachus's daughter:** Io, who became Isis; see on 1.77 "Memphitic . . . heifer."

Words inscribed on maple-wood tablets should test the waters;
    a suitable servant girl should receive the note sent.       470
Look closely; in what you'll read, figure out from the words
    themselves
    if he's faking or asking from the heart in real distress,
and write back after a brief delay: delay always spurs
    lovers on, provided it's only for a short time.
But don't either promise yourself too easily to the young man    475
    who's asking, or stonily refuse what he's after.
Make him fear and hope simultaneously; each time you write
    let the hope become more certain, and the dread less.
Girls, write elegant words, but ordinary, from common
    parlance: the normal form of speech is charming.      480
Ah, how often have words set a doubting lover on fire—
    and a barbarous tongue has ruined an excellent figure!
But since (although you're lacking in the honor of a fillet)
    you care about putting one over on your men,
use the hand of your maid or boy to furrow the tablets,    485
    and don't entrust your pledges to a *new* boy:    486
he who holds onto such things is a traitor, certainly—    489
    but still wields power like a thunderbolt from Aetna!    490
I've seen girls go white as a sheet from that sort of terror    487
    and suffer unending slavery in their misery.    488
In my opinion, deceit that repels deceit is legitimate;    491
    the laws permit bearing arms against armed men.
One hand should become skilled at shaping numerous figures
    (ah, damn those who make me give such warnings!);
it isn't safe to write back until the wax is erased,    495

469. **maple-wood tablets:** Compare this with the letter-sending advice given
to men at 1.437–70.
483. **fillet:** See on 1.31–32 "Get ye . . . foot."
490. **Aetna:** The Sicilian volcanic mountain under which the Cyclopes forged
Jupiter's thunderbolts.

so a single tablet doesn't show two hands.
Whenever you write, always refer to your lover as female;
   your notes should turn a "he" into a "she."

### ANGER (AND PRIDE) MANAGEMENT

If I might turn my attention from details to greater matters
   and spread my sails out full with billowing fold,        500
controlling irascible character is essential to beauty;
   fierce wrath looks good on beasts, shining peace on humans.
Wrath makes faces swell up, veins grow black with blood,
   eyes flash more savagely than a Gorgon's fire.
"Go away far hence, flute, you're not worth it to me!"      505
   said Pallas when she saw her face in the river.
You all, too—if you saw yourselves in the mirror mid-wrath,
   there's scarcely any who'd recognize her own face.
And pride is no less damaging when it shows on your face;
   Love should be lured in with gentle eyes.        510
Trust the expert—we hate immoderate disdain:
   often a silent face holds the seeds of hatred.
Look at the one who looks at you; smile at the one smiling softly.

496. **two hands:** This seems to mean that the tablet should not show samples of two different kinds of her (fake) handwriting, lest the ruse be discovered; but it could also be a warning not to let one tablet link her handwriting with his (if he writes back on the same tablet without erasing it completely).

504. **Gorgon's fire:** The Gorgons were three snaky-haired women whose glance could turn men to stone; with Minerva's help, Perseus cut off the head of one of them (Medusa), which eventually made it onto Minerva's shield (the aegis). Whereas the *praeceptor* considers the Gorgon's glance an anti-aphrodisiac, Freud's essay on "Medusa's Head" offers precisely the opposite interpretation of its petrificatory nature (while seeing Medusa's decapitation as an emblem of castration).

506. **Pallas . . . river:** Minerva invented the flute in order to imitate the wail of the remaining two Gorgons over the death of their sister Medusa. When the goddess saw what actually *playing* the flute did to her cheeks, however, she threw it away.

He's nodding at you? You give him the signal right back.
After such foreplay, that boy ditches his blunt practice weapons        515
    and brings out the sharp arrows from his quiver.
We hate the gloomy ones, too. Ajax may like Tecméssa;
    we cheerful people are charmed by happy women.
Andrómache, I would never ask you, or you, Tecméssa,
    to be my girlfriend—neither one of you two.                          520
In fact, I can hardly believe—though I'm forced to, because you
    gave birth—
    that you two actually had sex with your men!
Sure, that gloomiest of women would say to Ajax,
    "My darling!" and the words men always like!

## TREAT EACH MAN CORRECTLY (ESPECIALLY POETS)

Who forbids me to take examples from great things for smaller
    ones,                                                                  525
    and not to be afraid of the name of leader?
The good leader has this man rule a hundred with a vine-wood staff,
    gives that one cavalry, this one a flag to guard:
you all, too, look closely at the use for which each of us
    is suited, and put each in his proper place.                          530
The rich man should give gifts; the lawyer should give legal aid;
    the orator, of course, plead his client's case.

521. **though I'm forced to:** Actually, the *praeceptor* seems to spend an inordinate amount of time fantasizing about Andromache's sex life; see on 2.645 "Andromache."

526. **leader:** Latin *dux*, which leads the reader to believe the poet is about to say something about Augustus (though in fact this turns out to be a red herring). Since Latin has no definite or indefinite articles, *dux* could equally signify "leader," "a leader," or "the leader."

527–28. **this man . . . guard:** The centurion ("commander of 100 men"), the *praefectus equitum* (leader of the cavalry), and the *aquilifer* (standard-bearer) or *primuspilus* (senior centurion), respectively.

532. **client:** See on 1.88 "patron . . . client."

Those of us who do songs—we should send songs alone:
    *this* chorus, we're more suited for love than anyone!
We advertise far and wide the beauty that turns us on.      535
    Némesis is famous; Cynthia is famous.
The lands of the Evening Star and the Rising Sun know Lycóris,
    and many ask who my Corínna is.
Moreover, treachery is absent from sacred prophets;
    our art behaves in accordance with its character.      540
Neither ambition nor passion for possessions affects us;
    we scorn the Forum and live for bed and shade.
But we get attached easily; we're scorched by powerful heat,
    and we know how to love with a faith that's all too sure.
No doubt our genius is molded by our gentle art,      545
    and our character is appropriate to our hobby.
Go easy on Aónian prophets, girls: there's divinity
    in them, and they're fans of the Piérides.
There's a god in us, and commerce between us and heaven:
    that spirit comes from the ethereal home.      550
It's wickedness to hope for reward from learned poets!
    Woe is me, no girl is afraid of this wickedness.
Still, fake it, and don't let your expression broadcast your greed;
    a new lover will resist if he sees the net.

536–37. **Nemesis . . . Cynthia . . . Lycoris:** The (pseudonymous) girlfriends of the three "canonical" elegists (Tibullus, Propertius, and Gallus, respectively), famous from West to East.
538. **Corinna:** Ovid's main (pseudonymous) girlfriend in the *Amores*. But is she really famous if people cannot figure out who she is?
539. **prophets:** See on 1.29 "prophet."
547. **Aonian:** Aonia = Boeotia, home of the Muses and Bacchus; see on 1.312 "Aonian god."
548. **Pierides:** Muses (who were the "daughters of Pierus," a Macedonian king, in some versions).

## ADJUST FOR AGE

But a rider doesn't use the same bridle on a horse that has                    555
    just now felt the reins and one that's an artist;
nor should you take the same path to catch a heart that's steady
    with years as you would for youth that's still rather green.
This new recruit, who's just now entering the camp of Love—
    a new little prize who's just come into your bedroom—              560
should know only you, should always cling to you alone;
    that crop must be enclosed with a high fence.
Flee from a rival: as long as you alone have him, you'll win;
    kings and Venus don't do well with partners.
That veteran soldier, he'll love gradually and wisely;                         565
    he'll put up with lots the recruit will not.
He won't be breaking doorposts or burning them with fierce flames,
    or attacking his mistress's soft cheeks with his nails,
or tearing his own tunic—or his girl's tunic—
    nor will hair ripped out be a reason for tears.                    570
Those things are becoming for boys hot with youth and love;
    this man will calmly put up with savage wounds.
He will burn, ah!, with slow fires, like damp straw,
    like wood that's just been cut from a mountain ridge.
This love is surer, more serious, more fertile than the other;                 575
    with quick hand, pluck the fruit that's on its way out!

556. **artist:** Latin *artifex*, used of an animal only here in Latin literature.
560. **prize:** Latin *praeda*; see on 1.114 "prize."
562. **crop:** Though such imagery is common for women, figuring a *man* as a crop to be cultivated and/or protected is unusual, to say the least.
570. **hair ripped out:** See on 2.169 "I remember." The *praeceptor* would like to make clear that he has matured since the days of *Amores* 1.7.
576. **pluck the fruit that's on its way out:** See on 59 "be mindful of old age to come." When it comes to *males*, the (nearly) overripe fruit will, of course, be the best.

## The Utility of Rejection

Let's hand everything over (we've opened the gate to the enemy)
    and, in our faithless betrayal, let's keep faith.
Something too easily given won't nourish a long love well;
    the occasional rejection should season the fun.          580
He should lie in front of your gate; he should cry, "Cruel door!";
    he should make lots of pleas and lots of threats.
We can't take sweetness; let some bitter juice refresh us!
    Favoring winds will often make a boat sink.
This is what makes it difficult for wives to be loved:        585
    their men can go to them whenever they want!
Throw in a door and a guard to say stubbornly, "You can't"—
    once you're locked out, love will touch you, too!
(Put away the blunt swords now, time to fight with sharps.
    No doubt I'll be attacked with my own weapons.)       590
When falling into your net, and when freshly caught, the lover
    should hope that he alone has got your bedroom;
afterward, he should sense a rival, that the rights to your bed
    are shared: take away these arts and love gets old.
The valiant horse runs best, after the bar goes up,        595
    when he's got both some to pass and some to catch up to.
No matter how dead the flames are, injury resurrects them.
    Take me: I confess, I don't love unless I'm hurt!
Nevertheless, don't let his reason for pain be too obvious;
    let him be worried and think there's more than he knows.    600
The grim guardianship of a made-up slave gets him going,
    and the annoying concern of a too-harsh man.
Pleasure is not as welcome when it comes in safety;

578. **faithless betrayal:** Of men, that is, since he is telling all their secrets to
the Amazons (see on 2 "Penthesilea").
581. **"Cruel Door!":** See on 69 "locking out lovers."

even if you're freer than Thaïs, play scared.
Though you could use the door quite easily, let him in through     605
    the window, with many signs of fear on your face;
have a sly servant girl rush in and say, "We're dead!";
    you hide the trembling youth someplace or other.
Still, some carefree Venus should be mixed in with the fear,
    in case he doesn't think your nights are worth it.     610

## ADDITIONAL TRICKS

How a clever husband can be tricked, and a vigilant
    guard—I was just about to pass over these things.
The bride should fear her man! Guarding a bride should be valid!
    This is right! Laws, justice, and shame command it!
But for *you* to be kept safe, too, whose freedom has just been
    claimed—     615
    who could stand that? To deceive, approach my rites.

604. **Thaïs:** A famous Athenian courtesan (late fourth century BC) who traveled with Alexander the Great, and also a common name for prostitutes in Greek and Roman comedy.

607–8. **sly servant girl . . . trembling youth:** The servant-girl accomplice and the hidden youth are both stock figures in an adultery mime; see on 1.502 "playing the lover."

612. **just about to pass over:** See on 193 "How close I came."

615. **freedom has . . . been claimed:** Latin *vindicta redemit*, which literally means something like "the ceremonial claim (made by an advocate, called the *assertor*, that you were wrongfully held as a slave) has redeemed." Manumission was accomplished through this ceremonial claim and a touch with a rod (*festuca*); the woman thus freed, a *libertina* (freedwoman), would now be allowed to marry (slaves were not). The *praeceptor*'s assertion that he is writing only for such women is, naturally, disingenuous (see on 1.33 "safe Venus")—and if they were in fact his intended audience, they would hardly have appreciated his condescending implication that *their* marital fidelity was not worth preserving.

616. **rites:** See on 1.29 "prophet."

Though as many eyes as Argus had are carefully watching,
    if only your will is firm, you'll give them the slip.
As if the guard will keep you from being able to write,
    when time is allowed for you to take a bath!        620
When your accomplice is able to carry the tablets you've written
    by hiding them in her warm breast with a big bra!
When she can conceal the pages by binding them to her calf
    and carry your flirty notes between foot and shoe!
If the guard's onto these things, instead of paper, your accomplice   625
    should offer her back and carry your words on her body!
Also, a letter is safe and deceives the eyes if written in
    fresh milk: touch it with coal dust and you can read it.
A letter written with moist flax seed will deceive as well,
    and a blank tablet will carry a hidden message.        630
Acrísius took plenty of care to keep his girl safe;
    she still made him a grandfather through her guilt.
What's a guardian to do, when the City has so many theaters?
    When she happily goes to watch the teams of horses?
When she sits and worships the Phárian heifer with rattles
      and goes                                     635
    where her male attendants are forbidden to go?
When the Good Goddess shoos the eyes of men from her temple
    (except whatever ones *she* orders to come)?

617. **Argus:** See on 1.627 "bird of Juno."
618. **give them the slip:** See on 2.166 "I gave words." Once again, Ovid plays on the literal and figurative senses of *dare verba*, since he is counseling the women to "give the slip" by "giving words" written and conveyed in unusual ways.
631. **Acrisius:** See on 1.225 "descended from Danaë."
635. **Pharian heifer:** See on 1.77 "Memphitic . . . heifer" and 270 "Pharian fish."
637. **Good Goddess:** See on 244 "Good Goddess."

When—while the guard's outside, keeping the girl's clothes safe—
    many baths hide secret fun and games?                      640
When—as often as she needs—her sly friend gets sick,
    and (however sick she is) gives up her own bed?
When with its name the "adulterous key" teaches us what to do—
    and the door's not alone in providing the entrance you want?
The guardian's care can also be tricked with lots of Lyaéus     645
    (even from grapes that are picked in the mountains of Spain).
There are also some medications to produce deep sleep
    and press eyes shut, conquered by Léthean night.
It's fine to have your accomplice delay the pest with some long-lasting
    fun, and bed him herself to buy you time.                  650
But what's the point of this subterfuge and minute instructions
    when the guard can be bought off with the tiniest gift?
Believe me, gifts are what win over both men and gods:
    Jupiter himself is appeased by offerings.
What will the wise man do? The fool, too, loves a gift:     655
    he, too, will keep quiet if he gets a gift.
But the guard only needs to be bought once to last a long time:
    once he surrenders, he'll do it over and over.

643. **"adulterous key"**: Latin *adultera clavis*, a "duplicate key," which plays on the sense of *adultera* as both "adulterous" and "counterfeit" (see on 2.484 "adultery").

644. **door's not alone**: That is, the window will work too (and note the double entendre in "entrance").

645. **Lyaeus**: A title of Bacchus, meaning "the Loosener" (an appropriate epithet in this context).

646. **Spain**: A source of cheap wine—no need to waste the good stuff on slaves. The *praeceptor* is thrifty.

648. **Lethean**: See on 340 "Lethe's waters."

654. **offerings**: Latin *dona*, "gifts," can also mean both "offerings" and "bribes." The combination of religious grandeur, proverbial wisdom, and cynical practicality in this couplet is vintage Ovid.

BEWARE OF RIVALS
(AND SOME PERSONAL REVELATIONS)

I remember, I complained that companions ought to be feared;
    that complaint doesn't just pertain to men.         660
If you're too trusting, other women will pluck your joys;
    that rabbit will be hunted down by others.
Even that one who's eager to offer her place and her bed—
    believe me, we've been together more than once!
You all shouldn't have too pretty a maid as your servant:      665
    she's often taken the mistress's place for me!
What am I doing—am I crazy? Why meet the enemy with chest
    exposed and give evidence to betray myself?
The bird doesn't show the bird-catcher the best place to catch it;
    the doe doesn't teach the hated dogs to run.      670
Well, let utility deal with it. I'll pursue my plan faithfully:
    I'll give the Lémnian women swords to kill me.
See to it (and it's easy) that we believe we are loved:
    belief comes easy for those full of greedy desire.
The woman should gaze more lovingly at the young man, sighing  675
    deeply, and ask why he is coming so late;
tears should be thrown in, and made-up grief about a rival,
    and she should tear his face with her fingernails.
He'll have been persuaded long since: soon, he'll pity her
    and say, "Her care for me is torturing her!"      680
Especially if he's well groomed and likes what he sees in the mirror,
    he'll believe goddesses could fall in love with him.

---

659. **I remember, I complained:** See on 2.169 "I remember"; here the *praeceptor* "remembers" the advice he gave men in 1.739–54.

666. **she's often taken the mistress's place for me:** See on 1.382 "under my leadership . . . caught." As often, Ovid plays on the ambiguity of "mistress" as "her mistress" and "my mistress."

672. **Lemnian women:** The women of Lemnos (see on 2.579 "Lemnos") killed all their menfolk for infidelity (Hypsipyle alone spared her father).

THE SAD STORY OF PROCRIS

But whatever the injury is, let it bother you in moderation,
   and don't lose your head when you hear about a rival,
and don't be too quick to believe: of the harm in believing too
     quickly,                                      685
   Procris will be your all-too-serious example.
There lies not far from the purple hills of flowering Hyméttus
   a sacred spring and ground soft with verdant turf;
a forest—not deep—forms a grove; wild strawberry cloaks the grass;
   rosemary, laurel, and black myrtle waft their scent;       690
there was no lack of boxwood, thick with leaves, or delicate
   tamarisk, slender laburnum, and cultivated pine.

686. **Procris:** The death of Procris, the last and most elaborate mythological exemplum in the *Ars*, has a none-too-serious backstory involving adultery, bribery, and deception. There are many variants, but in one version, after marrying Cephalus, she is bribed to sleep with one Pteleon, then flees to King Minos (see on 1.290 "bull"). In exchange for another bribe—a preternaturally swift hunting dog and the unerring spear that will soon appear in the present episode—she cures Minos of an unfortunate venereal ailment (involving ejaculation of snakes, scorpions, and centipedes) and sleeps with him too, supplanting Pasiphaë in his affections (see *Rem.* 453). After she returns to Cephalus, he attempts (with some success) to seduce her in disguise, offering enormous bribes; she later attempts (with some success), disguising herself as a man, to seduce *him*, offering the fatal spear as a bribe. On the transformation of this seedy story into a tale of tragic pathos, see "When the *Praeceptor* Reads" in the introduction.
687. **Hymettus:** See on 2.423 "Hymettian."
688. **sacred spring:** A spring, grass, and shade are stock elements in the *locus amoenus* (pleasant place), a standard backdrop in Latin poetry for erotic encounters of all kinds (as well as for divine epiphanies or the creation of art).
692. **slender . . . cultivated:** Latin *tenuis* (slender) is a "Callimachean" buzzword often employed when poets wish to contrast their own elegant, learned, polished poems (like small clear springs) with the bloated bombastic epics of others (like swollen muddy rivers). Combined with "cultivated" (*culta*; see on 101 "grooming"), it gives this sylvan scene a distinctly aesthetic feel. Given

The gentle Zephyrs and the refreshing breeze sway the leaves
   of so many species, and ruffle the tips of the grass.
The resting place pleased Céphalus. Leaving his dogs and
    attendants,                                                                                                   695
   the weary youth would often recline on this ground,
and used to sing, "You who can relieve my heat,
   come, fickle breeze, to be received in my bosom!"
To his wife's fearful ears, some busybody reported
   (with lips that remembered all) the sounds he had heard.                 700
Procris, when she heard the name Aura, as if of a rival,
   went out of her mind and fell dumb at the sudden pain;
she paled, as after the grapes have been plucked the lingering leaves
   on a vine grow pale, harmed by the coming of winter,
and ripe Cydónian apples bending their branches low,                            705
   and cherries not yet good enough for us to eat.
When she's come to her senses, she tears the thin robe from her breast
   and wounds her undeserving cheeks with her nail;
in a flash, she flies out in the middle of the street, her hair disheveled,
   furious, like a Bacchant whipped up by the thyrsus.                         710

---

the close relationship between "grooming" and seduction in this poem, Procris
is not wrong to have her suspicions raised.

693. **Zephyrs:** West Winds. Another element to Procris's backstory: her sister
Orithyia was abducted by Boreas, the North Wind.

698. **breeze:** Latin *aura*; Procris, of course, cannot tell whether this is *aura*
the thing or a person/nymph/goddess named Aura (and she has a family
history of liaisons with all-too-humanoid "breezes"). Cephalus was in fact
lusted after by the dawn goddess Aurora (see on 84 "rosy goddess"), whom
the ancients connected etymologically with *aura*; the extent to which he re-
sisted her advances depends on who is telling the story.

705. **Cydonian:** See on 1.293 "Cnossian . . . Cydonian." "Cydonian apples"
were quinces, a pale fruit—but the choice of "Cydonian" may also hint at
Procris's dubious connection with Crete.

710. **Bacchant . . . thyrsus:** See on 1.190 "thyrsus" and 1.312 "Aonian god."
Women in the throes of passion and jealousy are often compared to Bac-
chants; in the *Ars*, however, such a simile is applied only to Pasiphaë.

When nearly there, she leaves her companions behind in the valley
    and bravely, secretly, tiptoes into the grove.
What were your thoughts as you hid there, nearly out of your mind,
    Procris? What fire was raging in your stunned heart?
Any minute (you were thinking), this Aura, whoever she was,      715
    would arrive, and present a shocking sight to your eyes!
Now you regret having come (for you really don't want to catch them),
    now you're glad; doubtful love is twisting your heart.
Urging you to believe, there's the place, and the name, and the spy,
    and that the mind always thinks its fears have come true.      720
When she sees the imprint of a body in the matted grass,
    her trembling heart strikes against her fearful breast.
And now the middle of the day had shrunk the slender shadows,
    and sunset and sunrise were equally far away.
Look, Céphalus returns to the woods, Cyllénian scion,      725
    and soothes his burning mouth with water from a spring.
Procris, you anxiously hide; he sprawls on the usual grass
    and says, "Gentle Zephyrs and breeze, come here!"
When the pleasing error of the name was made clear to the poor thing,
    her mind came back, true color came back to her face.      730
She rises, her eager body disturbing the leaves in her way,
    and moves, a wife, to go to her man's embrace:
he thinks he's seen a wild beast, and in youthful haste raises up
    his limbs: the shafts were there in his right hand—
what are you doing, wretch? She's not a beast, hold back your
      shafts!      735
    Miserable me! The girl's been pierced by your spear.

719. **there's the place:** Latin *locus est*, a classic beginning to the kind of digression that often culminates in an erotic encounter.
725. **Cyllenian:** See on 147 "Cyllenian tortoise shell"; Cephalus was a son of Mercury (in this version).
736. **girl:** Latin *puella*, the term used throughout the *Ars* for the lover's target; used inappropriately here of a married woman, it reminds the reader of the story's context.

"Woe is me!" she exclaims. "You've pierced a friendly heart.
    This place is always getting wounds from Céphalus.
I die before my time, but I've been wronged by no rival:
    Earth, this will make you rest lightly on my bones.                   740
My spirit is going away to the 'breezes' whose name I suspected.
    I'm slipping—oh! Close my eyes with your dear hand."
He held the dying body of his mistress in his gloomy
    bosom and bathed her savage wounds with his tears;
gradually slipping from her incautious breast, her spirit              745
    departs and is taken up by her wretched man's lips.

### Navigating Dinner Parties

But let's get back to work. It's time for my naked style,
    so my weary keel can make it into its harbor.
You're anxiously waiting for me to take you to a dinner party;
    you're begging for my advice in this matter too.                      750
Come late, and enter gracefully, when the lamps are lit:
    delay helps your case, delay is the greatest bawd;
even if you're hideous, to plastered men you'll seem beautiful,
    and night itself will give cover to your faults.
Take the food in your fingers (the way you eat counts for
        something);                                                         755
    don't smear it all over your mouth with a dirty hand.
Don't fill up at home beforehand, but stop before
    you're full; eat a little less than you can eat.

---

738. **wounds:** Procris's fate shows what happens when the metaphors of "hunting" and "Cupid's arrows" turn real.

743. **mistress:** Another love-elegy word (like *puella*) inappropriate for a married woman; see on 1.139 "mistress."

745. **spirit:** Latin *spiritus* means both "spirit" and "breath"; to catch the dying breath of a loved one was a gesture of affection.

747. **naked style:** Need I point out the double entendre here as the art of poetry intersects with the art of love?

If Priam's son should catch sight of Helen stuffing her face,
   he would despise her and say, "My plunder is stupid."          760
It's more suitable and appropriate for girls to drink:
   you don't go badly, Bacchus, with Venus's son.
This too—only as much as your head can take, so your mind
   and feet stay steady, and don't be seeing double.
A woman lying in a puddle of Lyaéus? Disgraceful.                765
   She's worthy to suffer any sex whatsoever.
Nor is it safe to lie there asleep when dessert's been served;
   many shameful things often happen through sleep.

INTIMATE DETAILS

I'm ashamed to teach any further—but kind Dióne says,
   "Any work that's shameful is my specialty."                    770
Let each be known to herself; take your cue about position
   from your body; the same technique doesn't work for everyone.
One who's got an exquisite face should lie face up;
   those with a pleasing behind should be seen from behind.
Milánion used to carry Atalánta's calves on his shoulders;        775
   that's the way they should be seen if they're good.
One who's petite should ride horse; because she was very tall,
   the Theban bride never rode the Hectórean horse.

760. **plunder:** Latin *rapina*, which can mean both "the act of forcibly carrying off" and "the thing forcibly carried off"; Paris could be criticizing either his own stupid behavior in snatching Helen or the stupidity of the booty herself.
765. **Lyaeus:** See on 645 "Lyaeus."
769. **Dione:** See on 2.593 "Dione."
771. **be known to herself:** See on 2.500 "to be known to himself."
775. **Milanion . . . Atalanta:** See on 2.185 "Nonacrian Atalanta." As a huntress and athlete, Atalanta would, presumably, have had good legs.
778. **Theban bride . . . Hectorean horse:** See on 2.645 "Andromache" (who was from Thebe, a city near Troy). This may well be Ovid's most ludicrous contrast between epic phraseology and pornographic subject matter. (One of Hector's primary Homeric epithets is "tamer of horses.")

The woman who wants to show off her long flank should lie with
   her neck
   bent back just a little, and press the sheets with her knees.    780
If one's got a youthful thigh, and her breasts are also flawless,
   the man should stand while she sprawls at an angle on the bed.
Don't think it's a disgrace to let down your hair like the Phylleían
   mother, and bend your neck back while your tresses go wild.
You as well, whose belly Lucína has marked with wrinkles,    785
   ride the horse turned backward, like the swift Párthian.
Venus has a thousand games; it's simple, and least work,
   when she lies, semi-reclined, on her right flank.
But neither the tripods of Phoebus nor the horned Ammon

783–84. **Phylleian mother:** This reference is a bit puzzling. Phyllus was the
town in Thessaly from which Laodamia came (see on 2.356 "Son of Phylacus"), so this could refer to her grieving friends. On the other hand, Phyllis
(see on 2.353 "Phyllis") was from Thrace, the traditional haunt of Bacchants
(see on 710 "Bacchant . . . thyrsus"), so this could be a reference to the unfettered hair (and loose sexual practices) of these crazed women.
785. **Lucina:** The goddess of childbirth.
786. **Parthian:** See on 1.210 "shoots . . . in retreat."
789. **tripods of Phoebus:** At Apollo's oracle at Delphi (see on 2.500 "to be
known to himself"), the priestess would sit on a tripod and, inspired by
gaseous exhalations from a crack in the ground (whose composition is not
known: theories include ethylene, benzene, carbon dioxide, etc.), would utter
gibberish that the priests would translate into polished, if riddling, hexameters. To the sentiment expressed here I cannot resist comparing part of A. E.
Housman's "Fragment of a Greek Tragedy":
    Not from the flight of omen-yelling fowls
    This fact did I discover,
    Nor did the Delphine tripod bark it out,
    Nor yet Dodona.
    Its native ingenuity sufficed
    My self-taught diaphragm.
789. **Ammon:** The African manifestation of Jupiter (represented with ram's
horns), whose oracle in Libya was largely nonfunctional by Ovid's day but
was still famous as a proverbial oracle.

will sing you anything truer than my Muse;                                      790
if anything can be trusted, believe my art, which I've made
    through long experience; my songs will establish trust.
The woman should relax and welcome Venus deep in her
    blood, and that business should please both parties equally.
Keep the sweet nothings coming, and the charming murmurs;                       795
    naughty words shouldn't stop in the middle of the game.
You as well, to whom nature's denied the sensation of Venus,
    fake delightful joys with lying sounds.
(Unhappy the girl for whom that place is dull and numb,
    where woman and man are supposed to get equal enjoyment!)                 800
When you're faking it, just be sure you're not found out;
    your motions, your very eyes, should make it believable.
Both the words and the gasps from your mouth should show what
      you like.
    Ah, I'm ashamed . . . but *that* part has secret signs.
She who demands a gift from her lover after Venus's joys                         805
    must want her prayers not to have any weight.
And don't throw open the windows and flood the bedroom with light:
    better that many things on your body lie hidden.

THE END

That's the end of my game. Time to get down off the swans
    who have drawn the yoke of my chariot with their necks.                   810
As once the young men did, so now the girls, my crowd,
    should inscribe on the spoils, "NASO WAS MY TEACHER"!

809. **swans:** These birds drew the chariot of Venus, which the poet has appro-
priated for his own use.
812. **NASO:** See on 2.744 "NASO."

# Remedia Amoris

Love just read the title and name of this book. He said,
   "War against me! This means war, I see!"
"Don't be so quick to accuse your prophet of wickedness, Cupid—
   I who so often carried the flag you gave me.
I'm not Týdeus's son, who wounded your mother and made her          5
   retreat to the clear sky with the horses of Mars.
Other young men often grow lukewarm. I've always loved;
   if you must know what I'm doing, I'm loving now too.
No, even better—I've taught the art of acquiring you!
   What used to be an impulse is now a science!                    10
Beguiling boy, I have betrayed neither you nor my *Arts*,
   nor is some new Muse unweaving past work.
If someone loves what he likes to love, let him burn away happily,
   keep sailing with his wind and enjoy the trip!
But if an unworthy girl's dominion is getting him down,             15
   the aid of my art should keep him from being a wreck.
Why has some lover knotted a noose around his neck
   and dangled—sad burden!—from a lofty beam?

5. **Tydeus's son:** Diomedes; this Greek hero wounded Venus when she tried
her hand at combat during the Trojan War.
11. **my *Arts*:** Or it "my arts"? Both, in a sense; Ovid likes to play on the title
of his poem (which he gives as both *Art* and *Arts*).

174

Why has another stabbed his own breast with rigid steel?
   A lover of peace, you've gotten a rep for murder!                    20
Whoever—if he won't stop—will perish through wretched love
   must stop! Then you'll be the author of no one's funeral.
Besides, you're a boy; the only thing you should do is play.
   So, play! A *soft* reign is appropriate for your age.
[For you were able to wage war with naked arrows,                       25
   but your weapons lack death-bringing blood.]
Your stepfather should be fighting with swords and piercing spears,
   a bloody conqueror wading through much slaughter;
*you* should be cultivating the arts we use safely—your mother's;
   *their* evil robs no mother of her children.                        30
Make it so the door's beaten down with nocturnal brawls
   and the doorpost is buried in decorative garlands!
Make young men and timid girls come together in secret
   and give her cautious man the slip by some art!
The lover should alternate between sweet nothings and tantrums        35
   at the harsh door, singing weepy things when locked out.
Those tears will satisfy you, without the reproach of death:
   your torch is not worthy to light the devouring pyre!"
That's what I said. Golden Love moved his jeweled wings
   and told me, "Complete the work you have proposed."                 40

IF ONLY I HAD BEEN THEIR TEACHER!

O deceived young men, come listen to my instructions,
   you whom Love has tricked on every side.

27. **stepfather:** Mars (not Cupid's legal stepfather, but one of his mother's lovers, at least).
34. **art:** Or *Art?*
36. **locked out:** See on 3.69 "locking out lovers."
38. **torch . . . pyre:** The *praeceptor* rings a humorous change on the analogy between the fires of love (or wedding torches) and those of the funeral pyre, commonplace in Latin poetry but played out most tragically in *Aeneid* 4 (Dido's passion and suicide).

Learn to be cured by the one through whom you learned to love;
    a single hand will deal your wound and heal it.
The same earth nourishes plants that are salutary and harmful,        45
    and roses often grow right next to nettles;
the spear that once had wounded the Herculéan foe—
    that Pélian spear brought healing to the wound.
(But whatever I say to men, girls, know that I'm saying to you
    as well: I'm supplying arms to opposing sides.        50
If any of those things isn't relevant to your needs,
    nevertheless, it can teach a lot by example.)
My useful proposition: to extinguish fierce flames,
    and not to have the heart be the slave of its sin.
Phyllis would have survived if she'd had *me* for a teacher;        55
    the path she took nine times she'd have taken much more.
Dido would have watched from the citadel as the Dardánian
    ships set sail—but not while she was dying!
Pain would not have armed the mother against her own womb—
    the one who spilled their shared blood for revenge on her man.    60
My art would have kept Téreus (though he found Phílomel hot)
    from turning into a bird because of his crime.

47. **Herculean foe:** Hercules's son Telephus was wounded by the spear of
Achilles on the way to Troy, then later (as the Delphic Oracle promised)
healed by rust from the same spear.
48. **Pelian spear:** See on 1.696 "Pelian spear."
55. **Phyllis:** See on 2.353 "Phyllis." Note that the list of Love's victims in this
passage does not include any who actually *have* been cured (who would they
be?).
57. **Dido:** See on 3.39–40 "He even . . . Elissa."
57. **Dardanian:** Son of Electra and Jupiter (and yet another source of Juno's
epic jealousy), Dardanus was an Italian prince who was also a mythical founder
of Troy (hence "Dardanian" = "Trojan"). In *Aeneid* 4, Dido refers to Aeneas
or things belonging to him as Dardanian with special bitterness after he has
left her.
59. **the mother:** Medea.
61. **Tereus:** See on 2.383 "this swallow."

Give me Pasíphaë: now she'll discard her love for the bull!
  Give me Phaedra: Phaedra's foul love will vanish!
Hand Paris over to me: Meneláus will hold onto Helen          65
  and Pérgamum won't fall, conquered by Dánaan hands!
If that undutiful Scylla had read my pamphlet, Nisus,
  the purple lock would still be stuck to your head!
Under my leadership, people, squash your destructive obsessions;
  under my leadership, ship and crew should sail straight!          70
Naso was your must-read back when you learned how to love;
  that same Naso will be your must-read now.
As public defender I'll bring relief to hearts oppressed by
  mistresses: everyone, clap for your liberation!
To you I pray at the start, Phoebus, inventor of poetry          75
  and of medicine: may your laurel be with us!
Give your aid to the prophet and equally to the healer:
  both of these disciplines are in your sphere.

## The Best Strategy: Nip It in the Bud

While you can—only moderate feeling flutters your heart—
  if you don't like it, stop that foot at the threshold.          80
Squelch those evil seeds of sudden disease while they're new,
  and right at the start, don't let your horse out the gate.
For delay gives strength: delay ripens tender grapes
  and turns the young blade into a vigorous crop.

63. **Pasiphaë:** For her story, see 1.289–366.
66. **Pergamum:** See on 1.478 "Pergamum."
66. **Danaan:** See on 2.735 "Danaan."
67. **Scylla:** See on 1.331 "daughter of Nisus."
71. **Naso:** See on 2.744 "NASO."
74. **liberation:** Latin *vindicta*; see on 3.615 "freedom has . . . been claimed."
The poet is playing with legal terminology and the double meaning of "mistress": see on 1.139 "mistress."
76. **laurel:** See on 2.495 "Laurel."
77. **prophet:** See on 1.29 "prophet."

The tree that provides abundant shade for those out strolling?          85
 Back when it was first planted, it was a shoot.
Then, it could have been plucked out from the topsoil by hand:
 now, it stands firm, grown to great height in its strength.
Do a quick mental check on what sort of thing you're in love with,
 and snatch your neck from a yoke that promises harm.          90
Resist at the beginning: medicine comes too late
 when evils have gathered strength through long delay.
But hurry, and don't let yourself off till some future time:
 the man who's not ready today will be less tomorrow.
Every love gives the slip and finds nourishment through delaying:      95
 tomorrow's always the best day for liberation.
Only a few rivers do you see sprung from great springs:
 most are multiplied by collecting water.
If you had sensed quickly how great a sin you were cooking up,
 Myrrha, you wouldn't be covering your face in bark.          100
I myself observed how a wound that at first had been curable,
 left alone, brought disaster through long delay.
But because it's so delightful to pluck the fruit of Venus,
 we're constantly saying, "Tomorrow it'll be the same."
Meanwhile, flames are creeping silently into our guts,          105
 and the evil tree is driving its roots still deeper.

## Plan B: After It's Taken Root

If, on the other hand, the time for first aid has gone by,
 and mature love has settled in a captive heart,
a greater work awaits; but just because I'm summoned
 later to the patient doesn't mean I'll desert him.          110

96. **tomorrow's always the best day for liberation:** That is, this is what the procrastinator tells himself, ignoring the Love Doctor's advice.
100. **Myrrha:** See on 1.285 "Myrrha."
109. **greater work:** See on 3.370 "the greater work."

The Poeántian hero *should* have cut out right away,
  with steady hand, that part where he'd been wounded;
nevertheless, they believe this man after many years
  was healed, and put the finishing touch on the war.
I who was hurrying to expel the disease at its birth       115
  am now advancing slowly to bring you late aid.
If you can, you should try to stamp out either fires that are new
  or ones that have collapsed through their own strength.
While madness is racing along, give in to the racing madness:
  every impulse is difficult to get near.       120
Foolish is that swimmer who, when he could be carried
  downstream at an angle, fights to go straight upstream.
The uncontrollable spirit—which art can no longer handle—
  rejects and despises the adviser's words?
I'll get a better approach when he'll allow his wounds       125
  to be touched, and will be ready to hear the truth.
Who but a fool would forbid a mother to weep at her son's
  funeral? That's no place to give her advice.
Once she has satisfied her grieving spirit with tears,
  that pain will be restrainable through words.       130
In general, medicine is the art of timing: giving
  wine at the right time helps; at the wrong time, it hurts.
In fact, by forbidding sins, you might even enflame and excite them
  if you don't fight against them at the right time.


111. **Poeantian hero:** Philoctetes (son of Poeas), a Greek hero who was bitten by a snake on the way to Troy and left behind on the island of Lemnos (see on 2.579 "Lemnos") because the stench of his wound was unbearable. When an oracle declared that the Trojan War could not be won without his bow (which had belonged to Hercules), however, the Greeks fetched him (after Ulysses stole his bow, Achilles's son Neoptolemus gave it back, and the deified Hercules instructed him to return to Troy, bow and all). He was healed by Machaon (see on 2.491 "Machaon's potions"), then fought a duel with Paris and won.

## AVOID LEISURE

Therefore, as soon as my art finds you in a curable state,                    135
    take my advice: above all, AVOID LEISURE.
That makes you fall in love and keeps you in love when it's made you;
    that's what causes and feeds the pleasing plague.
Take away leisure and Cupid's arrows are dead, as well as his
    torches—their flames go out and they lie there ignored.        140
As a plane tree rejoices in wine, as a poplar in water,
    as a marsh reed in muddy mucky soil,
so Venus loves leisure. Looking to put an end to love?
    Do things. (Love yields to things.) You'll be safe!
Lying around, unlimited sleep with no one to wake you,                        145
    dice, frying your brain with gallons of wine—
all these things break your spirit's backbone without a wound;
    cunning Love slips in when you're not looking.
That boy goes in pursuit of laziness. He hates doers.
    Give your idle mind work to keep it busy.                       150
There's courts! And laws! And friends for you to do things for!
    March through the gleaming camp of the urban toga!

## MAKE WAR, NOT LOVE!

Or else take up the young man's task of serving bloody
    Mars: now fun and games will beat a retreat!
Look, the fleeing Párthian, latest reason for a great                         155

---

141. **plane tree rejoices in wine:** The great natural historian Pliny the Elder (AD 23–79) says that wine was originally poured at the base of a plane tree to give it honor, but the custom was continued when it was discovered that the tree's roots benefited from the sousing; he quips that "we have taught even trees to drink wine" (*Natural History* 12.8).
152. **toga:** The toga, worn by freeborn Roman male citizens, represented one's status in society and symbolized civil (as opposed to military) activity.
155. **fleeing Parthian:** See on 1.210 "shoots . . . in retreat."

triumphal parade, now sees Caesar's arms in his camp:
  conquer the arrows of Cupid and Párthian at the same time,
    and bring the ancestral gods a double trophy!
No sooner is Venus wounded by the Aetólian spear
  than she gives her lover the command to wage war.                    160
You want to know why Aegísthus became an adulterer?
  The reason is obvious: because he was lazy.
Other men were fighting at Troy in an endless war;
  all of Greece had transferred its resources there.
If he wanted to spend time on wars, there were none being fought;   165
  if on courts, Argos was totally free of lawsuits.
To avoid having nothing to do, he did what he could: he loved.
  That's how that boy comes and that's how that boy stays.

## Try Farming!

Fields, too, delight the spirit, and zeal for farming;
  there's no care that won't give way to that care.                    170
Order bulls to submit their conquered necks to the burden
  to make the crooked plowshare wound the hard ground.
Bury the seeds of Ceres in the upturned soil
  so the field will return the investment with high interest.
Look at the branches so bent under the burden of apples               175
  their tree can hardly bear the weight it's produced;
look at the streams, gliding along with a pleasant murmur;
  look at the sheep, shearing the lush grass.
See the she-goats heading for the rocks and sheer cliffs:
  soon they'll be bringing full udders back for their kids.            180

156. **triumphal parade:** Which, of course, also happens to be an excellent
venue for flirting (see 1.213–28).
159. **Aetolian spear:** Diomedes was from Aetolia (a region in west-central
Greece); see on 5 "Tydeus's son."
160. **her lover:** Mars.
169. **Fields:** Nearly all the details of the idealized pastoral setting described in
this section hail from various kinds of erotic poetry.

The shepherd is warbling a song on pipes of varying length,
  his canine companions—hardworking crowd—at his side.
Somewhere else the deep forest is echoing with moos,
  a mother complaining that her calf is not there.
How about when the swarm flees from the smoke set beneath
    them                                                                           185
  so taking the honeycombs lightens the rounded baskets?
Autumn gives apples; summer is beautiful with the harvest;
  spring provides flowers; winter's relieved by fire.
At fixed seasons the countryman plucks ripened grapes
  and the new vintage flows beneath his bare foot;                                  190
at fixed seasons he cuts the grain and binds it in sheaves
  and harrows the earth he's shaved with a wide-toothed comb.
You yourself can plant a shoot in a watered garden,
  you yourself guide trickles of gentle water.
It's time for grafting: make a branch adopt a branch                                195
  and a tree stand covered with a foreigner's hair.
As soon as this pleasure has begun to soothe your spirit,
  feckless Love makes his exit on weakened wings.

## OR HUNTING! BIRD-CATCHING! FISHING!

Or cultivate a passion for hunting: Venus has often
  slunk off in disgrace, beaten by Phoebus's sister.                                200
Now with your clever hounds hunt rabbits pelting away,
  now stretch your nets out on the leafy ridge,
or terrify timid deer with the multicolored scare,
  or let the boar fall, gouged by your thrusting spear.
You'll be so weary at night that sleep, not care for your girl,                     205
  will seize you and soothe your limbs with delicious rest.
It's a milder passion—but still a passion—to capture birds

200. **Phoebus's sister:** Diana.
203. **scare:** Latin *formido*, a rope hung with bright feathers that was used to scare deer into hunting nets.

and go after that small quarry with nets or twigs,
   or hide a bronze hook beneath a morsel of food so a hungry
      fish will gulp it (bad plan) with greedy mouth.                    210
By these things or by others, while you're unlearning to love,
   you'll have to secretly deceive yourself.

## Or Travel!

Although you'll be held back by stubborn chains, just go
   far away, and persevere on a distant journey.
You'll weep, and think of the name of the girlfriend you left
      behind,                                                            215
   and often your foot will stick in the middle of the road.
But the less you want to go, remember to go all the more;
   bear up; force your unwilling feet to run.
Don't wish for rain, or let the foreign Sabbath delay you,
   or the Állia, infamous for its disaster;                             220
don't ask how many miles you've gone, but how many you still
   have left, and don't gin up detours to keep you close;
don't count the days, or keep looking back toward Rome, but flee!
   Through flight, the Párthian is still safe from his foe.

## I KNOW It's Tough

Someone may call my instructions harsh: harsh, I confess,              225
   they are—but you'll have to bear lots of pain to get well.
Often when I was sick, though I didn't want to, I drank bitter
   potions, and wasn't allowed to eat, though I begged.
To redeem your body, you'll suffer steel and fire, and not
   relieve your parched mouth with water when thirsty;                  230

208. **twigs:** See on 1.391 "limed."
219. **Sabbath:** See on 1.415 "Sabbath festival."
220. **Allia:** See on 1.413 "tearful Allia."
224. **Parthian:** See on 1.210 "shoots . . . in retreat."
229. **steel and fire:** Surgery and cautery.

to heal your soul, is there anything you'll refuse to suffer?
    But *that* part is more valuable than the body!

## A Journey of a Thousand Miles . . .

Still, the door is the most depressing part of my art;
    the one hard task is to endure the beginning.
You see how the first yoke chafes young bulls when they're
        captured                                                    235
    and the new saddle hurts the galloping steed?
Maybe you'll find it tough to leave your ancestral hearth—
    but still, you'll leave; and then you'll want to go back.
It's not the ancestral hearth that'll call you back, but love
    for your girlfriend, cloaking your sin in beautiful words.      240
Once you've gone, there's a hundred solaces for your obsession
    in countryside, companions, and long journey.
But don't think leaving is enough: stay away a long time,
    till the fire has lost its strength and turned to ashes.
If you rush to return before your mind has been steeled,          245
    Love will fight back and bear savage arms against you;
you'll come back hungry and thirsty from how much you were away,
    and that whole expanse will contribute to your ruin.

## Avoid Magic (Look at Medea and Circe)!

If anyone thinks baneful herbs from the land of Haemónia
    and magic arts can help, then he should deal with it.          250
That's the ancient path of sorcery. *My* Apollo
    offers innocent help through sacred song.
Under my leadership, no Shade will be pried from its tomb,
    no crone will crack the earth with her ill-omened song,

248. **expanse:** Latin *spatium*, which means both "extent of time" and "extent
of space." In the previous line, "how much you were away" could also refer
to both time and distance.
249. **Haemonia:** See on 2.99 "Haemonian arts."
254. **song:** See on 1.2 "song."

no crop will transfer itself out of one field into another,            255
    nor will Phoebus's orb grow suddenly pale.
Tiber, as always, will flow into the waters of the sea,
    Luna, as always, be carried by snowy horses.
Chanting won't make any hearts put away their obsessions;
    potent sulfur won't make Love flee in defeat.            260
How'd those herbs from the land of the Phasis help you, Cólchian,
    when you wanted to stay in your father's house?
How'd those grasses of Perses's daughter work for you, Circe,
    when the Nerítian ship was riding its wind?
You did everything to keep your clever guest from leaving:            265
    he'd decided on flight and gave it full sail.
You did everything to keep the fierce fire from burning you:
    Love stuck fast even in your unwilling heart.
You had power to change humans into a thousand shapes:
    you didn't have power to change the laws of your heart.            270
They say you even—when he already wanted to leave—
    detained the Dulíchian leader with these words:
"I don't pray now for what (I remember) I used to hope for

256. **Phoebus's orb:** Witches were thought to have the power to change the "complexion" of the sun (and moon).

258. **Luna . . . snowy horses:** That is, the moon will stay white.

260. **sulfur:** See on 2.330 "sulfur and eggs."

261. **Colchian:** Medea.

263. **Perses's daughter:** Latin *Perseides*, which could also mean "Perse's daughter." This could refer to Circe's mother, whom Hesiod calls Perseid; Circe herself, since Homer calls her mother Perse; or Hecate, goddess of witchcraft, whom Apollonius calls a daughter of the Titan Perses. The ambiguity shows off the poet's erudition.

264. **Neritian:** From Ithaca (Neritos is a mountain in Ithaca), homeland of Ulysses.

272. **Dulichian:** Another poetic substitution for Ithacan (Dulichium is a small island near Ithaca).

273. **I remember:** This looks like an "Alexandrian footnote" (see on 2.169 "I remember"), but the Circe of the *Odyssey* expresses no such wish. Circe's

at first, that you could wish to be my husband.
And yet, I thought I was worthy to become your wife,                    275
    as a goddess and a daughter of great Sun!
I beg you not to hurry: I'm asking for the gift of time;
    what smaller thing could my prayers possibly wish?
Also, you see how the sea is troubled—you should fear it;
    there'll be a better wind for sailing later.                    280
What's your reason for flight? No new Troy is rising here,
    nor anyone calling the allies back to arms.
Here there is love and peace, in which I'm the only one wounded,
    and you will be the king over this whole land!"
She was talking, Ulysses was untying his ship;                    285
    the wind carried off her useless words with his sails.
Circe burns, and runs to her accustomed arts:
    nevertheless, these didn't diminish her love.
Therefore, whoever you are who seek the aid of my art,
    withdraw your trust from sorceries and songs.                    290

## FIXATE ON HER FLAWS!

If some powerful cause keeps you in our mistress City,
    hear what my advice is in the City.
He's his own best champion who, when he's broken the chains

---

whole speech here, like the similar one of Calypso (2.123–42), is in fact more
reminiscent of Dido in *Aeneid* 4 (see on 2.127 "asking for The Fall of Troy").
Ovid is, among other things, showing off his awareness of how Virgil's Dido
alludes to the various women who tempt Ulysses in the *Odyssey*.
291. **mistress City:** Latin *domina Vrbs*, a striking phrase that conveys both
"Rome, which is the ruler of the world" (*urbs* is of the feminine gender, so
the adjective *dominus, -a, -um* describing it must take the feminine ending:
see on 3.23 "Virtue") and "Rome, who is your/our mistress" (see on 1.139
"mistress"). In his exile poetry, Ovid figures himself as the lover locked out
by his "mistress" Rome (see on 3.69 "locking out lovers").
293. **champion:** Latin *vindex*, the one who accomplishes *vindicta*: see on 74
"liberation" (more legal terminology involving slavery and emancipation).

that wound his heart, un-hurts himself once and for all;
even I will admire one who has that much spirit,                        295
    and say, "That one has no need of my advice."
But you for whom unlearning to love what you love is hard—
    you can't and you wish you could—you're the one I must teach.
Keep going over in your mind the deeds of the wicked girl
    and place every one of your losses before your eyes:                300
"She got that and that, but this plunder wasn't enough for her:
    her greed has made my house go up for sale!
Here's how she swore me an oath, how she tricked me under oath,
    letting me lie at her doorstep so many times!
She herself likes others, disdains to be loved by me;                  305
    the salesman, alas, gets the nights she doesn't give me!"
All these things should totally embitter your feelings;
    think about these, look here for the seeds of your hatred.
If only they could even turn you into an orator!
    Just be in pain, you'll be effortlessly eloquent.                   310

It Worked for Me, Sort of

My heart had gotten stuck recently on a certain girl;
    she really wasn't suitable to my spirit.
A sick Podalírius, I was cured by my own concoctions!
    (I know, the "sick doctor"—I was a disgrace.)
It helped to fixate constantly on my girlfriend's faults;              315
    doing this over and over worked my cure.
I used to say, "What terrible calves the girl has got!"
    (And yet, to tell the truth, they really weren't.)
"The girl's arms, how very unattractive they are!"
    (OK, to tell the truth, they really weren't.)                      320
"How short she is!" (she wasn't); "How much she demands from
    her lover!"
Now *that* was the biggest reason for me to despise her.

313. **Podalirius:** See on 2.735 "Podalirius."

## TURN VIRTUES INTO VICES

Also, bad things are very close to good ones: that error
     has often given virtues the name of vices.
As much as you can, make your girl's endowments something
          worse,                                                      325
     deceiving your judgment by a narrow distinction.
If she's full-breasted, call her "obese"; if she's dusky, "black";
     "skinny" can be the slender one's reproach.
One who isn't a prude can take the name of "slut";
     anyone who is modest can be a "prude."                          330
Better—whatever endowment your woman *doesn't* have,
     keep flattering her and begging her to display.
Insist that she sing, if the girl has no voice; make her dance,
     if she doesn't have a clue about moving her arms.
Barbarous in speech? Make her converse with you all the time.       335
     She never learned to strum strings? Demand the lyre.
She walks like a duck? Make her stroll. Her boobs are spilling over
     her whole top half? Let no bra cover this fault.
If her teeth are lousy, tell her stories to make her laugh.
     If her eyes are weak, say things to make her cry.               340
What'll also help: when she hasn't made herself up for anyone,
     suddenly fly to your mistress first thing in the morning.
We're blown away by grooming; jewels and gold cover everything;
     the actual girl is the smallest part of herself.
You may well ask, "With all this stuff—where's something to love?" 345
     Wealthy Love deceives the eyes with this shield.
Show up unexpected: you'll catch her unarmed, and be safe!
     Her faults will be the unlucky woman's downfall.

324. **virtues . . . vices:** This advice, of course, reverses that given in 2.657–62:
see on 2.657 "names."
329. **prude:** Latin *rustica*; see on 1.607 "rustic."
343. **grooming:** See on 3.101 "grooming."

(On the other hand, it's not safe to put *too* much trust in this
    teaching;
  beauty that charms without art takes many men in.) 350
Then, too, when she's smearing her visage with poisonous potions,
  go see your mistress's face: don't let shame hold you back!
You'll find jars with a thousand colors of all sorts of things—
  and grease that's sliding down into her warm bosom.
Phíneus, those concoctions have the stench of your table! 355
  They've made me sick to my stomach more than once.

## About Sex—No, Wait, about My Poetry

Now I'll expound for you what steps we should take in the middle
  of sex: Love must be routed from every direction.
Shame prevents me, of course, from expressing many of these,
  but use your wits to imagine more than I say. 360
For recently certain people have criticized my books;
  according to their strict standard, my Muse is a slut.
But as long as I'm this charming, and sung all over the world,
  the one or two who want to can pick at my work!
Envy disparages the genius of great Homer; 365
  Zoilus, whoever you are, you got *your* name from *him.*
Sacrilegious tongues have even shredded your song,
  you who led Troy to bring her conquered gods here.
Envy strikes peaks: winds blow through the highest points;
  thunderbolts sent by Jupiter's hand strike peaks. 370

---

355. **Phineus:** See on 1.339 "Phineus."
361. **certain people:** See "Ovid's Exile: Fact and Fiction" in the introduction.
366. **Zoilus:** A philosopher of the fourth century BC, known for his bitter
attacks on Homer, Plato, and others.
367. **your song:** The *Aeneid*; Ovid honors Virgil by not naming either him
or his poem (see on 3.338 "Latium has no more brilliant work than him").
370. **thunderbolts:** In the exile poetry, "Jupiter's thunderbolt" is the primary
metaphor for Augustus's edict sending Ovid into exile.

But you, whoever you are whom my free spirit offends,
    if you're wise, give each thing its proper measure.
Brave wars love to be narrated in Maeónian feet:
    what place can there be in those for fun and games?
Tragedians sound grand: wrath wears the tragic buskin;        375
    ordinary speech fits the comic slipper.
Freewheeling iambs should be drawn at advancing enemies—
    the fast kind or the kind that drags the last foot.
Beguiling Elegy should sing of Loves with their quivers,
    a fickle girlfriend having fun at her whim.        380
Achilles should not be sung in the measures of Callímachus;
    Homer, Cydíppe is not the one for your lips.

---

372. **measure:** Latin *numeri*, "measure" in the sense of both "quantity" and "poetic meter." An adage about moderation slyly shifts to a discourse on the meters appropriate to each genre.

373. **Maeonian feet:** That is, the hexameters of Homer (see on 2.4 "Ascran and Maeonian old men") and all epic poetry (see on 1.24 "the wound he's made").

375. **buskin:** Latin *cothurnus*, a laced boot worn by tragic actors to increase their height (it often stands metonymically for the genre of tragedy).

376. **comic slipper:** Latin *soccus*, the sock or slipper worn by comic actors (it often stands metonymically for the genre of comedy).

377. **iambs:** Metrical feet consisting of a short beat followed by a long one; iambic trimeter (three sets of two iambs) was the standard meter for invective.

378. **drags the last foot:** In one variety of iambic trimeter (called *scazōn*, "limping"), the final iamb was a spondee (long long) rather than an iamb (short long).

380. **girlfriend:** Does this refer to Elegy or to its (her) subject? Like the English, the Latin is ambiguous, and Ovid often personifies Elegy as a flirtatious goddess (e.g., *Amores* 3.1, where she appears to him in person, limp and all).

381. **Callimachus:** Callimachus did, in fact, write in both hexameters and elegiac couplets.

382. **Cydippe:** See on 1.457 "letter . . . Cydippe"; Callimachus wrote a poem about her.

Who could stand Thaïs playing the part of Andrómache?
  Whoever plays a Thaïs in Andrómache sins!
My art is all about Thaïs; my fun is emancipated.                    385
  I'm fillet-free; my art is all about Thaïs.
If my Muse is appropriate for frivolous material,
  I've won my case—she's being tried on false charges.
Devouring Envy, eat your heart out! I've got a great name now—
  and greater, if its feet just keep the same path.                 390
But you're in too big a hurry: if I live, you'll hurt worse;
  my years have still got many a song in store.
I like this, and my thirst for fame has grown with my honor;
  my horse is panting at the bottom of the hill.
Elegies say they owe the same amount to me                          395
  as Epic, noble genre, owes to Virgil.
That's all the answer I give to jealousy: pull in your reins
  more tightly, poet, and run in your own circle.

## Back to Sex: Take the Edge Off

So then, when it's sex and the work of youth you're after,
  and the time of the promised night is drawing near,               400
so the delight from your mistress won't snare you because your body's
  too swollen, I want you to do it with anyone first.
Find anyone to take the edge off your first pleasure;
  after the first, the next one will be sluggish.

383. **Thaïs:** See on 3.604 "Thaïs."
383. **Andromache:** See on 2.645 "Andromache." The *praeceptor*, of course, would never dream of reducing Andromache's tragic grandeur!
385. **emancipated:** Latin *libera*, playing on the sense of "free to do what it wants" and "freed from slavery," that is, dealing with freedwomen (*libertinae*); see on 3.615 "freedom has . . . been claimed."
386. **fillet-free:** See on 2.600 "hem."
386. **my art:** Or my *Art*? See on 11 "my *Arts*."
399. **So then:** Ovid is the master of ludicrous transitions, but this one takes the cake.

Venus deferred is the most enticing: sun feels good                    405
    in the cold, shade in the sun, water to thirst.

## FOCUS ON FLAWS

It's embarrassing, but I'll say it: join for sex in the way
    you think each one is least attractively joined.
It's not hard to do, since very few women admit the truth
    to themselves, and they don't think anything makes them
        look bad.                    410
Moreover, I command you to throw the windows wide open
    and let in the light to reveal their ugly limbs.
But just as soon as your pleasure has crossed the finish line
    and your whole bodies and minds are lying there pooped—
when you're so sick of it you could wish you'd never touched                    415
    a girl and don't think you'll touch one for a long time—
then make a note in your mind of every flaw in her body,
    and don't take your eyes off any of her faults.
Possibly someone will call these "small" (for, in fact, they are)—
    but while they don't help one by one, they do en masse.                    420
A puny viper kills an enormous bull with a bite;
    often a boar is held by a dog that's not big.
Just you take my instructions together, and fight with numbers:
    a giant heap will grow out of many grains.

## BUT BE FLEXIBLE

But since there are as many postures as personalities,                    425
    my precepts shouldn't have to spell everything out.
Things by which your sensibilities can't be offended
    will possibly be a reproach in another's judgment.
Because one man had seen the obscene parts on her exposed
    body, his love—which was in full flow—dried up;                    430
another's because, when the girl was getting up from the business
    of Venus, he saw shameful stains on the dirty bed.
If things like *that* could move you, you're just playing around;

the torches that enflamed your heart were lukewarm.
Once that boy pulls his bowstring taut with greater force,          435
    you wounded lot will be looking for more assistance.
What of that man who hid while his girl was passing . . . obscene stuff,
    and saw what even custom forbids us to see?
Gods forbid that we should advise anyone to do *that*!
    Such things shouldn't be proposed (even if they're helpful).          440

## HAVE A BACK-UP GIRLFRIEND (LIKE AGAMEMNON)

I also urge you to have two girlfriends at the same time
    (he who can have more than that is even stronger!);
when the heart is torn and runs in opposite directions,
    one love saps the power of the other.
Great rivers are diminished by flowing to lots of streams,          445
    and savage fires die out through removal of logs.
One anchor is not enough to hold down wax-smeared ships,
    nor is a single hook enough for swift waters;
he who has long ago procured for himself twin comforts
    has long ago become victor on the high Citadel!          450
But you, who made the mistake of entrusting yourself to one mistress—
    now, at least, you've got to find a new love.

438. **even custom forbids us to see:** That is, even the most basic standards for human behavior forbid us to watch another person defecating.
442. **stronger:** Latin *fortior*, which can mean both "stronger" and "braver." Here it appears to mean both "in a stronger position" and "having a greater endowment of testosterone [as evidenced by his bravery in being willing and by his strength in being able]."
448. **single hook . . . swift waters:** That is, in fast-moving water, two hooks may be required to keep a fish on the line—either two hooks for a single fish or one each for two separate fish (in the hope that at least one will stay on). Analogy with the two-anchored boat in the previous line would suggest the former, though the *Ars*'s ubiquitous "trolling for girls" metaphors would suggest the latter.
450. **victor . . . Citadel:** See on 2.540 "Jupiter's Citadel."

Minos lost his fire for Pasíphaë in Procris;
  beaten by wife Idaéa, the first wife lost;
Callíroë, who got a share of his bed, made sure that          455
  Amphílochus's brother not always love Phégeus's daughter;
Oenóne would have kept even Paris to the very end
  if her Oebálian rival hadn't hurt her.
The beauty of his wife would have pleased the Odrýsian tyrant—
  but the beauty of her locked-up sister was better.          460
Why am I wasting time on examples? Their multitude tires me!
  Every love is beaten by a new successor.
A mother can more bravely lose one child out of many than
  him for whom she weeps, "You were my only one!"

453. **Minos . . . Pasiphaë . . . Procris:** See on 3.686 "Procris." As with all the mythical examples in this section, an act of betrayal with horrific consequences becomes a recommendation.

454. **Idaea:** The second wife of Phineus (see on 1.339 "Phineus"), and quite the stepmother.

456. **Amphilochus's brother:** Alcmaeon; see on 3.13 "Oecles's son." As he was traveling the world seeking purification for the murder of his mother, Alcmaeon first married the daughter of Phegeus (Arsinoë or Alphesiboea), a king who purified him; but this purification was not entirely successful (the land was still barren because of him), so he eventually went to Acheloüs, a river god, who *really* purified him and gave him his daughter Calliroë. She hated her stepsons and had them put to death.

457. **Oenone:** The mountain nymph who was Paris's wife while he was still a shepherd, before the infamous Judgment. She warned him not to go off with Helen; when he disregarded her prophetic advice, she told him to return to her if he were ever wounded. He did, but she refused to heal him. Though she later repented, by that point he was beyond repair; after he died, she hanged herself.

457. **even Paris:** That is, though he was the womanizer par excellence.

458. **Oebalian:** Oebalus, king of Sparta (Oebalian often = Spartan), was father of Tyndareus, (mortal foster-)father of Helen.

459. **Odrysian tyrant:** Tereus (the Odrysians were a Thracian tribe, so Odrysia = Thrace); see on 2.383 "this swallow."

And lest you happen to think I'm writing new rules for you          465
    (would that the glory of that invention were mine!),
the son of Átreus saw this: indeed, what couldn't he see,
    who had the whole of Greece under his authority?
That victor loved Chryses's daughter, captured by his own Mars—
    but her senile father kept blubbering like a fool.          470
Why the tears, you hateful old man? They're great together!
    You're hurting your daughter by meddling, you blockhead!
When Calchas—shielded by Achilles—had ordered that she be
    returned, and she was received in her father's home,
the son of Átreus said, "There's one almost like her in beauty—          475
    even has the same name, except the first syllable.
Achilles will give her up to me on his own if he's smart;
    if not, he'll get a taste of my authority.
But if any one of you has a problem with this, Achaéans—
    it's something to hold a scepter in a strong hand!          480
For if I'm king and there isn't anyone for me to sleep with,
    Thersítes is welcome to take over my kingdom."
He spoke, took this one as great consolation for the previous,
    and put away his passion, repelled by new passion.

473. **Calchas:** The Greek priest who instructed Agamemnon to give up Chryseis; Achilles's protection of Calchas was one reason why Agamemnon chose to take Achilles's prize (Briseis) as replacement for his own.

476. **same name, except the first syllable:** Since the "-eis" ending on Chryseis/Briseis means "daughter of," this would be like our saying all disyllabic names ending in "-son" are essentially the same. In addition to being one of his funniest, this line shows Ovid's literary acumen: Agamemnon's fatuity, especially in managing people (think Dilbert's Pointy-Haired Boss), is a prominent theme in both epic and tragedy.

479. **Achaeans:** A common name for the Greeks in the *Iliad* (Achaea is in the northern Peloponnese).

482. **Thersites:** The ugliest of the Greeks (and therefore, by ancient standards, one worthy of utter scorn).

Therefore, make Agamémnon your model and get some new
  flames,                                                              485
  so your love will be pulled apart in different directions.
You want to know where to find them? Go and read my *Arts*;
  soon your boat will be overloaded with girls.

## PLAY IT COOL

But if my instructions are worth anything, if Apollo gives mortals
  any useful teaching through my lips,                               490
even if you're in the middle of Aetna, burning, wretched—
  be sure that, to your mistress, you're colder than ice.
Pretend you're fine, don't let her sense it if by chance you're
  in pain; when you ought to weep for yourself, laugh.
Now, I'm not ordering you to break off in the middle of passion;    495
  the orders of this commander are not so savage.
Pretend you're not what you are; imitate madness discarded;
  that's how you'll turn your play-acting into reality.
Often, to avoid drinking, I've wanted to look like I'm sleeping;
  while looking the part, my eyes have been conquered by sleep!     500
I've laughed at the dupe who, while he pretended to be in love,
  had fallen, that bird-catcher, into his own snare!
Love enters our hearts through practice; it's unlearned through practice.
  He who can pretend to be fine will be fine.
She's told you to come: come on the night she agreed on with you.   505
  You've come, and the door is locked? You'll grin and bear it.
Don't murmur sweet nothings to or throw tantrums at the doorpost,
  and don't lie on your side on the hard threshold.
Another day dawns: your words must be without complaints,
  and don't let your face show any signs that you're hurt.          510

485. **make Agamemnon your model:** Need I point out that this is quite possibly the worst advice ever given?
491. **Aetna:** See on 3.490 "Aetna."
492. **colder than ice:** Some manuscripts have "rather cold"; both readings have merit.

She'll stop putting on airs when she sees you're growing lukewarm
    (here's yet another service you'll get from my *Art*!).

## FOOL YOURSELF

Deceive yourself too, though: don't set yourself a deadline for when
    to stop loving; the horse often fights against the reins.
Utility should stay hidden. What you don't proclaim, will happen;   515
    the bird avoids the nets that are too obvious.
She mustn't be too pleased with herself, or scornful of you:
    buck up your spirit, so she'll yield to your spirit.
Maybe her door's open? Pass it by, even if you're called back.
    A night's given? Balk at coming on the given night.   520
Being patient is easy when, once the patience ceases,
    you're able to snatch some joys right away with ease.

## TRY OVERINDULGENCE

To think that anyone could call my instructions hard!
    Look, I'm even playing the part of a pander!
For personalities vary, so I'll vary my arts:   525
    a thousand forms of disease, a thousand remedies!
Certain bodies are scarcely healed by a sharp knife;
    many have found relief through potions and herbs.
You're too soft, you can't walk away, you're firmly bound,
    fierce Love is crushing your neck beneath his foot?   530
Stop fighting it! Allow the winds to carry your sails,
    and ply your oars wherever the waves invite you.
You need to slake that burning thirst that's making you a wreck.
    I give in. Go drink from the middle of the river.

512. **another service you'll get from my *Art***: That is, in addition to the boat-
load of girls referred to in 487–88. To deflate a puffed-up girl, follow the advice
in 1.715–18.
522. **with ease**: Latin *ex facili*, an expression that means "easily," but could
also mean "from an easy [girl]" (which is the implication either way).

But make it an even *bigger* drink than your stomach asks for,          535
    so that the water you've drunk comes back up your throat.
Go ahead, no one's stopping you—keep enjoying your girl!
    Let her carry away your nights and your days!
Get bored with the disease. Boredom can end things too.
    And also stay when you think you can do without,          540
till you've made yourself too full, and abundance erases love,
    and it's no fun to be in the house you're sick of.
Love also lasts a long time when nourished by lack of confidence;
    get rid of your fear if you want to get rid of this love.
One who's afraid she's not his, or that someone will steal her
      from him—          545
    Macháon's help will hardly make *him* well!
A mother of two will usually feel more love for the son
    in the army, because she's afraid he won't return.

## LETHEAN CUPID'S ADVICE:
## DON'T BE HAPPY, WORRY!

There's a venerable temple near the Colline Gate;
    lofty Eryx has given his name to this temple.          550
Léthean Love lives there—the one who makes hearts whole
    and douses his own torches in icy water.
That's where young men beg for forgetfulness of their desires,
    and any girl who's enthralled by a hardhearted man.
He spoke to me thus (I'm not sure whether it was the real          555
    Cupid or a dream—but I think it was a dream):
"O you who sometimes give anxious loves, sometimes take them away,
    Naso, add this, too, to your instructions.

546. **Machaon:** See on 2.491 "Machaon's potions."
550. **this temple:** The temple of Venus Erycina (see on 2.420 "Eryx"), near
the Colline Gate on the northeast side of the City.
551. **Lethean:** See on 3.340 "Lethe's waters."
558. **Naso:** See on 2.744 "NASO."

Let each one turn his mind to his troubles: he'll discard love.
  The god has given them, more or less, to everyone. 560
He who fears the Púteal, and Janus, and the quick Kalends—
  let him be tortured by the sum of his debt.
The one with a harsh father? Though everything else is going
  his way, let him keep his harsh father before his eyes.
This pauper is living with a wife whose dowry was lousy? 565
  Let him believe his wife is obstructing his destiny.
You've got some fine land, a fertile vineyard that gives abundant
  grapes? Be afraid your grapes will be blighted at birth!
Some man's got a ship coming home? Let him constantly think
  of the treacherous sea, and the shore littered with his losses. 570
One fears for his son the soldier, you for your nubile daughter:
  who doesn't have a thousand causes for grief?
Paris, so you could have hated your woman, you should have kept
  the funerals of your brothers before your eyes!"
He was saying more, but the image of the boy deserted 575
  my gentle dream—if in fact it was a dream.

560. **The god:** Not any specific personified god, but an all-embracing divinity essentially equivalent to "fate" or "fortune."

561. **Puteal:** A *puteal* was a circle of stones surrounding a wellhead or marking a sacred place; the Puteal Libonis (or Puteal Scribonianum) in the Comitium (the part of the Forum where people assembled for legislative or judicial purposes), which marked a spot where lightning had struck, was a gathering place for merchants and moneylenders.

561. **Janus:** A god with two faces (one facing forward, one backward), whose temple was another place for financial transactions. This could also be a reference to the Kalends of January (see next note).

561. **Kalends:** The Kalends (whence our "calendar") was the first day of each month, when debts and interest came due.

## AVOID SOLITUDE (LOOK AT PHYLLIS)

What should I do? Palinúrus is jumping ship in the middle
  of the waves: I'm forced to enter unknown waters.
Whoever you are who love—solitude harms! Avoid solitude!
  Where are you fleeing? You can be safer in a crowd.                580
You have no need for secrecy (secrecy feeds the madness);
  a crowd is going to be your best defense.
If you're alone you'll be sad; the face of the mistress you've left
  will stand before your eyes like she's there in person.
Therefore, night is sadder than the time of Phoebus:                585
  the crowd of companions to soothe your grief is gone.
Don't run away from conversation, don't lock your door
  and get all weepy, hiding your face in the shadows:
always have some Pýlades to look after Oréstes.
  That too is an important use for friendship.                       590
What was it that did Phyllis in, but the lonely woods?
  The cause of her death is clear: she was unaccompanied.
She was going about with her hair down, like the barbarous throng
  that performs the biennial rites of Edónian Bacchus;
and now she was gazing out to sea as far as she could,        _      595
  now lying there exhausted on the sandy ground;
"Demóphoön, you traitor!" she shouted to the deaf waves,
  and as she spoke, her words were broken by sobs.
There was a slender path, somewhat overcast with long shadows,
  where she would often make her way to the sea.                     600

577. **Palinurus:** The helmsman of Aeneas's ship (thrown overboard by Sleep
in *Aeneid* 5).
585. **time of Phoebus:** That is, daylight.
589. **Pylades . . . Orestes:** See on 1.745 "Pylades . . . Pallas."
591. **Phyllis:** See on 2.353 "Phyllis."
594. **Edonian:** The Edoni, a tribe on the border of Thrace and Macedonia,
were known for their orgiastic worship of Bacchus.

The wretch was treading her ninth road; she said, "Let him deal
    with it!"
  and sees the girdle she's wearing, and grows pale—
sees branches, too; she hesitates, balks at what she's daring,
    and fearfully brings her fingers to her neck.
I really wish you hadn't been alone then, Sithónian:        605
    the forest wouldn't have shed its hair and mourned Phyllis.
Take Phyllis's example: fear places that are too lonely,
    man hurt by your mistress and girl hurt by your man!

## But Also Avoid Contagion

Once, a young man had followed all my Muse's orders
    and was practically pulling in to the harbor of safety.      610
But when he fell among longing lovers, he had a relapse;
    Love picked up again the arrows he'd shelved.
If you're loving against your will, be sure to avoid contagion:
    this often tends to do harm to livestock, too.
As eyes take in the wounded, they're also wounded themselves,    615
    and many things do harm to our bodies in passing.
Sometimes water flows from a river running nearby
    into areas where the ground is hard and dry;
love flows in secretly, if you don't withdraw from your lover;
    we're all an ingenious crowd where this is concerned!    620

605. **Sithonian:** See on 2.137 "Sithonian."
606. **shed its hair:** Leaves were seen as the "hair" (*comae*) of trees (and "Phyllis" derives from Greek *phyllon*, "leaf"). Legend had it that trees grew up over Phyllis's grave and shed their leaves/hair, as grieving humans would cut their hair and dedicate the locks to lost loved ones.
620. **ingenious:** Latin *ingeniosus*, a deceptively difficult word to translate. Since *ingenium* means "natural talent or endowment, genius," *ingeniosus* can mean both "ingenious" in our sense ("clever," "skilled") and "naturally prone to"— that is, can convey both an active will and a passive disposition. Ovid likes to play on the different nuances, which allow him both to boast of his talent and to deny responsibility for its consequences ("It's not my fault, I was born

Another, likewise, had just been cured: proximity harmed him.
    He wasn't able to bear running into his mistress.
The scab was not well formed; the old wound opened again.
    My arts in this case couldn't claim success.
It's hard to stop a fire next door from reaching your house;      625
    keeping out of the neighborhood is most useful.
And don't go strolling in the same colonnade she frequents,
    and don't fulfill the same social obligations.
How does it help to reheat your lukewarm heart with reminders?
    If you can, you should live in a different world!      630
It's not easy to fast with a plate of food in front of you;
    leaping water incites a raging thirst.
It's not easy to hold back the bull when he's seen the cow;
    the strong horse always neighs at the mare he's spotted.

AVOID ALL WHO KNOW HER

When you've accomplished this, to reach the shore at last,      635
    it's not enough for you to have left just her:
say goodbye to her mother, and sister, and nurse (the accomplice),
    and anyone with any share in your mistress.
Her slave mustn't come, or her little handmaid, weeping fake tears
    and imploringly greeting you in the mistress's name;      640
and even if you're longing to know how she's doing, don't ask.
    Bear up. Holding your tongue will be to your benefit.
You too, who are busy explaining the reasons for ending your love
    and reciting many complaints about your mistress,
stop complaining: there's better revenge in keeping quiet,      645
    so she'll drain away out of your desires.

---

that way"). Though *ingenium* is common, in the works in this volume, *inge-niosus* appears only here and at *Tr.* 2.288 and 342.

630. **world:** Latin *orbis*, "circle"; this could mean both "social circle" (theoreti-cally possible) and "world" (totally impossible—which I think is actually the point).

I'd rather you keep quiet than say you've gotten over it;
    he who tells many, "I'm not in love," is in love.
But a fire is more reliably put out little by little
    than all at once: quit slowly, and you'll be safe.          650
A torrent tends to run higher than a regular river—
    but the one is short-lived, the other a constant stream.
Let love go unnoticed, gradually vanish into thin air,
    and, by gentle degrees, die a slow death.

## BUT DON'T BE TOO HOSTILE

But it's a crime to hate a girl you loved just now;        655
    that ending is suitable for savage spirits.
It's enough not to care: he who finishes love with hate
    either loves or will find it hard to stop being wretched.
Man and woman allies one minute, foes the next? Shameful!
    The Áppian herself disapproves of such quarrels.        660
Often men put them on trial, then love them: where no strife
    has occurred, free from reminders, Love wanders off.
By chance, I was with a young man; his mistress rode by in a litter;
    all his words were bristling with savage threats.

649–50. **a fire is more reliably put out little by little than all at once:** Really?
651. **higher:** Latin *altior*, which means either "higher" or "deeper."
658. **either loves or will find it hard to stop being wretched:** Like the English, the Latin is ambiguous: it could mean "either he's in love or he'll find it hard to stop being wretched" or "either he loves being wretched or will find it hard to stop (being wretched)."
659. **allies:** Latin *iuncti*, literally "joined" or "yoked"—a metaphor with military, erotic, or agricultural connotations, here nudged into its military sense by "foes" (*hostes*) later in the line.
660. **Appian:** See on 1.81–82 "temple of Venus . . . water."
663. **I was with:** Latin *adesse*, which could mean "I was acting as legal counsel for."

He was about to sue her. He said, "Come out of the litter!"          665
    She came. At the sight of his wife, he was struck dumb.
His hands fell, and the folded tablet fell from his hands;
    he took her in his arms and said, "You win!"
It's safer and more suitable to separate in peace,
    not head from the bedroom to the litigious Forum.          670
The gifts you gave—command her to keep them without dispute;
    that smaller loss tends to be for the greater good.
But with your whole mind, remember to cling to the weapons
        I give you
    if some coincidence brings you two together.

## Stand Firm against All Those Techniques I Taught You (and Them)

Now is there need for weapons! Here, bravest warrior, fight!          675
    By your spear must Penthesiléa be conquered!
Now, lover, you must remember the rival, the hard
    threshold, the vain words before all the gods!
Don't comb your hair because you're about to enter her presence,
    or try to show off with that flashy "relaxed toga" look:          680
don't take any care to please a girl who's not yours;
    now make sure that to you she's just one in a crowd.
But let me explain what stands in the way of my attempts
    most of all; each can learn from his own example.

665. **sue:** Latin *vador*, which the *OLD* defines, "(of a plaintiff) To accept sureties from (the other party) for his appearance or reappearance in court at an appointed date (sts. = to institute proceedings against)."
666. **wife:** Latin *coniunx* is most naturally translated "wife," though it can mean "fiancée" or "concubine"; as often, the intended audience for this poem is a bit fuzzy. This whole scene, however, resembles divorce proceedings more than anything else.
667. **folded tablet:** See on 1.383 "tablets." This one seems to be involved in the legal proceedings.
676. **Penthesilea:** See on 3.2 "Penthesilea."

We're slow to give it up, because we all hope that we're loved: 685
   we're a gullible lot, since each is attractive to himself.
But don't believe their words (what's more treacherous than those?)
   or that the eternal gods have any weight.
Beware of letting yourself be moved by the tears of girls:
   they've given their eyes careful instruction in weeping. 690
The heart of the lover is assailed by innumerable arts,
   like a rock pounded by seawater on all sides.
Don't reveal the reasons why you'd rather break up,
   and don't say what hurts, but keep nursing the hurt in secret.
And don't recount her sins, or she may explain them away; 695
   you yourself will help make her case better than yours.
He who is silent is strong! If he makes lots of accusations
   against his girl, he's begging to be made up to.

## MAKE COMPARISONS

I wouldn't dare to steal the boy's arrows like the Dulíchian
   or grab his torches and douse them in a river, 700
nor will I be clipping back his glowing wings,
   nor will my art make his sacred bowstring looser.
Whatever I sing is wisdom: obey the singer—and you,
   health-bringing Phoebus, be present and favor my project!
Phoebus is present: the lyre has sounded, the quiver has sounded! 705
   I know the god by his signs: Phoebus is present!
Compare the wool that's dyed in the cauldrons of Amýclae
   with Týrian purple: the former will be uglier.

688. **that the eternal gods have any weight:** That is, that her oaths by the gods mean anything.
691. **innumerable arts:** I wonder where those came from!
699. **Dulichian:** Ulysses (see on 272 "Dulichian"), who attempted to steal the bow of Philoctetes (see on 111 "Poeantian hero").
707. **Amyclae:** See on 2.6 "Amyclae." "Spartan purple" dye was famous, but less spectacular than Tyrian.
708. **Tyrian:** See on 2.297 "Tyrians."

You all, too—compare your girls to genuine beauties:
  each will begin to be ashamed of his mistress.                                   710
Either of the two could have seemed beautiful to Paris,
  but Venus beat them both compared to herself.
And not just appearance: compare personality too, and art
  (just don't let your love get in the way of judgment).

## AVOID REMINDERS

What I'll sing next is a little thing, but a little thing                          715
  that's made a big difference to many, myself among them.
Beware of keeping and rereading letters from a sexy girl;
  letters reread can move a determined heart.
Throw them all (you won't want to do it) into savage fires
  and say, "Let that be the pyre for my burning passion!"                          720
Théstius's daughter set her absent son on fire with the log,
  and you're afraid to give treacherous words to the flames?
If you can, get rid of her pictures, too; why be tormented
  by a mute image? That's what killed Laodamía.
Places, too, are often harmful. Flee places that share                            725
  the secret of your sex; they're a cause of pain.
"Here she was, here she lay, there's the bedroom we slept in,
  here's where she brought me joys that luscious night."
Love is rubbed raw again by reminders, the wound is split open
  anew: a tiny mistake is harmful to the weak,                                     730
like an *almost* extinguished cinder—if you touch it with sulfur
  it'll live, and grow from the smallest to the greatest fire;

711. **Either of the two:** Juno or Minerva.
721. **Thestius's daughter:** Althaea, queen of Calydon (in Aetolia, north of
the Gulf of Corinth). The Fates had said her infant son Meleager would die
when a log currently burning was entirely consumed; she extinguished the
flame and preserved the log. After the great Calydonian Boar Hunt, Melea-
ger killed Althaea's brothers (either accidentally or in anger); in vengeance,
she killed Meleager by burning the log, then committed suicide.
724. **Laodamia:** See on 2.356 "Son of Phylacus."

so, if you don't avoid whatever will revive your love,
    the flame that was nothing just now will blaze up anew.
The Argive ships could wish to have avoided Caphéreus        735
    and you, old man, who avenged your grief with fires;
the cautious sailor is glad to have sailed past Nisus's daughter:
    you beware of places you had too much fun!
Let these be Syrtes to you; avoid this Acroceraúnia;
    here dire Charýbdis vomits the water she's drunk.        740

## POVERTY HELPS

There are some things that can't be compelled through someone's
    orders,
    but often have brought relief when they happen by chance.
If Phaedra should lose her wealth, Neptune, you'll spare your grandson,
    nor will his horses be spooked by his grandfather's bull.
If you had made the Cnossian poor, she would have loved wisely:    745
    love craves luxury and is nourished by riches.
Why did Hécale and Irus have no takers?
    No doubt because he was a beggar and she was a pauper.
Poverty doesn't have the means to feed its love—
    though that's not worth your wanting to be a pauper.    750

735. **Caphereus:** A promontory on the coast of Argos (eastern Peloponnese) where Nauplius, in vengeance for the death of his son Palamedes, would shine false lights to lure to their death Greek sailors returning from Troy.
737. **Nisus's daughter:** Scylla; see on 1.332 "housing rabid dogs."
739. **Syrtes:** Dangerous shoals and shallows off North Africa.
739. **Acroceraunia:** A dangerous rocky promontory in northern Epirus (western Balkans).
740. **Charybdis:** A whirlpool in the strait between Italy and Sicily, regarded as a female monster.
745. **the Cnossian:** Ariadne; see on 1.527 "Cnossian girl."
747. **Hecale:** A poor old woman who shows hospitality to Theseus (the subject of a poem by Callimachus).
747. **Irus:** A beggar in the *Odyssey*.

## Avoid the Theater, Music, Dancing, and, above All, Poetry

But not to indulge in the theater *should* be worth it for you,
    until your heart is quite free and love retreats.
Zithers and flutes and lyres make the spirit weak,
    and speeches, and arms that move to their own rhythms.
Fictional lovers are constantly being acted there;                755
    the actor's art shows the pleasure of what you must shun.
I hate to say it, but I will: don't touch tender poets!
    I myself am removing my own endowments.
Flee from Callímachus—he's no enemy to love;
    along with Callímachus, Cöan, you're harmful too.          760
Sappho certainly made me better for my girlfriend,
    nor did the Muse of Teos teach strict morals.
Who could have read the poetry of Tibúllus in safety,
    or yours, whose work was Cynthia alone?
Who'll be able to leave hardhearted after reading Gallus?       765
    My songs, too, have something of that timbre.

## Don't Think about Rivals

But unless Apollo—guide of this work—is deluding his prophet,
    a competitor is the greatest cause of my trouble.
But you—don't go making up a rival for yourself;
    believe that she's lying alone in her own bed.             770
Oréstes was in love with Hermíone all the more fiercely

760. **Cöan:** Philetas; see on 3.329 "Cöan poet."
761. **Sappho:** See on 3.331 "Sappho."
762. **Muse of Teos:** Anacreon; see on 3.330 "Tëan . . . old man."
764. **yours:** Propertius.
771. **Hermione:** See on 1.745 "Pylades . . . Pallas." Hermione was betrothed to Orestes, but during the Trojan War her father, Menelaus, promised her to the son of Achilles (Neoptolemus/Pyrrhus)—whom Orestes subsequently killed.

because she'd begun to belong to another man.
What's the matter, Meneláus? You set off for Crete without
   your wife, and could stay away from your bride with no problem.
Now that Paris has snatched her, at last you can't go without        775
   your wife—another man's love has made yours grow!
After Briséis was stolen, Achilles wept for this too—
   that to the Plisthénian man she was giving pleasure.
He wasn't weeping for nothing, believe me—Atreus's son did
   what he'd be a ridiculous wimp not to do!        780
I certainly would have done it, and I'm no wiser than he:
   that was the biggest payoff for causing that stink.
As for his swearing by his scepter that he never touched
   Briséis—he figures his scepter isn't the gods.

## PASS BY HER DOOR (AND BE NICE TO YOUR RIVAL)

May the gods give you strength to pass by your abandoned
      mistress's        785
   threshold, and make your feet equal to the task!
You *can* do it—just cling to your will—you've got to keep going
   bravely, and to spur your horse to a gallop!


778. **Plisthenian man:** Agamemnon. In some traditions, Plisthenes is the son of Atreus and father of Agamemnon. That Agamemnon is usually called "son of Atreus" can be reconciled with this by the common use of "son of" to mean "descendant of"; Plisthenes's early death, which meant Agamemnon was raised by his grandfather; and the propensity of ancient writers for embracing contradictory traditions simultaneously (and showing off their knowledge of all of them).
782. **that stink:** That is, the monumental wrath of Achilles that drives the action of the *Iliad*.
784. **he figures his scepter isn't the gods:** The *praeceptor* has apparently forgotten that it was *Achilles* who swore by the scepter (*Il.* 1.233–39); Agamemnon swore two oaths that he had not slept with Briseis (*Il.* 1.132–32, 19.258–65), the second of which was by Jupiter and a host of other deities.

Keep thinking that the Lotus-Eaters, that the Sirens
    are dwelling in that cave, and add sails to your oars.                    790
Also, that man you were overly grieved to have as a rival—
    I wish you would cease to consider him an enemy.
But definitely—though you still hate his guts—say "Hi!" to him;
    once you can give him a kiss, it'll mean you're fine.

## On Food

See here—to leave no medical stone unturned, I'll even                    795
    tell you which foods to avoid and which to consume.
Onions—Daúnian, or imported from the Libyan coast,
    or Megárian—are disastrous, every one;
sexy arugula also should be avoided completely,
    and anything that prepares our bodies for Venus.                    800
Better for you to be eating rue (which sharpens the eyesight)
    and anything that *denies* our bodies to Venus.

## On Wine

You want to know my instructions about the gift of Bacchus?
    You'll be done with my advice sooner than you hope.
Wine prepares the spirit for Venus, unless you take                    805
    so much that the quantity drowns and deadens your heart.
Wind feeds a fire, but wind can also blow one out;
    a gentle breeze coaxes flames; a bigger one kills them.

789. **Lotus-Eaters:** In the *Odyssey*, Ulysses must escape from these addicts
to the lotus flower (which took away all desire to do anything but eat lotus
flowers).
789. **Sirens:** See 3.311–14.
794. **kiss:** Roman males commonly greeted their friends with a quick (non-
erotic) peck.
797. **Daunian:** The Dauni were a people of Apulia (southeast Italy); Daunian
is an erudite way of saying "homegrown."
798. **Megarian:** See on 2.421 "Alcathoüs."
799. **sexy arugula:** See on 2.422 "salacious herb."

Either don't drink at all, or drink so much that it drowns
    your cares: anything between those extremes is harmful.     810

## THE END (AGAIN)

I've finished this work! Hang garlands upon my weary keel;
    I've reached the harbor that was my destination.
Soon you'll render dutiful thanks to the sacred poet,
    woman and man who have been healed by my song!

814. **woman and man:** This phrase occurs four times throughout the *Ars* (2.478, 682, 728, 3.800), always in the context of "woman and man" having sex. Its appearance here is a final hint that those who actually expected a cure from the Love Doctor should ask for their money back.

# *Tristia*

BOOK 2

Why am I bothering with you, books, unlucky obsession,
    now that my talent has made me a miserable wreck?
Why am I looking for those damned Muses—my "crime"—again now?
    It's not enough to have earned that punishment once?
Songs made woman and man so eager to get to know me,        5
    which for me was an inauspicious omen;
songs made Caesar put a black mark on me and my morals—
    because of my *Art*, published so long ago.
Strip me of my hobby, you'll strip my life of "crimes";
    I give my verses the credit for making me guilty.        10

2. **talent:** Latin *ingenium*; see on *Rem.* 620 "ingenious."
3. **"crime":** Latin *crimen* can mean "crime," but also "accusation" or "reproach"—that is, something alleged but not necessarily committed. Much of Ovid's poetic strategy in the exile poetry depends on seeing his offense (whatever it was) as a *crimen* in the latter sense. With the scare quotes on "crime" I have tried to convey "what someone else calls a crime (even though it really wasn't all that bad)."
5. **Songs:** See on 1.2 "song."
5. **woman and man:** For the erotic connotations of this phrase, see on *Rem.* 814 "woman and man."
7. **black mark:** See on 2.664 "rigid censor."
10. **I give . . . the credit:** Latin *acceptum refero*, a banking idiom that appears elsewhere in Augustan poetry only at Horace *Epistle* 2.1.234. Horace refers to a sycophantic court poet named Choerilus who got a monetary reward for

This is the reward I get for my care, for my sleepless
    toils: my talent has won itself a punishment!
If I were wise, I'd be right to hate those learned Sisters,
    goddesses pernicious to their votary:
but now—such insanity is the comrade of my illness—       15
    I'm hitting my bad foot again on the same stone.
Yes, the beaten gladiator heads for the sand again,
    and the wrecked ship goes back to the swelling waves.

## Maybe There's a Chance for Me?

But maybe—it happened once for the ruler of Teuthras's kingdom—
    the very same thing could give me a wound and heal it,    20
the Muse who stirred up wrath also soften the wrath she stirred up:
    songs often win over mighty gods by prayer.
Even Caesar himself commanded the mothers and wives
    of Ausónia to chant songs to turret-crowned Ops;
he'd ordered them to be chanted for Phoebus Apollo, too,    25
    when he threw the games each generation sees once.

---

his doggerel; Ovid implicitly contrasts his own poetry (of excellent quality,
and punished rather than rewarded).

13. **learned Sisters:** The Muses.

16. **bad foot:** Ovid can never resist a pun on human and metrical "feet" (see
on 1.24 "the wound he's made").

19. **ruler of Teuthras's kingdom:** Telephus, adoptive son of Teuthras, king of
Mysia (in Asia Minor); see on *Rem.* 47 "Herculean foe."

23. **wives:** Latin *nurus*, literally "daughters-in-law"—a term that emphasizes
women's role as bearers of legitimate children.

24. **Ausonia:** Italy (from "Ausones," primitive inhabitants of southern Italy).

24. **turret-crowned Ops:** An Italian harvest goddess identified with the Great
Mother Cybele (see on 1.507 "Phrygian rhythms"), who was depicted with a
crown of towers (signifying the wealth of cities).

26. **games each generation sees once:** The Secular Games (*Ludi Saeculares*),
so called because they were held about once a century, so each generation
(*saeculum*) would see them only once. Augustus held them in 17 BC.

Following these examples, gentlest Caesar, I pray
  that your wrath may now be softened by my talent.
That wrath, of course, is just, and I won't deny I deserved it—
  shame has not so utterly fled from my lips—                    30
but, if I hadn't sinned, what would you have had to forgive?
  My doom has provided material for your mercy.

## Be Merciful, Like Jupiter

If Jupiter were to send his thunderbolts every time humans
  sin, in a short time he'll be unarmed:
now, after thundering and scaring the world to death with his
      roars,                                                     35
  he scatters the waters and brings the clear sky back.
It's right, therefore, that he's called the father and ruler of the gods,
  right the wide world has nothing greater than Jove.
You, too, since you're called the ruler and Father of the Fatherland,
  follow the lead of the god who has the same name.              40
You're doing this—nor could anyone, ever, hold the reins
  of his empire more moderately than you do!
You've often granted mercy to the defeated side,
  which it wouldn't have done for you if it had won.
I've even seen many men endowed with riches and honors          45
  who'd previously borne arms against your life;
the day that ended the war also ended your wrath about war,
  and both sides, at the same time, brought gifts to the temples;
and as your soldier rejoices because he has beaten the foe,
  so the foe has cause to rejoice he's been beaten!              50


33. **his thunderbolts:** Throughout the exile poetry, Ovid refers to the edict
that banished him as Jupiter's thunderbolt. See "The Illicit Sex Tour of Roman
Topography and Religion" in the introduction.
39. **Father of the Fatherland:** See on 1.197 "Father of the Fatherland."

## I Was Your Biggest Fan!

My case is better: no one has ever said that I followed
  hostile arms or the forces of the enemy.
By sea, by sky, by the powers of the third realm I swear,
  and by You, a manifest, visible god,
Greatest of Men, my soul was your devoted fan; I've          55
  been yours in my heart—the only way I could.
I wanted you to head for the heavenly stars—but late;
  I was a tiny part of the crowd that prayed that;
I offered pious incense for you, and one among all
  I helped along the public prayers with my prayers.         60
Why should I mention that my books—even *those*, my "crime"—
  are packed chock-full of your name in a thousand places?
Look at my greater work (which I've left still unfinished),
  the bodies transformed in unbelievable ways:
you'll find a triumphant pronouncement of your divinity there,  65
  you'll find indisputable pledges of my heart—
not that your glory could get any greater through my songs;
  it hasn't got any possible room to grow!
Jupiter has plenty of fame, but still, he likes
  to have his deeds told and to be material for song;        70
and when the battles of the Giant War are narrated,
  we can believe he's happy to hear his own praises.

53. **powers of the third realm:** That is, the underworld; Ovid varies the usual formula of "earth, sea, and sky" by referring to the tripartite division of the universe into the domains of Neptune (sea), Jupiter (sky), and Pluto (underworld). (The text here is uncertain, but this seems to be the best reconstruction.)

57. **but late:** See on 1.204 "the other will be."

63. **greater work:** The *Metamorphoses*, an epic at least in form (i.e., a long narrative poem in hexameters); see on 3.370 "the greater work."

71. **Giant War:** When the earthborn Giants attempted to attack Olympus, Jupiter defeated them with his thunderbolts. This so-called Gigantomachy is the quintessential topic of martial epic and often metonymically represents

Others celebrate you with speeches properly grand,
    and sing your praises with more abundant talent:
but still, as he does in the blood poured from a hundred bulls,    75
    a god delights in a puny offering of incense.

## Curse the One Who Read You My Frivolous Songs!

Oh! Savage, and an enemy crueler to me than all,
    whoever it was that read you my little playthings,
so that the songs that honor you along with our calendar
    couldn't be read with a more unclouded judgment!    80
But who could be my friend when you were angry with me?
    I was practically my own enemy then.
[When a house is shaken and has begun to collapse, the entire
    weight sinks down onto the weakest parts;
when Fortune opens up a crack and the roof gapes apart,    85
    it's pulled and comes crashing down through its own weight.]
Thus, I earned people's hatred by my song, and the whole crowd—
    as it should have—took its cue from your frown.

## But You Used to Approve of Me!

And yet, I remember, you used to approve of my life and morals,
    as I paraded by on the horse you had given.    90

---

that genre (especially when poets are speaking of the kind of poetry they don't, can't, or won't write).

75. **blood poured from a hundred bulls:** A hecatomb, from the Greek for "a hundred oxen"; this sort of enormous public sacrifice appears in, and was associated with, martial epic.

79. **songs . . . our calendar:** The *Fasti.*

89–90. **you used to approve . . . you had given:** Ovid refers to the process by which Roman *equites* (Knights; literally, "horsemen"), the second-highest social class (after senators), were confirmed as members of their order. The *recognitio* (approval) involved the censors' approval of the character and property (there was a minimum requirement of 400,000 sesterces, very roughly

[Even if that's no use now, and no credit is given for
    good behavior, still, I'd acquired no "crime";]
I hadn't done a bad job of deciding defendants' verdicts
    when judging cases on the Board of a Hundred Men.
I was a blameless judge of private disputes as well;         95
    even the losing side admitted I was fair.
I'm so unhappy! If these recent incidents hadn't hurt me,
    I could have been safe in your judgment more than once;
these latest events are destroying me, and a storm is plunging
    my ship—so often unscathed!—to the bottom of the sea.    100
And it's not just some little part of the flood, but every
    single wave, and Ocean, are heaped on my head.

## Why Did I See—What I Saw?
## I Was So Respectable . . .

Why did I see that—something? Why did I make my eyes guilty?
    Why was that fault made known to me, all unawares?
Actaéon didn't mean to see Diana naked;         105
    that didn't make him a prey for his dogs any less.
Yes, among the gods even Fortune must be atoned for;
    wounded divinity shows no mercy to Chance.

---

$100,000) for each *eques*; those who made the cut rode by in a public parade
on horseback (*transvectio equitum*, "carrying-past of the horsemen").

94. **Board of a Hundred Men:** An ancient court (actually comprising 105
men, three from each of the 35 Tribes) that decided property disputes.

103. **Why did I see that—something?:** On the mysterious nature of Ovid's
"crime," see "Ovid's Exile: Fact and Fiction" in the introduction.

105. **Actaeon:** In *Metamorphoses* 3.138–252, Ovid relates the story of this
hunter who, entirely by accident, came upon Diana bathing and was pun-
ished by being turned into a deer and torn apart by his own dogs.

108. **wounded divinity:** Latin *laesum numen*, recalling most obviously the
"wounded divinity" that spurs the epic wrath of Juno in Virgil's *Aeneid* (1.8).
Throughout the exile poetry, Ovid implicitly figures himself as an epic hero
persecuted by wrathful gods.

Naturally, that day evil error swept me away,
    my house—small, indeed, but stainless—was destroyed;      110
moreover, small in a way that could be called distinguished
    in ancestral land, second to none in nobility,
and not conspicuous for either wealth or poverty,
    a source of Knights not remarkable either way.
My house may be that small in property and in lineage,      115
    but surely my talent has raised it from obscurity:
although it would seem I used it too much in my youthful folly,
    still, the whole world has given me a great name,
and the throng of educated people knows Naso, and dares
    to count me among those men who are not despised.      120

## You've Been So Merciful!

This house, then, accepted by the Muses, has collapsed
    beneath a single "crime"—though not a small one:
but it has collapsed in such a way that it could rise up,
    if only the wrath of Caesar—who was injured—should mellow.
His clemency in the choice of my punishment was so great      125
    that it came in more lenient than I had feared:
my life was granted, and your wrath stopped short of death,
    O prince who make such sparing use of your strength!
Still more, my ancestral wealth—you didn't take that away—
    was added, as if life were too small a gift!      130

114. **Knights:** See on 89–90 "you used to approve . . . you had given."
119. **Naso:** See on 2.744 "NASO."
128. **prince:** Latin *princeps*, whose complicated history culminates in our word
"prince." From the basic meaning of "one who is first, instigator, founder,
leader," it comes to mean "first citizen" (*OLD* 3b), but *OLD* 6 has a useful
explanation: "adopted by Augustus as a title to emphasize the non-military
nature of his rule (cf. sense 3b), but later acquiring the connotation of an
autocratic ruler." Try fitting that into an English pentameter.

Nor did you condemn my deeds by decree of the senate,
   nor was my exile ordered by a chosen judge:
attacking me with grim words—quite appropriate for a prince—
   you yourself, as is right, avenged your injuries.
Furthermore, your edict, though severe and threatening,       135
   was gentle nevertheless in the name of my punishment:
for in it I am called a "banished man," not an "exile";
   its words are formulated to match my fortune.
Of course, for anyone who's sane and in his right mind,
   to have displeased such a man is the greatest punishment.     140
But it's common for divinity to be appeasable sometimes;
   it's common for clouds to disperse and bright day to return;
I myself once saw an elm loaded with tendrils of grapevines
   after fierce Jupiter's thunderbolt had struck it.

## YOU CAN'T KEEP ME FROM HOPING!

Even if you should forbid me to hope, I'll keep on hoping:     145
   this one thing can be done even if you prohibit it.

131. **Nor did you condemn my deeds by decree of the senate:** This line implies that the senate was Augustus's puppet ("*you* condemn") and that Ovid was important enough that such a decree (reserved for important cases) could have been appropriate.

132. **judge:** Latin *iudex*, which combines our roles of "judge" and "jury." While apparently praising Augustus's clemency, Ovid also makes it clear that he was denied trial by a jury of his peers (such as he himself had participated in: see 93–96).

133. **attacking me with grim words:** Latin *tristibus invectus verbis*, punning on the title *Tristia* (*tristis* can mean "sad" or "grim"). Augustus and Ovid both hurl *tristia verba* at one another.

137. **"banished man," not an "exile":** Latin *relegatus, non exul*, though Ovid when it suits his purpose often calls himself an "exile" (and "relegation poetry" would hardly have the same punch). There was an important legal distinction: *relegatio* (banishment) was a milder punishment that did not necessarily entail the loss of property or citizenship, and it could be revoked after a time.

When I look at you, gentlest prince, great hope rises up in me;
  when I look at my deeds, my hope sinks down;
and just as, when the winds are lashing the sea, their rage
  and fury is not continuously the same,                                    150
but sometimes they subside, and take a break, and calm down,
  and you could think they've laid aside their violence,
so my fears go away, and return, and are always changing,
  give me hope of appeasing you, then deny it.
Therefore, by the gods (may they give you long life—and they
    will,                                                                    155
  as long as they have any love for the name of Rome!),
and by the fatherland, safe and secure while you are its father,
  of which I was lately one small voice in the crowd,
so may your grateful City give you the love you deserve,
  since by your deeds and wisdom you're always earning it;                  160
so may Lívia live with you all the years of your marriage,
  she who was worthy of no spouse other than you—
and if she weren't there, a celibate life would be right for you,
  and there'd be no woman whose husband you could be;
so may your son be healthy—with you healthy too—and someday   165
  rule this empire, an old man along with an older one;
and as your grandsons—stars of the youth!—are doing already,
  so may they walk in your footsteps and in their father's;

159. **so may:** A typical kind of Roman prayer takes the form "So may X happen for you (as you) do Y for me!" This one is unusual in that the "so may" part extends for twenty lines.
162. **worthy of no spouse other than you:** Livia was married to Tiberius Claudius Nero, to whom she had already borne Tiberius and by whom she was heavily pregnant with Drusus, when Augustus took her for his wife in 38 BC (a scandal at the time).
165. **your son:** Tiberius (who would be Augustus's successor as emperor), Livia's son by her previous husband; Augustus had adopted him in AD 4.
167. **your grandsons—stars of the youth!:** Germanicus, son of Livia's son Drusus (the Elder), and Drusus (the Younger), son of Tiberius. "Stars" is an

so may Victory, who is always at home in your camp,
    show up now, too, and follow the flag she knows,                    170
flit about the Ausónian leader with her usual wings,
    and place the laurel wreath on his gleaming hair,
through whom you're waging war, in whose body you're fighting
      now,
    to whom you give your gods and mighty authority—
with half of yourself you're here in person watching the city,             175
    with half, you're far away waging violent wars—
so may he come back victorious to you from the conquered foe,
    straight and tall and radiant on garlanded horses:
spare me, I pray! Put away your thunderbolts, savage shafts—
    shafts, alas, this wretch knows all too well!                           180
Spare me, Father of the Fatherland, don't forget that name
    and rob me of my hope of appeasing you someday!
I'm not praying to return—although it's believable that
    the great gods often give things that exceed our prayers:
if you give me a gentler exile, and closer, as I ask,                        185
    the great part of my punishment will have been lightened.

## IT'S REALLY BAD HERE!

I'm enduring the extreme, cast out in the middle of foes;
    there's no exile who's farther from his fatherland.
I alone have been sent to the mouth of the seven-branched Hister,

---

allusion to the Dioscuri ("Sons of Zeus"), Castor and Pollux, identified with
the constellation Gemini ("Twins")—divinities who (among other things)
guided lost ships with their light.

171. **Ausonian leader:** Tiberius; see on 24 "Ausonia."

174. **authority:** Latin *auspicium*; see on 1.191 "authority."

178. **garlanded horses:** Those pulling his chariot in a "triumph," that is; see
on 1.213 "you" (the imagined triumph of Gaius).

189. **Hister:** Another name for the Danube river; Ovid often associates it
with his place of exile.

pressed by the icy pole of the Parrhásian virgin.                                  190
Though others have been expelled by you for more serious reasons,  193
   no one's been given a more remote land than I.                     194
There's nothing beyond this one—nothing but cold and foes,                          195
   and a wave of the sea that's congealed with clutching ice.
Up to this point is the Roman part of the sinister Euxine;
   Bastárnans, Saurómatans hold the land close by;
Cíziges, Colchi, the swarm of Matéreans, the Getes—                                 191
   the Danube's waters can barely keep them away!                     192
This is the very last land to come under Ausónian sway                              199
   and barely clings to the margin of your empire.                    200
Therefore, I beg, on my knees, please banish me somewhere safe,
   so peace won't be robbed from me along with my fatherland,
and I won't fear the races the Hister can barely hold back,
   or the foe be able to catch me, your own citizen.

190. **the icy pole of the Parrhasian virgin:** See on 2.55 "maiden of Tegea, the comrade of Boötes"; Callisto was from Parrhasia (part of Arcadia). On one level, this line is a fancy way of saying "far North." On another level, the story of Callisto, which Ovid recounts at length in both the *Metamorphoses* (2.409–530) and the *Fasti* (2.153–92) and alludes to frequently in the exile poetry, parallels Ovid's own story in numerous ways.

197. **sinister Euxine:** An untranslatable pun and oxymoron. Black Sea = Latin *Euxenus* = Greek "Hospitable to Strangers," an apotropaic euphemism (i.e., a nice name given to something bad in order to avert evil). Latin *sinister* means "on the left side" (an archaic meaning for English "sinister" as well), which was considered unlucky, giving rise to the meaning "ominous, menacing"; but Tomis was also on the "left side" of the Euxine for ships coming from Rome. "Sinister Euxine" thus means both "ominous Hospitable-to-Strangers Sea" and "left-hand side of the Black Sea."

198–91. **Bastarnans . . . Getes:** Various barbarian tribes. The poet would like to emphasize that the much-vaunted Pax Augusta ("Augustan Peace") is pretty tenuous in his neck of the woods.

199. **very last:** Latin *novissimus*, which can mean both "most remote" and "most recent."

199. **Ausonian:** See on 24 "Ausonia."

Right prohibits anyone born of Latin blood                              205
    to suffer barbarian chains while the Caesars live.

## YOU'RE SO BUSY!

Though two "crimes" have ruined me—a song and a mistake—
    I need to keep quiet about the guilt of the second one.
Caesar, it's more than my life is worth to reopen your wounds;
    to have grieved you once already is way too much.                    210
The first part of my case remains, that through a disgraceful
    song I'm charged with teaching filthy adultery.
It's right, then, that heavenly minds are in some way deceived,
    and many things are too trivial for your notice.
Just as Jupiter, keeping an eye on the gods and high heaven,        215
    doesn't have time to be around for the small stuff,
so, when you gaze upon the world that depends on you,
    lesser matters tend to escape your attention.
Sure, as Prince of the Empire, you would abandon your post
    and read poetry composed in unequal measures!                       220
The massive weight of the Roman name doesn't press you at all,
    and the burden upon your shoulders is so light,
that you could turn your divinity toward silly games,
    and scrutinize my pastimes with your own eyes!
Now you must subdue Pannónia, now Illýria,                               225
    now Raetic arms, now Thracian are causing terror,

220. **unequal measures:** See on 1.263 "unequal wheels."
225. **Now you must subdue:** Of the seven places mentioned in 225–30, only
Thrace and Raetia were securely under Roman control at the time Ovid was
writing. The passage thus functions both as a panegyric emphasizing the
extent of the Roman Empire and as a reminder of the present dangers threat-
ening it (which Ovid, on the fringes, experiences as very real).
225. **Pannonia:** Part of modern Austria and West Hungary; Rome was still
engaged in suppressing a revolt there that had begun in AD 6.
225. **Illyria:** See on 2.658 "Illyrian.
226. **Raetic . . . Thracian:** Along with Thrace, Raetia (modern day East

now the Arménian's pleading for peace, now the Párthian horseman
    with timid hand offers his bow and the flag he captured,
now Germany experiences you as a youth through your son,
    and a Caesar wages war on behalf of great Caesar.                    230
Finally, even in the greatest body of Empire that's ever
    existed, there's not a single part that's weak.
The City, too, and guardianship of your laws wears you out,
    and morals, which you want to be like your own,
nor do you get to enjoy the leisure you give the nations:                235
    you're waging unremitting wars against vices.

## So of Course You Didn't Have Time to Read My Songs!

So should I be surprised that amid this mass of such great
    matters you never unrolled the scroll of my jokes?
And yet, if by chance—as I would have preferred—you'd had the time,
    you would not have read any "crime" in my *Art*.                    240
Of course, I admit that it wasn't written with stern face,

---

Switzerland, the Tyrol, and Bavaria), which became a Roman province around
15 BC, was actually peaceful at the time of Ovid's writing.
227. **Armenian:** In his *Res Gestae* (Things Accomplished, a propagandistic
summary of his achievements), Augustus claimed that he *could* have made
Armenia a Roman province but chose instead to install kings friendly to
Rome, and that his son Gaius (see 1.177–94) had subdued a rebellion there.
But in fact, Armenia was unstable, and Gaius died (4 BC) from a wound he
received there.
227. **Parthian:** See on 1.179–80 "O buried Crassi and flag."
229. **Germany:** Germany was definitely not peaceful at the time of Ovid's
writing; in AD 9, the loss of three legions there by the commander Varus was
perhaps the most devastating military defeat the Romans had experienced
(though this was still in the future when Ovid wrote this line).
229. **through your son:** Tiberius (see 171–76).
241. **face:** Latin *frons*, which can refer both to the human forehead and to the
edge of a book-scroll, which showed the work's title.

not worthy to be read by so great a prince—
but still, it doesn't on that account advise and instruct
   Roman wives to break the commands of the laws.
And so you could have no doubt about its intended audience,     245
   Book One of three has the following four verses:
"Get ye far hence, slender fillets, badges of modesty,
   and you, long hem, who reach halfway down the foot:
I'll sing only what's lawful, and permissible affairs,
   and there will be nothing criminal in my song."     250
So didn't I strictly exclude every woman from this *Art*
   whose robe and fillet say that she's off limits?

## OBJECTION 1: THE BOOK COULD BE DANGEROUS (BUT SO COULD ANY BOOK!)

"But a matron can make use of arts not intended for her,
   can be sucked in even if she's not being taught."
A matron had better not read anything, then, since every     255
   song can make her more of an expert in sin.
Whatever she lays hands on—if she's looking for trouble—
   she'll make her instruction manual for vice.

244. **wives:** See on 23 "wives."
246. **the following four verses:** Readers who wish to refresh their knowledge about the significance of religious formulae, fillets, and hems by consulting 1.31–34 will also discover that Ovid is not *quite* quoting the verses he actually wrote.
250. **nothing criminal:** No *crimen* (see on 3 "'crime'").
253. **But:** Latin *at*, a conjunction frequently used in rhetorical discourse to signal that the author/speaker is imagining an objection his opponent might make (hence the quotation marks); the author/speaker then answers the objection in his own voice.
·253. **matron:** Latin *matrona* = "respectable married woman who would produce legitimate children."

She's picked up *The Annals*—there's nothing shaggier than that one;
   bet she'll read how Ília was made a mother.                                    260
Now she's picked up the "Mother of Aeneas's Race": she'll be asking
   how kind Venus got to be mother of Aeneas's race.
I shall explain below, if I may set things out in due order,
   that every genre of song can harm the soul.
But every book will not for that reason be charged with a "crime":    265
   there's nothing helpful that can't be hurtful as well.
What's more useful than fire? But anyone aiming to burn
   a house down equips his aggressive hands with fire.
Medicine sometimes restores health but sometimes takes it away,
   shows us plants that can heal and plants that can harm.    270
Both the robber and the cautious traveler strap on a sword,
   but one's wearing it for mugging, the other for safety.
Eloquence is learned to plead the cases of the just—
   and yet it protects the guilty and crushes the innocent.
Thus it will be agreed that a song, if read with pure mind,    275
   can't do harm to anyone—even mine.

259. *The Annals*: A long epic poem on the history of Rome by Ennius (see on 3.409 "Ennius"), of which we now have only fragments (though some are substantial). It included the story of Mars impregnating Ilia (a Vestal Virgin: see on 3.463 "Vesta") with the twins Romulus and Remus.
259. **shaggier**: Latin *hirsutus*, "hairy" or "shaggy," is one of many terms for human appearance that Ovid likes to apply to poetic style, here implying "primitive and unpolished"; see on 3.101 "grooming."
261. **"Mother of Aeneas's Race"**: The opening words of Lucretius's *De Rerum Natura*. Ancient poems were often referred to by their opening words.
262. **kind Venus**: These words begin the *second* line of Lucretius's poem. (Venus's "kindness" included her affair with Aeneas's father, Anchises.)
263. **I shall explain below**: This is the sort of didactic language Lucretius uses.

## OBJECTION 2: IT'S AN INVITATION TO SIN
## (BUT SO IS EVERYTHING!)

"It's an invitation to sin." He's wrong, whoever thinks this;
    he's attributing too much power to my writings.
But say I concede this: the shows, too, scatter the seeds
    of naughtiness. Have the whole theater thrown out!    280
The voting enclosures—they've given so many a cause for sin,
    when the sand of Mars is spread over the hard earth!
Throw out the Circus! The freedom of the Circus is dangerous:
    here a girl sits next to a man who's a stranger!
Since some women take a stroll there so they can meet their lovers,  285
    why is a single colonnade left open?
What place is more august than temples? She should avoid
    these too, unless she's ingeniously plotting her sin.
She's standing in Jupiter's temple: in Jupiter's temple, it will
    occur to her how many women that god made mothers!    290
Going to worship at Juno's temple next door, she'll be thinking
    how that goddess fumed about her copious rivals.
Taking a look at Pallas, she'll wonder why that virgin
    raised Erichthónius, who was born from "crime."

277. **an invitation to sin:** Need I point out that practically all of the venues
Ovid names in the passage are ones he recommended in *Ars* 1 (67–170) and
3 (387–96) as choice pickup spots?
280. **theater:** See on 1.89 "theater."
281. **voting enclosures:** Women were not of course allowed to vote, but they
were allowed to go to the gladiatorial contests sometimes held in these enclo-
sures (*saepta*).
282. **sand:** See on 1.164 "grim sand . . . Forum."
283. **Circus:** See on 1.136 "Circus."
286. **colonnade:** See on 1.67 "Pompey's shade."
287. **What place is more august than temples?:** See "The Illicit Sex Tour of
Roman Topography and Religion" in the introduction.
288. **ingeniously:** See on *Rem.* 620 "ingenious."
293. **Pallas:** Presumably either a temple or a cult statue of Minerva. Erichthon-
ius, mythical founder of Athens, was born from the premature ejaculation of

She's come into the temple of great Mars, your gift:                    295
　　the Avenger's coupled with Venus, her man's outside!
Sitting in Isis's temple, she'll ask why Saturn's daughter
　　drove her over the Iónian Sea and Bósporus.
With Venus, Anchíses; with Luna, the Látmian hero; with Ceres,
　　Iásion: they'll give her something to think about!                 300
*Everything* can corrupt a mind already in the gutter—                  301
　　yet everything is safe, in its proper place.                       302
Any woman who rushes in where the priest forbids her                    305
　　at once absolves him of guilt and incurs it herself.               306
The very first page of my *Art*—which was written for prostitutes
　　only!—                                                             303
　　shoos away the hands of freeborn women.                            304
Yet even so, it's not a crime to read tender verses;                    307
　　chaste women can read about lots they shouldn't do.
Often the matron of stern brow sees naked women
　　standing there on sale for all kinds of sex.                       310

---

Vulcan when he was attempting to rape Minerva (which the goddess wiped
off her thigh and threw on the ground, so the child was literally "earthborn").
**295. temple of great Mars, your gift:** See on 1.171 "mock naval battle."
**296. her man's outside:** A statue of Vulcan (god of fire), celebrating the foun-
dation of Rome's fire department, stood outside the temple. Ovid depicts
this as a cuckolded husband (see on 1.502 "playing the lover") or an *exclusus
amator* (see on 3.69 "locking out lovers").
**297. Isis's temple:** See on 1.77 "Memphitic . . . heifer."
**297. Saturn's daughter:** Juno.
**299–300. Anchises . . . Iasion:** Anchises, Endymion (= "the Latmian hero"),
and Iasion were all mortal lovers of goddesses, with mixed results. Iasion was
killed by Jupiter's thunderbolt (the god did not appreciate mortals sleeping
with goddesses). Anchises (father of Aeneas) was also blasted by thunder-
bolt, and though he survived, he was never the same. For Endymion, see on
3.83 "Latmian Endymion."

The eyes of Vestals look upon the bodies of whores,
   and that was no reason for punishing their boss.

## I Should Have Written
## Other Kinds of Poetry . . .

But why, you ask, is there too much naughtiness in my Muse,
   or why does my book persuade anyone to love?
Here I can only confess my sin and my manifest fault:          315
   I'm sorry about my talent—and my judgment.
Instead, Troy, which fell before the arms of the Argives—
   why wasn't it harassed again by my song?
Why did I shut up about Thebes, the mutual wounds
   of the brothers, and seven gates, each with its leader?      320
Nor did Warrior Rome not offer me lots of material—
   and singing the fatherland's deeds is a righteous task.
Finally, since you've filled everything with your merits, Caesar,
   I should have sung a single part of those merits,
and as the radiant light of the sun attracts every eye,       325
   so your exploits would have attracted my spirit.

## . . . But I'm Not Talented Enough for That!

But I'm unfairly accused! The field I plow is thin:
   *that* would've been a work for great fertility.


311. **Vestals:** See on 3.463 "Vesta."
312. **their boss:** Latin *dominus*, "master" (if this reading is correct—manuscripts and editors vary). It is not clear whether this means the "boss" of the prostitutes (their pimp) or of the Vestals (the Pontifex Maximus, "Greatest Priest"). Either role could fit the *praeceptor*.
316. **talent:** See on *Rem.* 620 "ingenious."
317. **Argives:** One of Homer's many terms for Greeks in the *Iliad*.
319. **Thebes:** See on 3.13 "Oecles's son."
327. **thin:** Latin *tenuis*; see on 3.692 "slender . . . cultivated." Ovid's *recusatio* ("refusal" to write epic) follows a common formula: "I *would* of course write

A little boat should not entrust itself to the sea
  because it dares to play in a puny lake.                          330
Possibly—I'm not sure—I'm good enough for the lighter
  verses, and I'm OK for little measures;
but if you command me to sing of the Giants, conquered by Jupiter's
  fire, the burden will cripple me in the attempt!
To write the gigantic deeds of Caesar requires a wealth             335
  of talent, lest the material surpass the work—
and yet I had dared! But it seemed I was detracting from you,
  and (this is impious!) causing a loss to your might.
I went again to my trivial work, my youthful songs,
  and with false love I inspired my own heart.                      340
I could wish I hadn't, but my doom was sucking me in,
  and I was ingeniously plotting my own punishment.

## You Can't Judge a Poet by His Books!

Woe is me! Why did I learn? Why did my parents teach me,
  and why did any writing attract my eyes?
It's this that turned you against me—because of my wanton *Arts*,   345
  which you thought were making a play for forbidden beds.
And yet it's not through my teaching that brides have learned to cheat:
  no one can teach a subject he barely knows!
I made my playthings and tender songs in such a way
  that not a single scandal has grazed my name;                     350

---

a big epic (or: I was busy writing one), but it turns out I'm just not talented
enough, so I'll stick to the small stuff."
333. **Giants:** See on 71 "Giant War."
337. **I had dared!:** In *Amores* 1.2.11–20, the poet claims that he "had dared"
to sing a Gigantomachy, but when his girlfriend shut her door, he dropped
Jupiter and the thunderbolt ("Jupiter, please forgive me: your weapons don't
help me at all; / the locked door has a greater bolt than yours," 19–20). His
claim here to have dared to write an epic for Augustus is perhaps not to be
taken at face value.
342. **ingeniously:** See on *Rem.* 620 "ingenious."

nor is there any husband, even among the plebs,
  who doubts his paternity because of my sin.
Believe me, my character's totally different from my song:
  my life is modest, but my Muse is playful.
The greatest part—all lies and fiction!—of my works          355
  has allowed itself more liberties than its author.
A book's a respectable pleasure, not evidence of the soul:
  it'll bring many things suited for soothing the ears.
Áccius would be savage, Terence a libertine,
  and those who sing fierce wars would all be warriors!        360

## OTHER WRITERS DON'T GET PUNISHED FOR WRITING DIRTY STUFF!

Finally, I'm not the only one who's composed tender loves:
  I'm the only one punished for a love composed!
What did the Tëan Muse of the Codger of Lyric ever teach,
  other than how to mix sex with a lot of wine?

351. **plebs:** Ovid refers here to the basic division of Roman society into the aristocratic "patricians," whose ancestry harked back to the original *patres* (fathers) of the Roman senate, and the "plebs" or "plebeians," common people who made up the majority of the population.

353. **my character's totally different from my song:** In arguing that he has not committed adultery and that his character is completely different from his poem, Ovid would appear to be tacitly admitting that his poem is, in fact, about adultery (which he denies, but never very convincingly).

357. **respectable pleasure:** A slight oxymoron. The primary meaning of *honestus* is "regarded with honor or respect"; *voluptas* (pleasure), which often has sexual connotations, is frequently contrasted in philosophical writings with "virtue" (*virtus*).

359. **Accius:** Lucius Accius (177–ca. 86 BC), writer of bloodthirsty tragedies. For this couplet to make sense, we must supply an "otherwise" (i.e., "If a book *were* evidence of the soul, then . . .").

359. **Terence:** Publius Terentius Afer (ca. 184–ca. 159 BC), writer of romantic comedies.

363. **Tëan Muse of the Codger of Lyric:** See on 3.330 "Tëan . . . old man."

What did Sappho of Lesbos teach, except how to love girls?            365
    But still, Sappho was safe, and he was safe too.
Nor did it do you harm, son of Battus, that you yourself
    often confessed your affairs to your reader in verse!
There's not one play of pleasant Menánder that's without love,
    and he's always being read by boys and virgins.                    370
What is the *Iliad* itself but a shameful adulteress
    fought over by her lover and her man?
What happens in it before the fire for Briséis, and how
    the snatching of the girl made the leaders wrathful?
Or what is the *Odyssey* but a woman, for the sake of love,            375
    courted by many suitors while her man's away?
Who but the Maeónian tells how Venus and Mars
    were bound, their bodies caught in that filthy bed?
How would we know, except by great Homer's testimony,
    two goddesses were burning hot for their guest?                    380

Look at Tragedy!

Tragedy beats every genre of writing in seriousness:
    it too gets all its material from love.
What's in *Hippólytus* but a stepmother blinded by lust?

365. **Sappho:** See on 3.331 "Sappho."
367. **son of Battus:** Callimachus. His home, Cyrene (in Libya), was founded by the legendary King Battus; "son of Battus" may mean actual descendant of Battus or just "from Cyrene."
369. **Menander:** See on 3.332 "the one . . . Geta's art."
373. **fire for Briseis:** The action of the *Iliad* does, in fact, open with Agamemnon taking Briseis from Achilles, who is or claims to be passionately in love with her.
377. **Maeonian:** Homer (see on 2.4 "Ascran and Maeonian old men"), who tells the story of the adultery of Venus and Mars (see 2.561–93) in *Odyssey* 8.
380. **two goddesses:** Calypso and Circe.

Cánace's known as a sister in love with her brother.
Well? Didn't Tantalus's ivory son, with Cupid driving                    385
   his chariot, abduct the Pisan with Phrygian horses?
When that mother dyed a sword with the blood of her sons,
   the pain arising from wounded love made her do it.
Love made sudden birds out of the king with his mistress,
   and the mother who even now laments for her Itys.                    390
If that accursed brother had not been in love with Aerópe,
   we wouldn't be reading about the Sun's horses turned back;
nor would impious Scylla have touched those tragic buskins
   if love had not cut off her father's lock.
You read *Eléctra*, and *Oréstes* (who was out of his mind),              395
   you're reading the "crime" of Tyndáreus's daughter and Aegísthus.
Why should I mention the austere conqueror of the Chimaéra,
   who was almost done in by his treacherous hostess?

384. **Canace:** When this daughter of Aeolus got pregnant by her brother Macareus, he persuaded Aeolus to marry his sons to his daughters—but Canace and Macareus did not get paired up, and she committed suicide. Euripides's (lost) tragedy *Aeolus* treated this theme.

385. **Tantalus's ivory son:** When Pelops's father Tantalus (see on 2.605 "tattletale Tantalus") served up Pelops in a banquet to the gods, they discovered this crime and put Pelops back together; his shoulder, however, had to be replaced with an ivory one, because Ceres (distraught over the loss of her daughter Proserpina) had inadvertently taken a bite.

386. **Pisan:** Hippodamia; see on 2.8 "Hippodamia."

387. **that mother:** Medea.

389. **sudden birds:** Tereus, Philomel, and Procne; see on 2.383 "this swallow."

393. **Scylla:** See on 1.331 "daughter of Nisus."

393. **buskins:** See on *Rem.* 375 "buskin."

397. **austere conqueror of the Chimaera:** Bellerophon. When King Proetus's wife tried and failed to seduce Bellerophon (hence his epithet "austere"), she accused him of raping her, and Proetus sent Bellerophon to King Iobates with a letter telling him to kill the bearer. Iobates instead posed Bellerophon the seemingly impossible task of killing the Chimaera (a fire-breathing monster part snake, part lion, part goat)—but he succeeded, subsequently marrying Iobates's daughter.

Why should I speak of Hermíone, or you, maiden daughter of
  Schoéneus,
  or you, Phoebus's priestess, loved by Mycéne's chief?                    400
Why Dánaë, Dánaë's daughter-in-law, and Lyaéus's mother,
  and Haemon, and her for whom two nights were rolled into one?
Why Pélias's son-in-law, or Theseus, or he who first
  of the Pelásgians off the boat touched Ílian soil?
To these can be added Íole, and Pyrrhus's mother; to these,             405
  Hercules's wife, and Hylas, and the Ílian boy.
I'd run out of time if I tried to go through all the tragic fires—
  my book could barely hold their naked names!

399. **Hermione:** See on *Rem.* 771 "Hermione."

399. **maiden daughter of Schoeneus:** Atalanta; see 2.185–92.

400. **Phoebus's priestess:** Cassandra.

401. **Danaë:** See on 1.225 "descended from Danaë."

401. **Danaë's daughter-in-law:** Andromeda; see on 1.53 "Perseus . . . Indians."

401. **Lyaeus's mother:** Semele (see on 3.251 "Semele" and 3.645 "Lyaeus").

402. **Haemon:** Son of Creon, king of Thebes; he killed himself after Creon ordered the execution of his fiancée, Antigone (the subject of Sophocles's *Antigone*).

402. **her for whom two nights:** Alcmena, mother of Hercules. Jupiter enjoyed his night with her so much that he stretched it out.

403. **Pelias's son-in-law:** Admetus; see on 3.19 "wife from Pagasae."

403–4. **first of the Pelasgians:** Protesilaus; see on 2.356 "Son of Phylacus" and 2.421 "Pelasgian" (here "Pelasgian" is just equivalent to "Greek").

405. **Iole:** Hercules's girlfriend (see on 3.156 "Alcides").

405. **Pyrrhus's mother:** Deidamia; see 1.681–706.

406. **Hercules's wife:** Deianira, who was jealous when Hercules brought home Iole. She was persuaded by the dying centaur Nessus (whom Hercules had shot with a poisoned arrow) to smear his blood on a cloak and give it to Hercules as a love charm. Hercules died from the poison (but was made into a god afterward).

406. **Ilian boy:** Ganymede, abducted by Jupiter's eagle to become the god's plaything.

## AND OTHER OFF-COLOR GENRES!

There's also tragedy that veers into dirty jokes,
    with lots of language that shows it has no shame;        410
nor does it hurt that author who gave us the tender Achilles
    that his measures emasculated manly deeds.
Aristídes connected himself with Milésian "crimes,"
    yet Aristídes wasn't kicked out of his city.
Neither the one who depicted destruction of mothers' seeds,    415
    Eúbius, founder of an unclean story,
nor he who just composed *Things Sybarític*, was exiled—
    nor those who wouldn't shut up about how they'd scored!
These stand mingled with monuments of learned men,
    and our leaders' gifts have made them public property.    420

409. **dirty jokes:** Satyr plays, one of which would be performed along with each tragic trilogy for some comic relief.

411. **that author:** Here Ovid's reference eludes us. Likely candidates are Sophocles, who wrote a satyr play on Achilles as the catamite of the satyrs and perhaps Hercules; and Sotades (mid-third century BC), who wrote on themes from Homer.

413. **Aristides:** Greek author who lived ca. 100 BC and wrote a collection of short, funny, erotic stories called *Milesian Tales* (the city of Miletus in Asia Minor was known for its luxurious decadence).

416. **Eubius:** This man seems to have written a didactic work on abortion, but he has not been identified.

417. **he who just composed *Things Sybaritic*:** Hemitheon of Sybaris, a Greek coastal city on the "instep" of Italy known for its licentiousness (as was the author). Though Hemitheon's dates are unknown, "just composed" suggests that he was a near contemporary.

419. **stand mingled with monuments of learned men:** Presumably, in libraries that also contain "serious" works.

420. **our leaders' gifts:** Victorious generals from the second century BC on sometimes dedicated public libraries, often filling them with books they had plundered. Augustus himself famously dedicated the Palatine Library in 28 BC.

### LOOK AT ROMAN LITERATURE!

So I don't mount my defense with foreign weapons alone—
    Roman literature, too, likes to play around.
Though serious Énnius sang of Mars in the proper voice—
    Énnius, greatest in talent (in art, a bit rough)—
and though Lucrétius explains the causes for scorching lightning    425
    and prophesies that the threefold world will fall,
still, that naughty Catúllus kept singing about his woman,
    the one who had the pseudonym of "Lésbia";
and not content with *her*, he went on about lots of loves,
    in which he himself confessed his own adultery!    430
Little Calvus showed equal and similar promiscuity,
    outing his affairs in various meters.
Cinna's one of this flock too, and Anser, hornier than Cinna,    435
    and the light works of Cornifícius—and Cato.    436

---

423. **Ennius:** See on 259 "*The Annals.*"

426. **threefold world will fall:** In accordance with Stoic doctrine (though he himself was an Epicurean), Lucretius predicts the destruction of the world ("threefold" in consisting of earth, sea, and sky) by fire, followed by its rebirth—an infinite, phoenix-like cycle.

431. **Little Calvus:** Gaius Licinius Calvus (ca. 82–53 BC), a poet of Catullus's circle, known for his diminutive size.

435. **Cinna:** Gaius Helvetius Cinna (ca. 90–44 BC), whose learned mini-epic *Smyrna* (on Myrrha's affair with her father: see on 1.285 "Myrrha") was admired by Catullus (poem 95).

435. **Anser:** The Latin word for "goose" and also the name of a poet who wrote praises of Mark Antony. He appears not to have been friends with the other poets mentioned—a goose among swans.

436. **Cornificius:** Quintus Cornificius (d. 42), who wrote among other things a mini-epic *Glaucus* (on the sea god's love for Scylla and rejection of Circe).

436. **Cato:** Publius Valerius Cato, a member of Catullus's poetic circle. He wrote a *Lydia*, a book of poems about either a woman named Lydia or the country Lydia (in Asia Minor).

Why mention Tícida's or Mémmius's songs, utterly 433
   shameless in both subject matter and language? 434
And those in whose books sometimes with the pseudonym
    "Perílla," 437
   sometimes Metélla is read under her real name? 438
He, too, who led the Argo into the Phasis's waters 439
   couldn't shut up about his own sexual adventures! 440
Nor are the songs of Horténsius, or Sérvius, any less wicked.
   Who'd hesitate to follow such big names?
Sisénna translated Aristídes, and it did him no harm
   to leaven his history-writing with dirty jokes.


433. **Ticida:** This appears to be one Lucius Ticida (d. 46 BC), who—apparently, along with others—wrote love poems to Metella (see 437–38).
433. **Memmius:** Gaius Memmius, dedicatee of Lucretius's poem. Catullus was on his staff when he governed Bithynia (coincidentally, the place of Ovid's exile).
437. **"Perilla":** The feminine form of Perillus (see on 1.653 "Phalaris")—an appropriate pseudonym for a woman who roasts and is roasted.
438. **Metella:** This is probably the wife of Publius Cornelius Lentulus Spinther, a notorious adulteress—and very likely the daughter of Catullus's "Lesbia," Clodia Metelli (daughters of Metellus would be named "Metella").
439. **who led the Argo:** Varro Atacinus; see on 3.335–36 "fleece . . . Phrixus."
441. **Hortensius:** Probably Quintus (?) Hortalus Hortensius (d. 42), the friend to whom Catullus addresses his poems 65 and 66; his father (of the same name) was a famous orator and rival of Cicero.
441. **Servius:** Probably Servius Sulpicius, son of a famous consul (51 BC) of the same name and father of the poetess Sulpicia (whose handful of elegies are the only ones by a Roman woman to survive from antiquity).
442. **follow such big names:** Though the ostensible meaning is that Ovid thought it was safe to follow these role models, there may also be a little joke here on *following* big *names*, since Hortensius and Servius turned to poetry rather than achieving the political status of their more famous same-named fathers.
443. **Sisenna:** Probably Lucius Cornelius Sisenna (praetor 78 BC), who wrote a history of the Social War ("War of the Allies," 91–88 BC, between Rome and other Italian communities) and also translated the *Milesian Tales* of

AND OTHER ELEGISTS!

Gallus wasn't censured for celebrating Lycóris,                                    445
  but for not keeping his mouth shut when he was drunk.
Tibúllus thinks it's hard to trust in his mistress's oaths
  because she swears the same things about him to her man.
He also confesses he taught her how to deceive her guardians,
  and now, poor man, he's flummoxed by his own art.              450
He remembers often pretending to judge his mistress's jewel
  or seal as an excuse to touch her hand;
he says how he often communicated with fingers and nods
  and doodled a silent message on the round table;
he teaches about the best juices for removing a bruise              455
  from the body when the mouth has left its mark;
finally, he begs the too-unsuspecting husband
  to keep an eye on him too, so she'll sin less!
He knows who's being barked at, since he himself is pacing,
  alone, and keeps coughing in front of the locked door.              460
He gives all kinds of instructions in affairs of this sort,
  and teaches young brides the art of deceiving their men.
But this didn't do him any harm! Tibúllus is read and pleases,
  and he became famous when you were already the prince!

---

Aristides (see on 413 "Aristides"). He probably worked on these (or perhaps other) "dirty jokes" alongside his serious *History* (it would have been strange to insert them into the *History*, though the Latin allows that possibility).

445. **Gallus:** The way Ovid describes Gallus's fatal gaffe here leads the reader to see Augustus as a capricious tyrant who has it out for poor poets.

445. **Lycoris:** Pseudonym of a famous mime actress named Volumnia, with the stage name Cytheris; she was Mark Antony's mistress before she was Gallus's.

447. **Tibullus:** The strategies Ovid summarizes here are mainly expounded in Tibullus 1.6.

452. **seal:** Latin *signum*; Romans often wore "signet" rings, whose unique "sign" they would press into a drop of warm wax to seal a letter or other document (whence our "signature").

You'll find similar instructions in beguiling Propértius—                    465
    but there's no trace of a black mark by his name!
I was their successor (since generosity bids me
    conceal the eminent names of living men).
I had no fear, I confess, that where so many ships had all sailed
    in perfect safety, a single one would be wrecked.                    470

## AND OTHER "ARTS"!

Other people have written *Arts* about games of dice—
    in our grandfathers' day, that was no small "crime"!—
how much the bones are worth, how to land the highest score
    with your roll, and to avoid the disastrous Dogs;
what combinations the dice have, and when a lone counter's
      challenged,                    475
    how best to throw, and to move when the throw is made;
how the soldier of a different color advances straight
    when the piece between two enemies is lost,
so he knows to follow and fight and recall the man before him
    and retreat in safety, not without an escort;                    480

465. **Propertius:** The element of erotodidaxis ("teaching seduction strategies") in Propertius's work is minimal; Ovid exaggerates it here to suit his purposes (but does not actually point to any examples).

467. **generosity:** A less charitable interpreter might say "conceit." Ovid likes to position himself as the fourth and final member of the elegiac canon—and literary history, to be fair, does confirm his assessment.

471. **other people have written *Arts*:** Didactic works in verse about the various activities Ovid describes do not survive, though undoubtedly many were written as erudite displays of wit.

471. **games of dice:** Augustus was fond of gambling, which was indeed frowned on by the more severe and old-fashioned Romans; Ovid may be inserting a slight dig here at the emperor's peccadillo in an attempt to show the triviality of his own.

473. **bones:** See on 2.205 "knucklebones."

475. **dice:** See on 2.203 "ivory dice."

477. **soldier:** See on 2.207 "bandit."

how a small board is laid out with stones in sets of three,
    and the object is to get your pieces in a line;
and other games (I won't go into all the details here)
    that constantly waste that precious resource, our time.
Look! Someone else is singing of shapes and throws of balls;     485
    this man and that teach the art of swimming and hoops.
Others have written works on coloring the complexion;
    someone writes rules about banquets and entertaining;
another demonstrates the best clay for making cups
    and teaches what kind of jar is right for clear wine.     490
In the smoky month of December, that's what we do for fun—
    and no one has been damned for composing such things.
This is what tricked me into writing non-sad songs—
    but the punishment that followed my jokes was sad.
Of course—not that I'm complaining!—out of so many writers,    495
    just one has been found whom his own Muse wrecked: myself!

## AND MIMES!

What if I'd written mimes, with all their filthy jokes,
    which always depict the "crime" of forbidden love,
a polished adulterer laying his plans assiduously
    and a crafty bride giving her stupid man the slip?    500

---

481. **small board:** See on 3.365 "three pebbles."
487. **works on coloring the complexion:** See on 3.205 "that work."
491. **smoky month of December:** The Saturnalia, a festival beginning December 17 and lasting up to a week, was (like our Christmas) the biggest and most fun of Roman holidays, involving various kinds of merrymaking, role-playing, and relaxation of standards (such as masters serving their slaves). It was "smoky" because fires were lit.
493. **non-sad:** Latin *non tristia*, playing on the title of the present poem (*Tristia*, "Sad Things"). See on 133 "attacking me with grim words."
497. **mimes:** See on 1.502 "playing the lover."
499. **polished:** Latin *cultus*, "well-groomed"; see on 3.101 "grooming."

The nubile virgin, the matron, man and boy all watch these—
  along with the majority of the senate!
It's not enough that ears are polluted with dirty words:
  eyes get used to enduring plenty of smut.
When the lover has bamboozled the husband with some new
    trick,                                                                    505
    he gets the loud applause and wins the big prize!
[The worse it is, the more lucrative is the stage for the poet;
  the praetor pays no small sum for such big "crimes"!]
Look over the expenditures for your shows, Augustus:
  you'll see you paid big money for many such things.                         510
You watched them yourself, and often put them on to be watched—
  your majesty is so obliging everywhere!—
and with your own eyes—the ones the entire world enjoys—
  you saw adulteries on the stage without flinching.
If it's right to write mimes, which imitate shameful behaviors,               515
  then my material merits a lesser punishment.

## AND PANTOMIMES! AND PAINTINGS!

Or is it the case that their stage makes this kind of writing safe,
  and the theater has given mimes their freedom?
My songs, too, have often been set to dance for the people,
  and even your eyes have often been captured by them!                       520
And, of course, in our homes, as the bodies of ancient heroes
  gleam, depicted by the hand of the artist,
similarly, there's a little tablet somewhere to illustrate
  various positions and types of sex.

508. **praetor:** In 22 BC, Augustus put praetors (the second-highest political office, after consuls) in charge of expenditures for public entertainment, which was paid for out of the public treasury.
519. **My songs . . . set to dance:** See on 3.351 "Artists of the flank, spectacles of the stage."
523. **little tablet:** Pompeii offers several examples of such illustrative works (along with the heroic and mythological subjects Ovid names).

As Télamon's son sits with his face confessing his wrath          525
   and the barbarian mother's got evil in her eye,
so Venus, dripping, wrings out her wet hair with her fingers,
   and is seen barely covered by her maternal waves.

### AND EVEN VIRGIL!

Others trumpet wars equipped with bloody weapons;
   some sing the deeds of your family, some your own;          530
grudging Nature confined me within a narrow space,
   and gave my talent very little strength.
And yet, that blessed author of your *Aeneid* brought
   his Arms and the Man right into the Týrian bed—
and from his entire corpus there's not a single part          535
   that people read more than this pact of illicit love.
This same man, in his youth, had played with the tender fires
   of Phyllis and Amarýllis in pastoral verse.

525. **Telamon's son:** Ajax.
526. **barbarian mother:** Medea.
527. **wrings out her wet hair:** See on 3.401 "Venus . . . Apelles of Cos."
528. **maternal waves:** Venus was born from the sea, her "mother."
531. **narrow space:** See on 327 "thin."
534. **Arms and the Man:** This is surely one of Ovid's naughtiest (mis)read-ings, turning the famous opening words of Virgil's *Aeneid* into a double entendre about the hero's "manly equipment." And yet, it is quite believable that book 4 of the *Aeneid* was then, as it is now, the most-thumbed portion of the poem (one remembers that St. Augustine himself wept over Dido's sorrow, *Confessions* 1.13).
534. **Tyrian:** Dido fled with her people to Carthage (in North Africa) from Tyre (in Asia Minor) after her brother killed her husband.
538. **Phyllis and Amaryllis:** Country girls who inspire shepherds' passions in Virgil's *Eclogues;* see on 2.267 "Amaryllis."

## My Sin Was So Long Ago!

I, too, sinned in that kind of writing—ages ago;
　　a fault not new is suffering a new punishment!　　　　540
I'd published the songs, and still passed by you, many times,
　　a Knight un-criticized, when you were censuring faults.
Thus, those writings I thought—fool that I was!—wouldn't hurt me
　　as a youth are hurting me now as an old man.
The vengeance for that ancient book has come flooding in late, 545
　　and the punishment's far removed from the time it was earned.

## And I Have Written Serious
## (and Panegyrical) Stuff!

But lest you think that my entire oeuvre is frivolous,
　　I've often given my ship substantial sails.
I wrote six books of *Fasti*, and as many again,
　　and each book came to an end along with its month;　　　550
this work, which was recently inscribed with *your* name, Caesar,
　　and consecrated to you—my doom broke it off.
I've given the royal scepter to tragic kings, too,
　　and the solemn buskin has the language it should;
I've also sung (although the project lacked the finishing　　555

540. **fault not new:** That is, both "not new in the history of writing" (since everyone writes about illicit sex) and "not recently written" (since the *Ars* was published ten years ago).

541. **passed by you:** See on 89–90 "you used to approve . . . you had given."

551. *your* **name, Caesar:** The *Fasti* as it currently stands is dedicated to Germanicus Caesar, Augustus's great-nephew, whom Ovid hoped could bring about his return from exile; but the poem was clearly modified after Augustus's death in AD 14, with the original dedication to Augustus moved to book 2 (15–18). This is but one of many postexilic revisions, despite Ovid's claim here that his exile broke off work on the poem (though how many of these revisions were done after *Tristia* 2 was written is impossible to say).

553. **tragic kings:** Ovid wrote a *Medea* tragedy, of which only two fragments now remain.

554. **solemn buskin:** See on *Rem.* 375 "buskin."

touch) the bodies changed to new appearances.
If only you'd call your spirit back from wrath for a while,
    and have a few of these read to you in your free time—
the few in which I brought this work rising from the world's
    first origin, Caesar, all the way down to your times!          560
You'll see what passion you yourself have inspired in me,
    with what devotion of spirit I sing you and yours!

## My Songs Have Harmed No One!

I haven't slashed at anyone with a scathing song,
    nor has my verse accused anyone of "crimes."
I've generously avoided wit that's dripping with gall;          565
    not one letter is tinged with a poisoned joke.
With so many writings by so many thousands of our people,
    there's only one his Callíope wounded: myself!
Therefore, I divine that not a single citizen
    is glad, but many have grieved, about my misfortunes.        570
I can't believe anyone has kicked me while I'm down,
    if I get any thanks for my generosity.

## My Final Prayer.

By these things and others I pray your divinity can be turned,
    O father, O care and salvation of your fatherland!
Not to return to Ausónia—except, perhaps, someday,              575
    when you'll be won over by the length of my punishment;
I beg for a safer exile, and a little more peaceful,
    so that my punishment will match my offense.

556. **bodies changed to new appearances:** The *Metamorphoses*. Ovid likes to exaggerate the "unfinished" nature of his masterpiece, imitating the "unfinished" *Aeneid*.
566. **letter:** Latin *littera*, "letter of the alphabet," which can also mean "epistle" and "literature/any written document."
568. **Calliope:** As the Muse of epic poetry, the highest of genres, Calliope gets to stand for the Muses in general.
575. **Ausonia:** See on 24 "Ausonia."

# Bibliography

Abbott, Claude Colleer, ed. 1955. *The Correspondence of Gerard Manley Hopkins and Richard Watson Dixon*. New York: Oxford University Press.

Acosta-Hughes, Benjamin. 2009. "Ovid and Callimachus: Rewriting the Master." In Knox 2009:236–51.

Ahern, Charles F. 1990. "Ovid as *Vates* in the Proem to the *Ars Amatoria*." *CP* 85: 44–48.

Alexander, William H. 1958. "The *Culpa* of Ovid." *CJ* 53:319–25.

Ancona, Ronnie, and Ellen Greene, eds. 2005. *Gendered Dynamics in Latin Love Poetry*. Baltimore: Johns Hopkins University Press.

Anderson, William S. 1990. "The Example of Procris in the *Ars Amatoria*." In Griffith and Mastronarde 1990:131–45.

Armstrong, Rebecca. 2005. *Ovid and His Love Poetry*. London: Duckworth.

Avery, Maurice W. 1936. "Ovid's Apologia." *CJ* 32:92–102.

Barchiesi, Alessandro. 1997. *The Poet and the Prince: Ovid and Augustan Discourse*. Berkeley: University of California Press.

———. 2001a. *Speaking Volumes: Narrative and Intertext in Ovid and Other Latin Poets*. London: Duckworth.

———. 2001b. "Teaching Augustus through Allusion." In Barchiesi 2001a:79–103.

———. 2006. "Women on Top: Livia and Andromache." In Gibson et al. 2006: 96–120.

Bowditch, Phebe Lowell. 2005. "Hermeneutic Uncertainty and the Feminine in Ovid's *Ars Amatoria*: The Procris and Cephalus Digression." In Ancona and Greene 2005:271–95.

Boyd, Barbara Weiden. 2002. *Brill's Companion to Ovid*. Boston: Brill.

———. 2009. "*Remedia Amoris*." In Knox 2009:104–19.

Boyle, A. J. 2003. *Ovid and the Monuments: A Poet's Rome*. Bendigo, Victoria: Aureal Publications.

Braden, Gordon. 2009. "Ovid and Shakespeare." In Knox 2009:442–54.

Brunelle, Christopher. 2000–2001. "Form vs. Function in Ovid's *Remedia Amoris*." *CJ* 96:123–40.

———. 2005. "Ovid's Satirical Remedies." In Ancona and Greene 2005:141–58.

Cahoon, Leslie. 1988. "The Bed as Battlefield: Erotic Conquest and Military Metaphor in Ovid's *Amores*." *TAPA* 118:293–307.

Casali, Sergio. 1997. "*Quaerenti plura legendum*: On the Necessity of 'Reading More' in Ovid's Exile Poetry." *Ramus* 26:80–112.

———. 2006. "The Art of Making Oneself Hated: Rethinking (Anti-) Augustanism in Ovid's *Ars Amatoria*." In Gibson et al. 2006:216–34.

———. 2009. "Ovidian Intertextuality." In Knox 2009:341–54.

Caston, Ruth. 2006. "Love as Illness: Poets and Philosophers on Romantic Love." *CJ* 101:271–98.

Claassen, Jo-Marie. 1994. "Ovid's Exile: Is the Secret Out Yet?" Review of R. Verdière, *Le secret du voltigeur d'amour ou le mystère de la relegation d'Ovide* (Brussels, 1992). *Scholia* 3:107–11.

———. 1999a. *Displaced Persons: The Literature of Exile from Cicero to Boethius*. Madison: University of Wisconsin Press.

———. 1999b. "The Vocabulary of Exile in Ovid's *Tristia* and *Epistolae ex Ponto*." *Glotta* 75:134–71.

———. 2001. "The Singular Myth: Ovid's Use of Myth in the Exilic Poetry." *Hermathena* 170:11–64.

———. 2009. "*Tristia*." In Knox 2009:170–83.

Conte, Gian Biagio. 1989. "Love without Elegy: The *Remedia Amoris* and the Logic of a Genre." *Poetics Today* 10:441–69.

Currie, H. M. 1981. "Ovid and the Roman Stage." *ANRW* 2.31.4:2701–42.

Dalzell, Alexander. 1996. *The Criticism of Didactic Poetry: Essays on Lucretius, Virgil, and Ovid*. Toronto: University of Toronto Press.

Davis, Peter J. 1995. "*Praeceptor Amoris*: Ovid's *Ars Amatoria* and the Augustan Idea of Rome." *Ramus* 24:181–95.

———. 1999. "Instructing the Emperor: Ovid, *Tristia* 2." *Latomus* 58:799–809.

———. 2006. *Ovid and Augustus: A Political Reading of Ovid's Erotic Poems*. London: Duckworth.

Davisson, Mary H. T. 1993. "*Quid Moror Exemplis?*: Mythological *Exempla* in Ovid's Pre-Exilic Poems and the Elegies from Exile." *Phoenix* 47:213–37.

———. 1996. "The Search for an *Alter Orbis* in Ovid's *Remedia Amoris*." *Phoenix* 50:240–61.

Dillon, John. 1994. "A Platonist *Ars Amatoria*." *CQ* 44:387–92.

Dimmick, Jeremy. 2002. "Ovid in the Middle Ages: Authority and Poetry." In Hardie 2002:264–87.

Downing, Eric. 1990. "Anti-Pygmalion: The Praeceptor in *Ars Amatoria*, Book 3." *Helios* 17:237–49.

———. 1993. *Artificial I's: The Self as Artwork in Ovid, Kierkegaard, and Thomas Mann*. Tübingen: Max Niemeyer Verlag.

Durling, Robert M. 1958. "Ovid as *Praeceptor Amoris*." *CJ* 53:157–67.

Dyson, Julia T. 2007. "The Lesbia Poems." In Skinner 2007:254–75.

Edwards, Catharine. 1996. *Writing Rome: Textual Approaches to the City*. Cambridge: Cambridge University Press.

Ezquerra, Antonio Alvar. 2010. "Ovid in Exile: Fact or Fiction?" *Annals of Ovidius University Constanta—Philology* 21:107–26.

Fantham, Elaine. 1989. "Mime: The Missing Link in Roman Literary History." *CW* 82: 153–63.

———. 2009. "Rhetoric and Ovid's Poetry." In Knox 2009:26–44.

Farrell, Joseph. 1999. "The Ovidian Corpus: Poetic Body and Poetic Text." In Hardie et al. 1999:125–41.

———. 2009. "Ovid's Generic Transformations." In Knox 2009:370–80.

Favro, Diane. 1996. *The Urban Image of Augustan Rome*. Cambridge: Cambridge University Press.

Fear, Trevor. 2000. "The Poet as Pimp: Elegiac Seduction in the Time of Augustus." *Arethusa* 33:217–40.

Fish, Jeffrey. 2004. "Physician, Heal Thyself: The Intertextuality of Ovid's Exile Poetry and the *Remedia Amoris*." *Latomus* 63:864–72.

Fitton Brown, A. D. 1985. "The Unreality of Ovid's Tomitan Exile." *LCM* 10:19–22.

Forbis, Elizabeth P. 1997. "Voice and Voicelessness in Ovid's Exile Poetry." *Latomus: Studies in Latin Literature and Roman History* 8:245–67.

Fulkerson, Laurel. 2004. "Omnia Vincit Amor: Why the *Remedia* Fail." *CQ* 54: 211–23.

———. 2012. "Sad Ovid, Angry Augustus." *Latomus: Studies in Latin Literature and Roman History* 16:339–66.

Fyler, John M. 2009. "The Medieval Ovid." In Knox 2009:411–22.

Gale, Monica R. 1997. "Propertius 2.7: *Militia Amoris* and the Ironies of Elegy." *JRS* 87:77–91.

Galinsky, Karl. 1996. *Augustan Culture: An Interpretive Introduction*. Princeton, NJ: Princeton University Press.

Gardner, Hunter H. 2008. "Women's Time in the *Remedia Amoris*." In Lively and Salzman-Mitchell 2008:68–85.

Gibson, Bruce. 1999. "Ovid on Reading: Reading Ovid. Reception in Ovid *Tristia* II." *JRS* 89:19–37.

Gibson, Roy K. 2000. "Book Endings in Greek Poetry and *Ars Amatoria* 2 and 3." *Mnemosyne* 53:588–91.

———. 2003. *Ovid: Ars Amatoria Book 3*. Cambridge: Cambridge University Press.

———. 2009. "The *Ars Amatoria*." In Knox 2009:90–103.

Gibson, Roy K., Steven Green, and Alison Sharrock, eds. 2006. *The Art of Love: Bimillennial Essays on Ovid's Ars Amatoria and Remedia Amoris*. Oxford: Oxford University Press.

Gold, Barbara K. 2012. *A Companion to Roman Love Elegy*. Malden, MA: Wiley-Blackwell.

Goold, G. P. 1983. "The Cause of Ovid's Exile." *ICS* 8:94–107.

Graf, Fritz. 2002. "Myth in Ovid." In Hardie 2002:108–21.

Green, Carin M. C. 1996. "Terms of Venery: *Ars Amatoria* 1." *TAPA* 126:221–63.

Green, Peter. 1982a. *Ovid: The Erotic Poems*. London: Penguin.

———. 1982b. "*Carmen et Error: Prophasis* and *Aitia* in the Matter of Ovid's Exile." *CA* 1:202–20.

———. 2005. *Ovid: The Poems of Exile. Tristia and the Black Sea Letters*. Berkeley: University of California Press.

Green, Steven J. 2006. "Lessons in Love: Fifty Years of Scholarship on the *Ars Amatoria* and *Remedia Amoris*." In Gibson et al. 2006:1–20.

Greene, Ellen. 1998. *The Erotics of Domination: Male Desire and the Mistress in Latin Love Poetry*. Baltimore: Johns Hopkins University Press.

Griffith, Mark, and Donald J. Mastronarde, eds. 1990. *Cabinet of the Muses: Essays on Classical and Comparative Literature in Honor of Thomas G. Rosenmeyer*. Atlanta: Scholars Press.

Habinek, Thomas. 1998. *The Politics of Latin Literature: Writing, Identity, and Empire in Ancient Rome*. Princeton, NJ: Princeton University Press.

Habinek, Thomas, and Alessandro Schiesaro, eds. 1997. *The Roman Cultural Revolution*. Cambridge: Cambridge University Press.

Hall, E., and R. Wyles, eds. 2008. *New Directions in Ancient Pantomime*. Oxford: Oxford University Press.

Hall, John Barrie. 1995. *P. Ovidi Nasonis Tristia*. Stuttgart: B. G. Teubner.

Hallett, Judith P. 2012. "Authorial Identity in Latin Love Elegy: Literary Fictions and Erotic Failings." In Gold 2012:269–84.

Hardie, Philip, ed. 2002. *The Cambridge Companion to Ovid*. Cambridge: Cambridge University Press.

———. 2006. "*Lethaeus Amor*: The Art of Forgetting." In Gibson et al. 2006:166–90.

Hardie, Philip, Alessandro Barchiesi, and Stephen Hinds, eds. 1999. *Ovidian Trans-formations: Essays on Ovid's Metamorphoses and Its Reception*. Cambridge: Cambridge Philological Society.

Harrison, Stephen. 2002. "Ovid and Genre: Evolutions of an Elegist." In Hardie 2002:79–94.

Hejduk, Julia D. 2008. *Clodia: A Sourcebook*. Norman: University of Oklahoma Press.

———. 2009. "Ovid and Religion." In Knox 2009:45–58.

———. 2010. "'To R. B.': Hopkins' Ovidian Letter from the Black Sea." *IJCT* 17:53–59.

———. 2011a. "Death by Elegy: Ovid's Cephalus and Procris." *TAPA* 141:285–314.

———. 2011b. "Facing the Minotaur: *Inception* (2010) and *Aeneid 6*." *Arion* 19: 93–104.

Helzle, Martin. 1988. "Ovid's Poetics of Exile." *ICS* 13:73–83.

Henderson, A. A. R. 1979. *P. Ovidi Nasonis: Remedia Amoris*. Edinburgh: Scottish Academic Press.

Heyworth, S. J., ed. 2007. *Classical Constructions: Papers in Memory of Don Fowler, Classicist and Epicurean*. Oxford: Oxford University Press.

Hinds, Stephen. 1998. *Allusion and Intertext: The Dynamics of Appropriation in Roman Poetry*. Cambridge: Cambridge University Press.

———. 2006. "Booking the Return Trip: Ovid and *Tristia 1*." In Knox 2006:415–40.

———. 2007. "Ovid Among the Conspiracy Theorists." In Heyworth 2007:194–220.

Hollis, Adrian S. 1977. *Ovid: Ars Amatoria Book I*. Oxford: Clarendon Press.

Holzberg, Niklas. 2002. *Ovid: The Poet and His Work*. Translated by G. M. Goshgarian. Ithaca, NY: Cornell University Press.

———. 2006. "Playing with his Life: Ovid's 'Autobiographical' References." In Knox 2006:51–68.

Ingleheart, Jennifer. 2006a. "Ovid's Error: Actaeon, Sight, Sex, and Striptease." *Omnibus* 52:6–8.

———. 2006b. "What the Poet Saw: Ovid, the Error and the Theme of Sight in *Tristia 2*." *MD* 56:63–86.

———. 2006c. "Ovid, *Tristia 1.2*: High Drama on the High Seas." *G&R* 53:73–91.

———. 2008. "*Et mea sunt populo saltata poemata saepe* (*Tristia 2.519*): Ovid and the Pantomime." In Hall and Wyles 2008:198–217.

———. 2010. *A Commentary on Ovid, Tristia, Book 2*. Oxford: Oxford University Press.

———, ed. 2011. *Two Thousand Years of Solitude: Exile after Ovid*. Oxford: Oxford University Press.

James, Heather. 2009. "Ovid in Renaissance English Literature." In Knox 2009: 423–41.

James, Sharon L. 2003a. "Her Turn to Cry: The Politics of Weeping in Roman Love Elegy." *TAPA* 133:99–122.

———. 2003b. *Learned Girls and Male Persuasion: Gender and Reading in Roman Love Elegy*. Berkeley: University of California Press.

———. 2008. "Women Reading Men: The Female Audience of the *Ars Amatoria*." *CCJ* (= *PCPhS*) 54:136–59.

———. 2012. "Elegy and New Comedy." In Gold 2012:253–68.

Janka, Markus. 1997. *Ovid, Ars Amatoria: Buch 2; Kommentar*. Heidelberg: Universitätsverlag C. Winter.

Johnson, Patricia J. 1997. "Ovid's Livia in Exile." *CW* 90:403–20.

Johnson, W. R. 2009. *A Latin Lover in Ancient Rome: Readings in Propertius and His Genre*. Columbus: Ohio State University Press.

Keith, Alison M. 1994. "*Corpus Eroticum*: Elegiac Poetics and Elegiac Puellae in Ovid's *Amores*." *CW* 88:27–40.

Kellum, Barbara. 1997. "Concealing/Revealing: Gender and the Play of Meaning in the Monuments of Augustan Rome." In Habinek and Schiesaro 1997:158–81.

Kennedy, Duncan F. 1993. *The Arts of Love: Five Studies in the Discourse of Roman Love Elegy*. Cambridge: Cambridge University Press.

———. 2000. "Bluff Your Way in Didactic: Ovid's *Ars Amatoria* and *Remedia Amoris*." *Arethusa* 33:159–76.

———. 2006. "*Vixisset Phyllis, si me foret usa magistro*: Erotodidaxis and Intertextuality." In Gibson et al. 2006:54–74.

Kenney, E. J. 1961. *P. Ovidi Nasonis Amores, Medicamina Faciei Femineae, Ars Amatoria, Remedia Amoris*. Oxford: Oxford University Press.

Kenney, E. J., and A. D. Melville. 1990. *Ovid: The Love Poems*. Translated by A. D. Melville. Oxford: Oxford University Press.

Knox, Peter E. 2004. "The Poet and the Second Prince: Ovid in the Age of Tiberius." *MAAR* 49:1–20.

———, ed. 2006. *Oxford Readings in Ovid*. Oxford: Oxford University Press.

———, ed. 2009. *A Companion to Ovid*. Malden, MA: Wiley-Blackwell.

Labate, Mario. 2006. "Erotic Aetiology: Romulus, Augustus, and the Rape of the Sabine Women." In Gibson et al. 2006:193–215.

Leach, Eleanor Winsor. 1964. "Georgic Imagery in the *Ars Amatoria*." *TAPA* 95: 142–54.

Lev Kenaan, Vered. 2008. "Platonic Strategies in Ovid's Tales of Love." In Lively and Salzman-Mitchell 2008:142–62.

Lively, Genevieve. 2006. "Ovid in Defeat? On the Reception of Ovid's *Ars Amatoria* and *Remedia Amoris*." In Gibson et al. 2006:318–37.

Lively, Genevieve, and Patricia Salzman-Mitchell, eds. 2008. *Latin Elegy and Narratology: Fragments of Story*. Columbus: Ohio State University Press.

Mader, Gottfried. 1991. "Panegyric and Persuasion in Ovid, *Tr.* 2.317–336." *Latomus* 50:139–49.

Martin, Charles. 2009. "Translating Ovid." In Knox 2009:469–84.

McGinn, Thomas A. 1998. *Prostitution, Sexuality, and the Law in Ancient Rome*. Oxford: Oxford University Press.

McKeown, J. C. 1979. "Augustan Elegy and Mime." *PCPhS* 25:71–84.

———. 1995. "*Militat omnis amans*." *CJ* 90:295–304.

McNelis, Charles. 2009. "Ovidian Strategies in Early Imperial Literature." In Knox 2009:397–410.

Merriam, Carol U. 2011. "She Who Laughs Best: Ovid, *Ars Amatoria* 3.279–90." *Latomus* 70:405–21.

Miller, John F. 1983. "Callimachus and the *Ars Amatoria*." *CP* 78:26–34.

———. 1993. "Apostrophe, Aside and the Didactic Addressee: Poetic Strategies in Ars Amatoria III." *MD* 31:231–41.

———. 1997. "Lucretian Moments in Ovidian Elegy." *CJ* 92:384–98.

———. 2006. "Ovidian Allusion and the Vocabulary of Memory." In Knox 2006: 86–99.

Miller, Paul Allen. 2004. *Subjecting Verses: Latin Love Elegy and the Emergence of the Real*. Princeton, NJ: Princeton University Press.

———. 2007. "Catullus and Roman Love Elegy." In Skinner 2007:399–417.

Murgatroyd, P. 1984. "Amatory Hunting, Fishing and Fowling." *Latomus* 43:362–68.

———. 1995. "The Sea of Love." *CQ* 45:9–25.

Murgia, Charles E. 1986a. "Influence of Ovid's *Remedia Amoris* on *Ars Amatoria* 3 and *Amores* 3." *CP* 81:203–20.

———. 1986b. "The Date of Ovid's *Ars Amatoria* 3." *AJP* 107:74–94.

Myerowitz, Molly. 1985. *Ovid's Games of Love*. Detroit: Wayne State University Press.

Myers, K. Sara. 1996. "The Poet and the Procuress: The *Lena* in Latin Love Elegy." *JRS* 86:1–21.

———. 1999. "The Metamorphosis of a Poet: Recent Work on Ovid." *JRS* 89: 190–204.

Nagle, Betty Rose. 1980. *The Poetics of Exile: Program and Polemic in the* Tristia *and* Epistulae ex Ponto *of Ovid*. Brussels: Latomus.

Nickbakht, Mehran A. 2005. "Further Evidence of the Original Outline of Ovid's *Ars Amatoria* (1.771–2)." *Mnemosyne* 58:284–86.

Nugent, Georgia. 1990. "*Tristia* 2: Ovid and Augustus." In Raaflaub and Toher 1990: 239–57.

O'Gorman, Ellen. 1997. "Love and the Family: Augustus and the Ovidian Legacy." *Arethusa* 30:103–23.

Oliensis, Ellen. 1998. "Return to Sender: The Rhetoric of *Nomina* in Ovid's *Tristia*." *Ramus* 26:172–93.

Otis, Brooks. 1970. *Ovid as an Epic Poet*. 2nd ed. Cambridge: Cambridge University Press.

Owen, S. G. 1924. *P. Ovidii Nasonis Tristium Liber Secundus*. Oxford: Oxford University Press.

Pollini, John. 2012. *From Republic to Empire: Rhetoric, Religion, and Power in the Visual Culture of Ancient Rome*. Norman: University of Oklahoma Press.

Raaflaub, Kurt A., and Mark Toher. 1990. *Between Republic and Empire: Interpretations of Augustus and His Principate*. Berkeley: University of California Press.

Richlin, Amy. 1992. *The Garden of Priapus: Sexuality and Aggression in Roman Humor*. Rev. ed. Oxford: Oxford University Press.

Rolfe, J. C. 1914. *Suetonius: Vol. I*. Cambridge, MA: Harvard University Press.

Rosati, Gianpiero. 2006. "The Art of *Remedia Amoris*: Unlearning to Love?" In Gibson et al. 2006:143–65.

Rosenmeyer, P. A. 1997. "Ovid's *Heroides* and *Tristia*: Voices from Exile." *Ramus* 26:29–56.

Sharrock, Alison R. 1994a. *Seduction and Repetition in Ovid's Ars Amatoria 2*. Oxford: Oxford University Press.

———. 1994b. "Ovid and the Politics of Reading." *MD* 33:97–122.

———. 1995. "The Drooping Rose: Elegiac Failure in *Amores* 3.7." *Ramus* 24:150–82.

———. 2002. "Ovid and the Discourses of Love: The Amatory Works." In Hardie 2002:150–62.

———. 2006. "Love in Parentheses: Digression and Narrative Hierarchy in Ovid's Erotodidactic Poems." In Gibson et al. 2006:23–39.

———. 2012. "Ovid." In Gold 2012:70–85.

Skinner, Marilyn B., ed. 2007. *A Companion to Catullus*. Malden, MA: Blackwell.

———. 2011. *Clodia Metelli: The Tribune's Sister*. Oxford: Oxford University Press.

Solodow, Joseph B. 1977. "Ovid's Ars Amatoria: The Lover as Cultural Ideal." *WS* 11:106–27.

Starr, Raymond J. 1987. "The Circulation of Literary Texts in the Roman World." *CQ* 37:213–23.

Syme, Ronald. 1978. *History in Ovid.* Oxford: Clarendon Press.

Thibault, John C. 1964. *The Mystery of Ovid's Exile.* Berkeley: University of California Press.

Toohey, Peter. 1996. *Epic Lessons: An Introduction to Ancient Didactic Poetry.* London: Routledge.

Treggiari, Susan. 1991. *Roman Marriage:* Iusti Coniuges *from the Time of Cicero to the Time of Ulpian.* Oxford: Clarendon Press.

Volk, Katharina. 2002. *The Poetics of Latin Didactic: Lucretius, Vergil, Ovid, Manilius.* Oxford: Oxford University Press.

Watson, Lindsay C. 2007. "The Bogus Teacher and his Relevance for Ovid's *Ars Amatoria.*" *RhM* 150:337–74.

Watson, Patricia. 1983. "Mythological Exempla in Ovid's *Ars Amatoria.*" *CP* 78: 117–26.

———. 2002. "*Praecepta Amoris*: Ovid's Didactic Elegy." In Boyd 2002:142–65.

Welch, Tara. 2005. *The Elegiac Cityscape: Propertius and the Meaning of Roman Monuments.* Columbus: Ohio State University Press.

———. 2012. "Elegy and the Monuments." In Gold 2012:103–18.

Wiedemann, Thomas. 1975. "The Political Background to Ovid's *Tristia* 2." *CQ* 25:264–71.

Wilkinson, L. P. 1955. *Ovid Recalled.* Cambridge: Cambridge University Press.

Williams, Gareth. 1994. *Banished Voices: Readings in Ovid's Exile Poetry.* Cambridge: Cambridge University Press.

———. 2002a. "Ovid's Exilic Poetry: Worlds Apart." In Boyd 2002:337–81.

———. 2002b. "Ovid's Exile Poetry: *Tristia, Epistulae ex Ponto* and *Ibis.*" In Hardie 2002:233–45.

Wright, Ellen F. 1984. "Profanum sunt genus: The Poets of the *Ars Amatoria.*" *PQ* 63:1–15.

Zanker, Paul. 1988. *The Power of Images in the Age of Augustus.* Translated by Alan Shapiro. Ann Arbor: University of Michigan Press.

Ziolkowski, Theodore. 2009. "Ovid in the Twentieth Century." In Knox 2009: 455–68.

# Index

Page numbers in [ ] indicate periphrastic references that have not been glossed in the notes: e.g., "king of the gods" for "Jupiter"; "Tyndareus's daughter" for "Clytemnestra" (this would also be listed under "Tyndareus"). "City" (= village, town, city, city-state) and "region" (= area, state, kingdom, province) are used somewhat loosely; I have avoided "country" because the word's modern connotations might give a misleading impression of ancient political geography. Numbers in **boldface** indicate extended discussions or appearances.

E. A. Thompson
*Romans and Barbarians: The Decline of the Western Empire*

H. I. Marrou
*A History of Education in Antiquity*
*Histoire de l'Education dans l'Antiquité*, translated by George Lamb

Jennifer Tolbert Roberts
*Accountability in Athenian Government*

Erika Simon
*Festivals of Attica: An Archaeological Commentary*

Warren G. Moon, editor
*Ancient Greek Art and Iconography*

G. Michael Woloch
*Roman Cities: Les villes romaines* by Pierre Grimal, translated and
edited by G. Michael Woloch, together with A Descriptive
Catalogue of Roman Cities by G. Michael Woloch

Katherine Dohan Morrow
*Greek Footwear and the Dating of Sculpture*

John Kevin Newman
*The Classical Epic Tradition*

Jeanny Vorys Canby, Edith Porada,
Brunilde Sismondo Ridgway, and Tamara Stech, editors
*Ancient Anatolia: Aspects of Change and Cultural Development*

PLAUTUS
JOHN HENDERSON, translator and commentator
*Asinaria: The One about the Asses*

PATRICE D. RANKINE
*Ulysses in Black: Ralph Ellison, Classicism, and
African American Literature*

PAUL REHAK
JOHN G. YOUNGER, editor
*Imperium and Cosmos: Augustus and the Northern Campus Martius*

PATRICIA J. JOHNSON
*Ovid before Exile: Art and Punishment in the "Metamorphoses"*

VERED LEV KENAAN
*Pandora's Senses: The Feminine Character of the Ancient Text*

ERIK GUNDERSON
*Nox Philologiae: Aulus Gellius and the Fantasy of the Roman Library*

SINCLAIR BELL and HELEN NAGY, editors
*New Perspectives on Etruria and Early Rome*

BARBARA PAVLOCK
*The Image of the Poet in Ovid's "Metamorphoses"*

PAUL CARTLEDGE and
FIONA ROSE GREENLAND, editors
*Responses to Oliver Stone's "Alexander": Film, History, and Cultural Studies*

AMALIA AVRAMIDOU
*The Codrus Painter: Iconography and Reception of
Athenian Vases in the Age of Pericles*

SHANE BUTLER
*The Matter of the Page: Essays in Search of Ancient and Medieval Authors*

ALLISON GLAZEBROOK and
MADELEINE HENRY, editors
*Greek Prostitutes in the Ancient Mediterranean, 800 BCE–200 CE*

NORMAN AUSTIN
*Sophocles' "Philoctetes" and the Great Soul Robbery*

SOPHOCLES
A verse translation by DAVID MULROY, with introduction and notes
*Oedipus Rex*

JOHN ANDREAU and RAYMOND DESCAT
*The Slave in Greece and Rome*
*Esclave en Grèce et à Rome*, translated by MARION LEOPOLD

AMANDA WILCOX
*The Gift of Correspondence in Classical Rome: Friendship in Cicero's*
*"Ad Familiares" and Seneca's "Moral Epistles"*

MARK BUCHAN
*Perfidy and Passion: Reintroducing the "Iliad"*

SOPHOCLES
A verse translation by DAVID MULROY,
with introduction and notes
*Antigone*

GEOFFREY W. BAKEWELL
*Aeschylus's "Suppliant Women": The Tragedy of Immigration*

ELIZABETH PAULETTE BAUGHAN
*Couched in Death: "Klinai" and Identity in Anatolia and Beyond*

BENJAMIN ELDON STEVENS
*Silence in Catullus*

HORACE
Translated with commentary by DAVID R. SLAVITT
*Odes*